D0722419

America's Military Past

AMERICAN GOVERNMENT AND HISTORY INFORMATION GUIDE SERIES

Series Editor: Harold Shill, Chief Circulation Librarian, Adjunct Assistant Professor of Political Science, West Virginia University, Morgantown

Also in this series:

AMERICAN EDUCATIONAL HISTORY—*Edited by Timothy Walsh and Michael W. Sedlak**

IMMIGRATION AND ETHNICITY—*Edited by John D. Buenker and Nicholas C. Burckel*

PROGRESSIVE REFORM—*Edited by John D. Buenker and Nicholas C. Burckel**

PUBLIC ADMINISTRATION—*Edited by John E. Rouse, Jr.**

PUBLIC POLICY—*Edited by William J. Murin, Gerald Michael Greenfield, and John D. Buenker**

SOCIAL HISTORY OF THE UNITED STATES—*Edited by Donald F. Tingley*

U.S. CONSTITUTION—*Edited by Earlean McCarrick**

U.S. CULTURAL HISTORY—*Edited by Philip I. Mitterling*

U.S. FOREIGN RELATIONS—*Edited by Elmer Plischke**

U.S. POLITICS AND ELECTIONS—*Edited by David J. Maurer*

U.S. RELIGIOUS AND CHURCH HISTORY—*Edited by Garth Rosell**

URBAN HISTORY AND URBANIZATION—*Edited by John D. Buenker, Gerald Michael Greenfield, and William J. Murin**

WOMEN AND FEMINISM IN AMERICAN HISTORY—*Edited by Donald F. Tingley and Elizabeth Tingley**

*in preparation

The above series is part of the
GALE INFORMATION GUIDE LIBRARY

The Library consists of a number of separate series of guides covering major areas in the social sciences, humanities, and current affairs.

General Editor: Paul Wasserman, Professor and former Dean, School of Library and Information Services, University of Maryland

Managing Editor: Denise Allard Adzigian, Gale Research Company

America's Military Past

A GUIDE TO INFORMATION SOURCES

Volume 7 in the American Government and History Information Guide Series

Jack C. Lane

*Professor of History
Rollins College
Winter Park, Florida*

Gale Research Company
Book Tower, Detroit, Michigan 48226

Library of Congress Cataloging in Publication Data

Lane, Jack C   1932-
    America's military past.

    (American government and history information guide
series ; v. 7) (Gale information guide library)
    1. United States—History, Military—Bibliography.
I. Title. II. Series.
Z1249.M5L36 [E181]   016.973   74-11517
ISBN 0-8103-1205-0

Copyright © 1980 by
Jack C. Lane

No part of this book may be reproduced in any form without permission in
writing from the publisher, except by a reviewer who wishes to quote brief
passages or entries in connection with a review written for inclusion in a
magazine or newspaper. Manufactured in the United States of America.

For my son Alan
and
For my daughter Anne

154188

VITA

Jack C. Lane is professor of history at Rollins College, Winter Park, Florida. He received his B.A. from Oglethorpe University (1958), M.A. from Emory University (1959), and Ph.D. from the University of Georgia (1963).

Lane has authored two books: CHASING GERONIMO (University of New Mexico Press, 1970) and ARMED PROGRESSIVE: GENERAL LEONARD WOOD (Presidio Press, 1978). He has also written several articles on American military history. Lane holds membership in the Organization of American Historians, American Military Institute, and InterUniversity Seminar on Armed Forces and Society.

CONTENTS

Contents

INTRODUCTION

This is a comprehensive bibliography. A complete one--one that would include all books and articles on American military history--would require several volumes. It would also be a futile endeavor because much of the literature on America's military past has been either militarily operational and/or self-serving or purely descriptive narrative. I have attempted, therefore, to collect the major works in the field--those that are not only the most interesting, but also those that attempt some analysis and evaluation in the process of telling a good story. Moreover, I have concentrated on works dealing with American land and air forces without including any naval sources for the very good reason that Myron Smith, THE AMERICAN NAVY, 1789-1941, has provided us recently with a complete bibliography of sources on naval history. In addition, I have not included dissertation titles because these have been collected and published by Allan Millett and B. Franklin Cooling (see entry 282). In each issue of MILITARY AFFAIRS, the editor publishes the most recent publications in military history and in each February issue updates the dissertation list.

Those interested in a more complete listing of sources for each of America's past wars should consult the following:

Buchanan, Russell. THE UNITED STATES IN WORLD WAR II. 2 vols. New York: Harper, 1963.

>   Contains a comprehensive bibliographical essay that is dated but still the most complete.

Rees, David. KOREA: THE LIMITED WAR. New York: St. Martin's, 1964. 511 p.

>   Contains an unannotated bibliographical list that is dated but still the best.

Shaffer, Ronald. THE UNITED STATES IN WORLD WAR I: A SELECTED BIBLIOGRAPHY. Santa Barbara, Calif.: ABC-Clio, 1978. 224 p.

>   Contains 2,900 English-language entries divided into nine chapters, but only an author index.

Nevis, Allan, et al. CIVIL WAR BOOKS: A CRITICAL BIBLIOGRAPHY. 2 vols. Baton Rouge: Louisiana State University Press, 1970.

> Contains a critical annotated list of published books. For articles on the Civil War, see the appropriate issues of CIVIL WAR HISTORY.

Connor, Seymour, and Faulk, Odie. NORTH AMERICA DIVIDED: THE MEXICAN WAR, 1846-1848. New York: Oxford University Press, 1971. 300 p.

> Contains a comprehensive list of books, articles, and pamphlets with useful annotated critical comments.

Cosmos, Graham. AN ARMY FOR EMPIRE: THE UNITED STATES ARMY IN THE SPANISH-AMERICAN WAR. Columbia: University of Missouri Press, 1971. 334 p.

> Contains an unannotated, somewhat less than comprehensive, list of books. Nevertheless, it is the best in print.

Higginbotham, Don. THE WAR OF AMERICAN INDEPENDENCE. New York: Macmillan, 1971. 509 p.

> Contains a selected and critical bibliography of American revolutionary war literature.

Mahon, John. THE WAR OF 1812. Gainesville: University of Florida Press, 1972. 476 p.

> Contains a comprehensive list that is noncritical and unannotated.

Leitenberg, Milton, and Burns, Richard D. THE VIETNAM CONFLICT. Santa Barbara, Calif.: ABC-Clio, 1973. 149 p.

> Unannotated but a complete bibliography of the Vietnam War to 1973.

Overall, I have approached the subject chronologically, but in the first part I have provided a topical arrangement that I believe gives both depth and breadth to the bibliography. Even within the chronological framework I have tried to suggest that wars have been part of larger historical developments.

The relatively large number of entries in the section in chapter 1 entitled "Military Historiography" indicate the interest that military historians have had in the nature of their field. Allan Millett (see entry 280) has argued that no interpretative patterns in military history have appeared to date. I have identified two general approaches and at the same time suggested the need for two others (see entry 275), but I would have to agree that military history has yet to reach the rich interpretative level of other fields of American history.

Still, the reader will find among these pages some of America's most significant historical literature, from such classics as Francis Parkman's narrative of colonial wars and Douglas Freeman's studies of Lee and Lee's commanders to brilliant recent accounts as Don Higginbotham's work on the Revolutionary

War and Russell Weigley's study of American strategic policy. These and many others indicate the traditionally high quality of military historical literature that could serve as standards for future military historians who may one day give us a historiographical tradition as well.

I would like to express my appreciation to Rollins College for awarding me the Weddell Professorship which has helped defray travel and clerical expenses incurred in working on the project. I would also like to thank the Mills Memorial Library staff for their aid in finding obscure works, and several Rollins students, especially Donna Seals and Lydia Chandler, who helped in the search for books. And finally, to the members of my family, I greatly appreciate how they both endured and encouraged this endeavor.

Chapter 1

FOUNDATIONS OF THE AMERICAN
MILITARY EXPERIENCE

A. GENERAL ACCOUNTS AND SOURCES

1   Albion, Robert G. INTRODUCTION TO MILITARY HISTORY. New
York: Appleton, 1929. 485 p.

A summary of American military history through World War I.

2   Anders, Leslie. "Retrospect: Four Decades of American Military
Journalism." MILITARY AFFAIRS 41 (1971): 62-66.

Surveys the field of military journalism since the 1930s, focusing particularly on how MILITARY AFFAIRS was the leading journal.

3   Bernardo, C. Joseph, and Bacon, Eugene H. AMERICAN MILITARY
POLICY: ITS DEVELOPMENT SINCE 1775. Harrisburg, Pa.: Military Service, 1955. 512 p.

A study of American military policy from a predominantly military point of view. Supports Emory Upton's conclusion concerning the weakness of American military policy. (See entry 105.)

4   Brackett, Albert G. HISTORY OF THE UNITED STATES CAVALRY
FROM THE FORMATION OF THE FEDERAL GOVERNMENT TO THE
1ST OF JUNE, 1863. 1865. Reprint. Westport, Conn.: Greenwood, 1975. 337 p.

Covers period to the Civil War. Still a useful source for
historians interested in the U.S. Cavalry.

5   Brady, Cyrus T. AMERICAN FIGHTS AND FIGHTERS: STORIES OF
THE FIRST FIVE WARS OF THE UNITED STATES, FROM THE WAR OF
REVOLUTION TO THE WAR OF 1812. New York: McClure, Phillips,
1900. 326 p.

A popular, yet historically interesting, account of early battles and leaders.

6   Burt, Richard, and Kemp, Geoffrey. CONGRESSIONAL HEARINGS
     ON AMERICAN DEFENSE POLICY, 1947-1951: AN ANNOTATED
     BIBLIOGRAPHY. Manhattan: University Press of Kansas, 1974.
     377 p.

     Focuses on Armed Services Committees and Appropriation Sub-
     committees. Includes complete list of witnesses and a short
     summary of their testimony.

7   Carter, William H. THE AMERICAN ARMY. Indianapolis: Bobbs-
     Merrill, 1915. 296 p.

     Considered one of the best descriptions of America's peace-
     time army and professional development, 1900-1914.

8   Cooling, Franklin. "A History of U.S. Army Aviation." AEROSPACE
     HISTORIAN 21 (1974): 102-9.

9   Craig, Hardin. A BIBLIOGRAPHY OF ENCYCLOPEDIAS AND DIC-
     TIONARIES DEALING WITH MILITARY, NAVAL, AND MARITIME
     AFFAIRS, 1577-1965. Houston: Fondren Library, Rice University,
     1965. 101 p.

     Useful as a research tool.

10   Cunliffe, Marcus F. "The American Military Tradition." In BRITISH
     ESSAYS IN AMERICAN HISTORY, edited by Harry Cranbrook and
     Charles Hill, pp. 207-24. London: Arnold, 1957.

     An important essay by the leading English historian of Ameri-
     can military affairs. Ideas more fully developed in SOLDIERS
     AND CIVILIANS (below).

11   _____. SOLDIERS AND CIVILIANS: THE MARTIAL SPIRIT IN
     AMERICA, 1775-1865. Boston: Little, Brown, 1968. 499 p.

     Covers the genesis of American military traditions and its ef-
     fects on civilian life. Emphasizes influence from society on
     the American military establishment.

12   Curti, Merle E. PEACE OR WAR: THE AMERICAN STRUGGLE 1636-
     1936. New York: Garland, 1972. 374 p.

     An account of antiwar movements, both organized and indi-
     vidual, in America from colonial times to 1936. Scholarly,
     well written, almost a classic in the field.

13   Decker, Leslie E., and Seager, Robert, eds. AMERICA'S MAJOR
     WARS: CRUSADERS, CRITICS, AND SCHOLARS. 2 vols. New York:
     Addison-Wesley, 1973.

Selected essays providing an introduction to the study of debates on American wars. Selections represent opinions on
both sides of the issue for each major war.

14   Downey, Fairfax D. SOUND OF GUNS: THE STORY OF AMERICAN
ARTILLERY. New York: McKay, 1956. 337 p.

Informal account of America's artillery from the Revolution to
atomic missiles. Weaves an interesting story out of a technical subject.

15   Dupuy, R. Ernest, and Baumer, William H. LITTLE WARS OF THE
UNITED STATES. New York: Hawthorn, 1968. 226 p.

Narrative account covering small American wars from the
quasiwar with France in 1798 to interventions in Caribbean
in the twentieth century. No analysis of the causes or evaluation of the small wars.

16   Dupuy, R. Ernest, and Dupuy, Trevor N. MILITARY HERITAGE OF
AMERICA. New York: McGraw-Hill, 1956. 794 p.

A detailed study from the military-lessons point of view.
Contains good annotated bibliography, though dated.

17   Edmonds, James E. FIGHTING FOOLS. New York: Appleton-Century-Crofts, 1938. 373 p.

Uptonian view of America's military past by a former citizen-
soldier, covering Spanish-American War through World War I.

18   Galvin, John R. AIR ASSAULT: THE DEVELOPMENT OF AIRMO-
BILE WARFARE. New York: Hawthorn, 1969. 365 p.

Traces the development of the concept and practice of verti-
cal envelopment from World War II to its ultimate successes
with helicopters in Vietnam.

19   Ganoe, William A. A HISTORY OF THE UNITED STATES ARMY.
New York: Appleton-Century-Crofts, 1924. 609 p.

The first comprehensive history of the U.S. Army. Based on
Uptonian thesis of past failures and tends to be more chronicle than history.

20   Gurney, Gene. PICTORICAL HISTORY OF THE UNITED STATES
ARMY IN WAR AND PEACE FROM COLONIAL TIMES TO VIETNAM.
New York: Crown, 1966. 815 p.

Collection of prints, photographs and sketches pictorially de-
picting American military history, including such military matters as uniforms, campaign banners, and equipment.

21   Haskin, William L., and Rodenbaugh, Thomas F. THE ARMY OF THE
      UNITED STATES. New York: Maynard, Merrill, 1896. 688 p.

      Collection of histories of regiments and staff bureaus, 1890–95.

22   Head, Richard G., and Rakke, Ervin J., eds. AMERICAN DEFENSE POL-
      ICY. Baltimore: Johns Hopkins University Press, 1973. 676 p.

      Collection of essays on American defense posture after World
      War II. Political science oriented.

23   Heinl, Robert D. SOLDIERS OF THE SEA: THE UNITED STATES
      MARINE CORPS., 1775–1962. Annapolis, Md.: U.S. Naval Insti-
      tute, 1962. 692 p.

      A less than detached, objective account by a former marine.

24   Herr, John K., and Wallace, Edward S. THE STORY OF THE
      UNITED STATES CAVALRY. Boston: Little, Brown, 1953. 275 p.

      Sympathetic, informal account of the U.S. Cavalry from the
      revolutionary period to the decision to dismount the cavalry
      during World War II.

25   Herring, Pendleton. THE IMPACT OF WAR: OUR DEMOCRACY UN-
      DER ARMS. New York: Farrar, Rinehart, 1941. 306 p.

      Studies the impact of war on American democratic principles
      and the role of the military in a democratic culture. Organ-
      ized historically and topically.

26   Hicken, Victor. THE AMERICAN FIGHTING MAN. New York:
      Macmillan, 1969. 496 p.

      Account of the attitudes and characteristics of U.S. military
      servicemen since the Revolution. Attributes universal char-
      acteristics to them: independent, hostile to discipline, loyal,
      and confident of victory.

27   Higham, Robin, ed. A GUIDE TO THE SOURCES OF UNITED STATES
      MILITARY HISTORY. Hamden, Conn.: Archon Press, 1975. 559 p.

      Nineteen bibliographic chapters by experts on various military
      topics or periods. Topics include science, medicine, and
      museums as historical sources. Each chapter lists over three
      hundred selected items and contains a critical bibliographic
      essay.

28   Huidekoper, Frederick L. THE MILITARY UNPREPAREDNESS OF THE
      UNITED STATES. New York: Macmillan, 1915. 735 p.

Account in the Uptonian vein that American military history is the story of past mistakes. More important as a historical source (significant for what it says about the period) than as a detached history of American land forces.

29   Hutton, C. Powell. "From Centurians to Praetorians: A Comparison of French and American Army Experiences." ESSAYS ON NEW DI-MENSIONS IN MILITARY HISTORY 4 (1976): 158–68.

30   Jacobs, Bruce. HEROES OF THE ARMY: THE MEDAL OF HONOR AND ITS WINNERS. New York: Norton, 1956. 240 p.

Gives background on the creation of the Medal of Honor and then tells the story, in a straightforward manner, of twenty Medal of Honor winners. Also includes a list of all winners.

31   Kelly, Thomas E. THE U.S. ARMY AND THE SPANISH AMERICAN WAR ERA. Carlisle Barracks, Pa.: U.S. Army Military History Research Center, 1974. 151 p.

Bibliography of material on the Spanish American War in the Military History Research Center. Material is organized by units with all regular and volunteer units represented.

32   Knorr, Klaus, ed. HISTORICAL DIMENSIONS OF NATIONAL SECU-RITY PROBLEMS. Lawrence: University Press of Kansas, 1976. 387 p.

Essays by four historians and four political scientists giving historical perspectives on national security policy.

33   Kredel, Fritz, and Todd, Frederich. SOLDIERS OF THE AMERICAN ARMY, 1775-1954. Chicago: Regnery, 1954. [unpaged].

Drawings of American uniforms by Kredel with text by Todd, covering American military history from the eighteenth century to post World War II.

34   Kreidberg, Marvin A., and Henry, Merton G. HISTORY OF MO-BILIZATION IN THE UNITED STATES ARMY, 1775-1945. Washing-ton, D.C.: Department of Army, 1955. 721 p.

Comprehensive account of American mobilization, based on extensive archival sources. Interpretations from the military-lessons genre.

35   Lea, Homer. THE VALOR OF IGNORANCE. New York: Harper, 1909. 343 p.

A lurid, widely read study of the author's view of the dangers to American security because of the decline of militancy in the society. Useful as a historical source.

36   Leckie, Robert. THE WARS OF AMERICA. New York: Harper, 1968. 1,052 p.

A general survey of all American wars including Vietnam to 1967. Short on analysis and long on narrative. Most appealing to the general reader.

37   Leonard, Thomas C. ABOVE THE BATTLE: WAR-MAKING IN AMERICA FROM APPOMATOX TO VERSAILLES. New York: Oxford University Press, 1978. 260 p.

Discusses how generations of Americans between 1865 and 1918 found war not only acceptable but learned to live with it and its consequences. Contains valuable new interpretations.

38   Lyons, Gene, and Masland, John. EDUCATION AND MILITARY LEADERSHIP: A STUDY OF THE R.O.T.C. Princeton, N.J.: Princeton University Press, 1959. 283 p.

Detailed critical analysis of the problems of military education in the United States in adjusting to Cold War exigencies, focusing on the ROTC program.

39   McGregor, Morris J., and Nalty, Bernard C., eds. BLACKS IN THE U.S. ARMED FORCES. 13 vols. New York: Scholarly Resources, 1974.

Basic documents which span the years, 1639-1973. Contains most of the essential documents for a study of this topic.

40   Matloff, Maurice, ed. AMERICAN MILITARY HISTORY. Washington, D.C.: U.S. Office of the Chief of Military History, 1969. 701 p.

ROTC textbook, much superior to one published in 1956.

41   Matthews, William, and Wecter, Dixon. OUR SOLDIERS SPEAK, 1775-1918. Boston: Little, Brown, 1943. 325 p.

First-hand accounts from American Wars from the Revolution to World War I.

42   May, Ernest, ed. THE ULTIMATE DECISION: THE PRESIDENT AS COMMANDER IN CHIEF. New York: Braziller, 1960. 200 p.

Collection of essays by competent authorities dealing with the responsibilities of the president as commander in chief, from Madison to Eisenhower.

43   Merrill, James M. SPURS TO GLORY: THE STORY OF THE UNITED STATES CAVALRY. Chicago: Rand McNally, 1966. 302 p.

An account of selected episodes involving the American Cavalry, 1833-1917.

44   Millis, Walter. ARMS AND MEN: A STUDY IN AMERICAN MILITARY HISTORY. New York: Putnam, 1956. 382 p.

First interpretative examination of the development of American military policy from the colonial period to the 1950s. Marred only by the author's antiwar bias.

45   Moley, Raymond, Jr. THE AMERICAN LEGION STORY. New York: Duell, Sloan and Pearce, 1966. 443 p.

Story of America's largest and most influential veteran's organization. Author sympathetic to most of the Legion's aims but not uncritical.

46   Nevins, Allan, et al., comps. CIVIL WAR BOOKS: A CRITICAL BIBLIOGRAPHY. 2 vols. Baton Rouge: Louisiana State University Press, 1967-69.

Useful bibliography, mostly topically organized, critically annotated.

47   O'Connor, Raymond G., ed. AMERICAN DEFENSE POLICY IN PERSPECTIVE: FROM COLONIAL TIMES TO THE PRESENT. New York: Wiley, 1965. 377 p.

Collection of documents on American military history.

48   _____, ed. READINGS IN THE HISTORY OF AMERICAN MILITARY POLICY. Lawrence: University of Kansas Press, 1962. 256 p.

49   Palmer, John McA. AMERICA IN ARMS: THE EXPERIENCES OF THE UNITED STATES WITH MILITARY ORGANIZATION. New Haven, Conn.: Yale University Press, 1941. Reprint. New York: Arno, 1979.

A classic study of American military policy by an officer convinced that a democracy must build a citizen, rather than a professional army.

50   _____. WASHINGTON, LINCOLN, WILSON: THREE STATESMAN. Garden City, N.Y.: Doubleday, 1930. 417 p.

Comparative account of American military policy with three presidents as the focus. Defends militia system over a large standing regular army.

51   Palmer, Williston B. THE EVOLUTION OF THE MILITARY POLICY
      OF THE UNITED STATES. Carlisle Barracks, Pa.: U.S. Army Infor-
      mation School, 1946. 72 p.

52   Peterson, Harold L. ROUND SHOT AND RAMMERS. Harrisburg,
      Pa.: Stackpole, 1956. 128 p.

      A survey of the artillery in America from the colonial period
      to the Civil War. Useful diagrams and sketches of artillery
      pieces.

53   Pratt, Fletcher. BATTLES THAT CHANGED HISTORY. Garden City,
      N.Y.: Doubleday, 1956. 384 p.

      Guide to battles through history, including American battles
      in the Revolutionary War, the Civil War, and the Second
      World War.

54   Reinhardt, George C., and Kintner, William R. THE HAPHAZARD
      YEARS: HOW AMERICA HAS GONE TO WAR. Garden City, N.Y.:
      Doubleday, 1960. 242 p.

      Popular history of American wars.

55   Robinson, Fayette. AN ACCOUNT OF THE ORGANIZATION OF
      THE ARMY OF THE UNITED STATES. 2 vols. Philadelphia: Butler,
      1848.

      Includes biographies of officers of all grades. Mostly valu-
      able as a historical work.

56   Sharpe, Philip. THE RIFLE IN AMERICA. New York: Morrow,
      1938. 641 p.

57   Slovaker, John. THE U.S. ARMY AND DOMESTIC DISTURBANCES.
      Carlisle Barracks, Pa.: U.S. Army Military History Research Collec-
      tion, 1970. 56 p.

      List of approximately five hundred documents located at the
      U.S. Military History Research Center. Strong on pre-Civil
      War and post-World War II periods, but weak on the period
      from 1866 to 1920.

58   _____. THE U.S. ARMY AND THE NEGRO. Carlisle Barracks,
      Pa.: U.S. Army Military History Research Collection, 1971. 97 p.

      A bibliography of sources on the army and the negro commun-
      ity located at the U.S. Military History Research Center and
      the U.S. Army War College Library. Covers the period from
      the Revolutionary War to Vietnam.

59   Sofaer, Abraham D. WAR, FOREIGN AFFAIRS AND CONSTITU-
        TIONAL POWER: THE ORIGINS. Cambridge, Mass.: Ballinger,
        1976. 533 p.

        First volume of a projected three volume study of the war-
        making powers of Congress and the President. Covering the
        years to 1829, argues that from the beginning the presidents
        assumed large powers in the use of military force to the point
        of war or near war: Adams in 1798, Monroe in 1818, and
        Jefferson and Madison in the neutral rights controversy.

60   Spaulding, Oliver L. THE UNITED STATES ARMY IN WAR AND
        PEACE. New York: Putnam, 1937. 541 p.

        History of the U.S. Army from colonial period to 1920. Fo-
        cuses on U.S. army and military campaigns with some material
        on the peacetime army. Dated but one of the first historical
        studies.

61   Steele, Matthew F. AMERICAN CAMPAIGNS. 2 vols. Washington,
        D.C.: Government Printing Office, 1909. Reprint. Washington,
        D.C.: Combat Forces Press, 1951.

        Standard work on American military operations from Queen
        Anne's War through the Spanish-American War. Contains
        maps and orders of battle for major wars.

62   Walton, William. THE ARMY AND NAVY OF THE UNITED STATES.
        2 vols. Boston: Barrie, 1889-95.

        Particularly useful for its description of the American frontier
        army.

63   Weigley, Russell. HISTORY OF THE AMERICAN ARMY. New York:
        Macmillan, 1967. 688 p.

        Latest and most complete work on the American Army as an
        institution. First to establish the thesis of American military
        history as a struggle between those who championed a regular
        army of professionals and those who supported a citizen army.

64   Williams, T. Harry. AMERICANS AT WAR: THE DEVELOPMENT OF
        THE AMERICAN MILITARY SYSTEM. Baton Rouge: Louisiana State
        University Press, 1960. 138 p.

        Brief but incisive interpretation of American military policy.

65   Wood, Leonard. OUR MILITARY HISTORY: ITS FACTS AND FALLA-
        CIES. Chicago: Reilly and Britton, 1916. 240 p.

        Sees military history in Uptonian terms, but proposes citizen

army solution. Wood's military thought mostly superficial
and derivative, but book is useful as a primary source.

66   Zogbaum, Rufus. HORSE, FOOT, AND DRAGOON. New York:
      Harper, 1888. 176 p.

      Description of post Civil War frontier army with illustrations
      by author who visited many frontier posts.

B. MILITARY THOUGHT

67   Ackley, Charles W. THE MODERN MILITARY IN AMERICAN SOCI-
      ETY: A STUDY IN THE NATURE OF MILITARY POWER. Philadel-
      phia: Westminster, 1972. 400 p.

      General survey of American military thought on the nature of
      military power, focusing on the period after World War II.

68   Adams, Charles F. STUDIES MILITARY AND DIPLOMATIC, 1775-
      1865. New York: Macmillan, 1911. 424 p.

      Mostly military studies covering such selected topics as revo-
      lutionary battles, the Battle of New Orleans, and "some
      phases of the Civil War." Dated but still useful.

69   Ambrose, Stephen. "Emory Upton and the Armies of Asia and Europe."
      MILITARY AFFAIRS 28 (1964): 27-32.

      Argues that within the military establishment Upton's ARMIES
      OF ASIA AND EUROPE (see entry 106) was as important and
      as influential as THE MILITARY POLICY OF THE UNITED
      STATES (see entry 105).

70   Bigelow, John, Jr. THE PRINCIPLES OF STRATEGY. Rev. ed.
      Philadelphia: Lippincott, 1894. 362 p.

      An early textbook based on Sherman's strategy against civilian
      populations.

71   Brown, Richard C. "General Emory Upton: The Army's Mahan."
      MILITARY AFFAIRS 17 (1953): 125-31.

      Argues that through his writings on military science and with the
      posthumous publication of his MILITARY POLICY OF THE
      UNITED STATES (see entry 105), Upton fulfilled the same
      intellectual role for the army that Mahan did for the navy.

72   Conn, Stetson. "Changing Concepts of National Defense in the United
      States; 1937-1947." MILITARY AFFAIRS 28 (1964): 1-8.

Argues that American concept of national defense shifted from one based purely on defense to one of military alliance during the decade 1937-47.

73   Donnelly, Charles H. "Evolution of United States Strategic Thought." MILITARY REVIEW 39 (1959): 12-24.

A useful review of American strategic thought after World War II, though somewhat biased toward the lessons-learned school of thought.

74   Dulles, Eleanor L., and Crane, Robert D., eds. DETENTE: COLD WAR STRATEGIES IN TRANSITION. New York: Praeger, 1965. 307 p.

A collection of essays on strategic thought after World War II.

75   Earle, Edward M. MAKERS OF MODERN STRATEGY: MILITARY THOUGHT FROM MACHIAVELLI TO HITLER. Princeton, N.J.: Princeton University Press, 1943. 553 p.

Scholarly essays on military thinkers, including American figures: Alexander Hamilton (chapter 6); Alfred Thayer Mahan (chapter 17).

76   Ekirch, Arthur J. "The Idea of a Citizen Army." MILITARY AFFAIRS 17 (1953): 30-56.

Argues for the citizen soldier army as most acceptable in a democratic society.

77   Evans, Gordon H. "The New Military Strategy." CURRENT HISTORY 47 (1964): 77-80.

Discusses the shift from massive retaliation of the Eisenhower administration to the "damage-limiting" nuclear strategy of the Kennedy administration.

78   Falk, Stanley L. "Disarmament in Historical Perspective." MILITARY REVIEW 44 (1964): 36-48.

Briefly traces disarmament efforts of the past and then looks at several kinds of disarmament processes and finally discusses various international efforts to achieve it.

79   Fleishman, Gordon K. "The Myth of the Military Mind." MILITARY REVIEW 44 (1964): 3-8.

Argues there is no distinct military mind; that the American officer comes from a cross-section of American society and therefore reflects its views and attitudes.

80   Gillmore, Russell. "'The New Courage': Rifles and Soldier Individualism, 1876-1918." MILITARY AFFAIRS 40 (1976): 97-102.

Rifle worksmanship seen as peculiarly American in that it reflected American sense of individualism. Focuses on how the
rifle movement culminated in American policy during World
War I.

81   Greene, Fred. "The Military View of American National Policy,
1904-1940." AMERICAN HISTORICAL REVIEW 66 (1961): 354-99.

Discusses how military planners found little guidance on policy from the executive department and therefore developed
their own view of American national policy in the interwar
period.

82   Guttman, Allen. "Political Ideals and the Military Ethic." AMERI-
CAN SCHOLAR 34 (1965): 221-38.

Argues that, although often accused of being conservative,
even reactionary, the American professional soldier does not
resemble much the conservative model. The soliders' views
generally reflect liberal American society.

83   Halleck, Henry W. ELEMENTS OF MILITARY ART AND SCIENCE.
New York: Appleton, 1863. 449 p.

Earliest coherent, systematic analysis of military theory by an
American officer. Work shows the influence of Jomini on
American military thought.

84   Harsh, Joseph L. "Battlesword and Rapier: Clausewitz, Jomini and
the American Civil War." MILITARY AFFAIRS 38 (1974): 133-38.

Discusses the influence of Jomini and Clausewitz on Civil
War strategy. Concludes that Jomini's theory suggested paci-
fication of the South while Clausewitz suggested military force.
Both sides opted for the latter.

85   Hays, John, and Hattendorf, John, eds. THE WRITINGS OF STEPHEN
LUCE. Newport, R.I.: Naval War College, 1975. 262 p.

Six key essays by one of America's earliest military thinkers.

86   Hurley, Alfred F. MAJOR BILLY MITCHELL: CRUSADER FOR AIR
POWER. New York: Franklin Watts, 1964. 180 p.

87   Jones, Archer. "Jomini and the Strategy of the American Civil War."
MILITARY AFFAIRS 34 (1970): 127-31.

Shows how Jomini's strategic theories influenced, or failed
to influence, American Civil War strategy.

88   Kahn, Herman. ON THERMONUCLEAR WAR. Princeton, N.J.:
Princeton University Press, 1960. Reprint. New York: Free Press,
1969. 668 p.

Pioneering study which helped shape American nuclear strategic
thought in the 1950s.

89   Levine, Issac D. MITCHELL: PIONEER OF AIR POWER. New York:
Duell, Sloan and Pearce, 1958. 420 p.

90   Logan, John A. THE VOLUNTEER SOLDIER OF AMERICA. New
York: Peale, 1887. Reprint. New York: Arno, 1979. 706 p.

Diatribe against the undemocratic characteristics of the regular army, and plea for a citizen army by a former volunteer
general in the Civil War.

91   Mahan, Alfred Thayer. RETROSPECT AND PROSPECT; STUDIES IN
INTERNATIONAL RELATIONS, NAVAL AND POLITICAL. Boston:
Little, Brown, 1902. 309 p.

Collection of magazine articles by the well-known late nine-
teenth-century military theorist covering such topics as naval
expansion and international relations.

92   Mahan, Dennis H. ADVANCED-GUARD, OUTPOST AND DETACH-
MENT SERVICE OF TROOPS, WITH ESSENTIAL PRINCIPLES OF TAC-
TICS AND GRAND STRATEGY. New York: Wiley, 1869. 305 p.

Example of early American military thought. One of the
first arguments for the professionalization of the officer corps.

93   Maxim, Hudson. DEFENSELESS AMERICA. New York: Hearst International, 1915. 318 p.

Example of pre-World War I preparedness thought. Useful as
a source on the period prior to World War I.

94   Millis, Walter, ed. AMERICAN MILITARY THOUGHT. Indianapolis:
Bobbs-Merrill, 1966. 564 p.

An anthology of primary sources demonstrating how Americans have tended to think about war, military policy, and
the military factor in a free society.

95   Morton, Louis. "National Policy and Military Strategy." VIRGINIA
QUARTERLY REVIEW 36 (1960): 1-17.

Traces the efforts to achieve a balanced national defense
policy from World War I through the Korean War. Concludes
that a balance between military and political policy was
achieved after World War II.

96   O'Connor, Raymond. "The U.S. Marines in the Twentieth Century:
        Amphibious Warfare and Doctrinal Debates." MILITARY AFFAIRS 38
        (1974): 97-102.

        Traces the development of this concept of warfare from the
        idea of "expeditionary" through the concept of amphibious.
        Argues the doctrine arose as a response to the needs of the
        navy.

97   Pohl, James W. "The Influences of Antoine Henri de Jomini on Win-
        field Scott's Campaign in the Mexican War." SOUTH-WEST HISTOR-
        ICAL QUARTERLY 77 (1973): 85-110.

        Argues that Jomini was held in high regard by American pre-
        Civil War officers because a disciple of Jomini, Gen. Win-
        field Scott, had successfully tested Jomini's theories during
        the Mexican campaigns.

98   Posvar, Wesley W. AMERICAN DEFENSE POLICY. Baltimore: Johns
        Hopkins University Press, 1965. 471 p.

        Covers post-World War II military defense thought.

99   Puleston, William D. THE LIFE AND WORKS OF CAPTAIN ALFRED
        THAYER MAHAN. New Haven, Conn.: Yale University Press, 1939.
        351 p.

        Study of Mahan's military thought.

100   Sellen, Robert Walker. "The Just Man Armed: Theodore Roosevelt
        on War." MILITARY REVIEW 39 (1959): 53-64.

        An interesting, though somewhat superficial, account of
        Roosevelt's attitudes toward war and preparedness.

101   Smith, Dale O. U.S. MILITARY DOCTRINE: A STUDY AND AP-
        PRAISAL. New York: Duell, Sloan and Pearce, 1955. 256 p.

        Thesis is that air power has replaced ground forces. Study
        is weak on American military policy.

102   Stuart, Reginald C. "Thomas Jefferson and the Function of War:
        Policy or Principle." CANADIAN JOURNAL OF HISTORY 11 (1976):
        155-71.

Argues that Jefferson and founding fathers believed in just wars but also wars as instruments of policy.

103   Tarlton, Charles D.   "The Styles of American International Thought: Mahan, Bryan, and Lippmann." WORLD POLITICS 17 (1965): 584-614.

A discussion of three different styles of international thought that emerged in America just prior to World War I as represented by Alfred Mahan, William Jennings Bryan, and Walter Lippmann.

104   Tone, William T.W.   ESSAY ON THE NECESSITY OF IMPROVING OUR NATIONAL FORCES. New York: Kirk and Mercein, 1819. 112 p.

Early plea for American preparedness based on a European experiment theory by a veteran of Napoleon Bonaparte's army.

105   Upton, Emory. THE MILITARY POLICY OF THE UNITED STATES. Washington, D.C.: Government Printing Office, 1911. 495 p.

First study of American military policy, depicts policy as a series of disastrous mistakes. Influenced American military thought for several generations.

106   _____. THE ARMIES OF ASIA AND EUROPE. New York: Appleton, 1878. 446 p.

Although concerned with foreign armies, greatly influenced thinking of American military in the late nineteenth century.

107   Weigley, Russell F. THE AMERICAN WAY OF WAR: A HISTORY OF UNITED STATES MILITARY STRATEGY AND POLICY. New York: Macmillan, 1973. 584 p.

A scholarly analysis and interpretation of the development of military strategy. Argues that nation's wealth and its unlimited war aims led it to adopt a strategy of annihilation.

108   _____. "The Military Thought of John M. Schofield." MILITARY AFFAIRS 23 (1959): 77-84.

Discusses thought of Schofield as demanding that a nation's military strategy need not always be one of annihilation, but must be adjusted to meet the nation's goals.

109   _____. TOWARDS AN AMERICAN ARMY: MILITARY THOUGHT FROM WASHINGTON TO MARSHALL. New York: Columbia University Press, 1962. 297 p.

A scholarly study of American military thought, focusing on the struggle between the advocates of a citizen armed force and those who wanted a professional regular force.

C. CIVIL-MILITARY RELATIONS

110   Ambrose, Stephen E., and Barber, James A., eds. THE MILITARY AND AMERICAN SOCIETY. New York: Free Press, 1972. 322 p.

A collection of essays and readings on military issues in modern American society. The readings are by prominent historians, sociologists, and political scientists; the essays by Ambrose and Barber.

111   Baker, Newton D. "Newton D. Baker On Executive Influence in Military Legislation." AMERICAN POLITICAL SCIENCE REVIEW 50 (1956): 700-701.

A letter from Baker to Howard White, author of a book on executive influence on the military (see entry 174), commenting on civil-military relations since the Civil War and reflecting on his experience as Secretary of War in the First World War.

112   Blum, Albert A. DRAFTED OR DEFERRED: PRACTICES PAST AND PRESENT. Ann Arbor: Bureau of Industrial Relations, University of Michigan, 1967. 249 p.

A survey of America's conscription policies, focusing on the post-World War II period.

113   Brogan, Dennis W. "The United States: Civilian and Military Power." In SOLDIERS AND GOVERNMENTS: NINE STUDIES IN CIVIL-MILITARY RELATIONS, edited by Michael Howard, pp. 167-85. London: Eyre and Spottiswoode, 1959.

114   Challener, Richard D. ADMIRALS, GENERALS, AND AMERICAN FOREIGN POLICY, 1898-1914. Princeton, N.J.: Princeton University Press, 1973. 433 p.

Describes the interrelationship between military, naval, and foreign affairs during the period near the turn of the twentieth century.

115   Clotfelter, James. THE MILITARY IN AMERICAN POLITICS. New York: Harper, 1973. 244 p.

Analysis of recent American civil-military relation. Finds no conspiracy between industry, Congress, and military, but rather areas of common agreement and interest.

116   Cochran, Charles L., ed. CIVIL-MILITARY RELATIONS: CHANG-
       ING CONCEPTS IN THE SEVENTIES. New York: Free Press, 1974.
       366 p.

       Collection of essays by former and present Annapolis faculty
       members on contemporary civil-military relations. Nine es-
       says deal with the American situation.

117   Coles, Harry, ed. TOTAL WAR AND COLD WAR: PROBLEMS IN
       THE CIVILIAN CONTROL OF THE MILITARY. Columbus: Ohio State
       University Press, 1962. 300 p.

       A collection of eleven essays dealing with civil control of
       the military under varying circumstances. Included are es-
       says on problems of high command during World War II.

118   Davis, James W., and Dolbeare, Kenneth. LITTLE GROUPS OF
       NEIGHBORS: THE SELECTIVE SERVICE SYSTEM. Chicago: Markham,
       1968. 276 p.

       Provides important insights into the operation of America's
       post-World War II conscription system. Employs organizational
       analysis approach.

119   Dearing, Mary R. VETERANS IN POLITICS: THE STORY OF THE
       G.A.R. Baton Rouge: Louisiana State University Press, 1952. 523 p.

       Discusses the voting patterns of soldiers during the Civil War
       and then concentrates on the political activity of veterans
       working through the Grand Army of the Republic from 1864–
       1949.

120   Derthick, Martha. THE NATIONAL GUARD IN POLITICS. Cam-
       bridge, Mass.: Harvard University Press, 1965. 202 p.

       A study of the National Guard as a successful pressure group,
       with a useful historical survey of the guard in politics, from
       1870 to 1962. Weak on the military capabilities of the guard.

121   DeWeerd, Harvey. "The Federalization of the Army." MILITARY AF-
       FAIRS 6 (1942): 143–52.

122   Dillard, Hardy C. "Power and Persuasion: The Role of Military Gov-
       ernment." YALE REVIEW 42 (1953): 212–25.

       General discussion of the historical development of military
       governments, establishing the prevailing concepts and ap-
       proaches. Applies these to American military governments in
       World War II and Korea.

123   Eagleton, Thomas F. WAR AND PRESIDENTIAL POWER: A CHRON-
ICLE OF CONGRESSIONAL SURRENDER. New York: Liveright,
1974. 240 p.

Senator from Missouri tells the complex story of the constitutional and recent relationship between Congress and the executive in the area of war making.

124   Edinger, Lewis J. "Military Leaders and Foreign Policy-Making."
AMERICAN POLITICAL SCIENCE REVIEW 57 (1963): 392-405.

Surveys the social science literature on civil-military relations, analyzing the various concepts and models and discussing methodological problems.

125   Ekirch, Arthur. THE CIVILIAN AND THE MILITARY. New York:
Oxford University Press, 1936. 340 p.

A study of antimilitarism in American history, summarizing
American antimilitaristic thinking. Believes the tradition has
been well established but recently has been threatened by
the warfare state.

126   Gabriel, Ralph H. "American Experience with Military Government."
AMERICAN HISTORICAL REVIEW 49 (1943): 630-43.

Historical survey of American experiences with military government, focusing on the experience during the Mexican War
and in the Philippines.

127   Girard, Jolyon P. "Congress and Presidential Military Policy: The
Occupation of Germany, 1919-1923." MID-AMERICA 56 (1974):
211-20.

Discusses the struggle between Congress and the executive
branch over the retention of American forces in Europe after
World War I. Congress finally pressured Harding to remove
them.

128   Hacker, Barton C. "The United States Army as a National Policy
Force: The Federal Policing of Labor Disputes, 1877-1898." MILI-
TARY AFFAIRS 33 (1969): 255-64.

Argues that the army's involvement in labor disputes as a
national police force broke down its physical isolation from
society, but increased society's distrust of the army.

129   Halle, Louis J. "Civil-Military Relations: Historical Case Studies.
III. 1898: The United States in the Pacific." MILITARY AFFAIRS
20 (1956): 76-80.

130   Halperin, Morton H. "The President and the Military." FOREIGN
AFFAIRS 50 (1972): 312–24.

Argues that in deciding on defense matters, the military presents the President with special problems because he has little
control over membership in that bureacracy and they have a
virtual monopoly on military information.

131   Hanning, Hugh. THE PEACEFUL USES OF MILITARY FORCES. New
York: Praeger, 1967. 325 p.

Uses statistical approach to discuss the use of the military for
nonmilitary purposes. Includes a chapter on the United
States.

132   Hartz, Louis, and Hardin, Charles M. "The United States." In
CIVIL-MILITARY RELATIONS: BIBLIOGRAPHICAL NOTES ON AD-
MINISTRATIVE PROBLEMS OF CIVILIAN MOBILIZATION, edited by
Pendleton Herring. Chicago: Public Administration Service, 1954.

133   Hassler, Warren W. THE PRESIDENT AS COMMANDER IN CHIEF.
Menlo Park, Calif.: Addison-Wesley, 1971. 168 p.

Short monograph on the American executive's war and emer-
gency powers and his role as civilian head of the military.

134   Hauser, William L. AMERICA'S ARMY IN CRISIS: A STUDY IN
CIVIL-MILITARY RELATIONS. Baltimore: Johns Hopkins University
Press, 1973. 242 p.

Compares present trends in the United States Army to the experiences of the German Army after World War II, the French
Army after Algiers, and the British Army after empire. Suggests American Army undergoing a similar experience.

135   Haynes, Richard. THE AWESOME POWER: HARRY S. TRUMAN AS
COMMANDER IN CHIEF. Baton Rouge: Louisiana State University
Press, 1973. 359 p.

Careful study of Truman's employment of power as commander
in chief. Praises Truman's dedication, mildly critical of some
of his decisions.

136   _____. A LIGHT OF VIOLENCE: THE HOUSTON RIOT OF 1917.
Baton Rouge: Louisiana State University Press, 1976.

The story of the all-black 24th Infantry Regiment and its assault on Houston to avenge the beating of a black soldier.

137   Herring, Pendleton. THE IMPACT OF WAR: OUR AMERICAN DE-
MOCRACY UNDER ARMS. New York: Farrar and Rinehart, 1941.
306 p.

Survey of the influence of war on American society from the early national period to 1941. Analyzes the whole role of the military in American culture from the influence of the War Department to industrial mobilization.

138   Higham, Robin, and Brandt, Carol, eds. THE UNITED STATES ARMY IN PEACETIME. Manhattan: Kansas State University Press, 1975.

Ten essays on such topics as the army and popular culture, on the army and the economy in Iowa as a case study, on flood and disaster relief, and public health.

139   Howard, Michael. "Civil-Military Relations in Great Britain and the United States, 1945-1948." POLITICAL SCIENCE QUARTERLY 75 (1950): 35-46.

Compares and contrasts the problems of civil-military relations in the United States and Great Britain as a way of better understanding both.

140   Huntington, Samuel P. "Civilian Control and the Constitution." AMERICAN POLITICAL SCIENCE REVIEW 50 (1956): 676-99.

Discusses how the concept of civilian control of the military has changed over the years since independence and how "objective" civilian control has never been achieved.

141   _____. THE SOLDIER AND THE STATE: THE THEORY AND POLITICS OF CIVIL-MILITARY RELATIONS. Cambridge, Mass.: Harvard University Press, 1957. 534 p.

Seminal study of the American military establishment and an analysis of the most effective method of achieving civilian control. Argues for more thorough professionalization.

142   Huzar, Elias. THE PURSE AND THE SWORD: CONTROL OF THE ARMY BY CONGRESS THROUGH MILITARY APPROPRIATIONS. Ithaca, N.Y.: Cornell University Press, 1950. 417 p.

Effort to show how military budgets influence military appropriations, military policy, and administration. Thesis is that in recent years Congress has abdicated its responsibilities.

143   Jackson, Charles O., and Johnson, Charles W. "The Urban Frontier: The Army and the Community of Oak Ridge, Tennessee, 1942-1947." MILITARY AFFAIRS 41 (1977): 8-15.

Story of the corps of engineers' role as town developers and administrators of the atomic bomb production site of Oak Ridge.

144   James, D. Clayton. "The Commander Civil-Military Administrator: MacArthur in Japan, 1945-1951." ESSAYS ON NEW DIMENSIONS IN MILITARY HISTORY 4 (1976): 91-104.

145   Johnson, Charles W. "The Army, The Negro and the Civilian Conservation Corps, 1933-1942." MILITARY AFFAIRS 36 (1972): 82-87.

Discusses army's role in implementing the nondiscriminatory article placed in the Civilian Conservation Corps Act. Thinks that the army was only vaguely aware of the need for change in racial relations.

146   Karsten, Peter. SOLDIERS AND SOCIETY: THE EFFECTS OF MILITARY SERVICE ON AMERICAN LIFE. Westport, Conn.: Greenwood, 1978. 339 p.

Uses case studies to show how war affects military and non-military life in the United States. Topics cover recruitment, combat, training, homecoming and the effects on the serviceman's family.

147   Kemble, Robert. THE IMAGE OF THE ARMY OFFICER IN AMERICA: BACKGROUND FOR CURRENT VIEWS. Westport, Conn.: Greenwood, 1973. 289 p.

Cultural-historical study of America's conceptions of and attitudes toward the military profession. Emphasizes complexity of thought rather than a simplistic dualism of military-antimilitary conflict.

148   Kyre, Martin, and Kyre, Joan. MILITARY OCCUPATION AND NATIONAL SECURITY. Washington, D.C.: Public Affairs, 1968. 198 p.

Useful survey of the military administration of occupied territory from the Mexican War through Vietnam. Emphasizes relationship between domestic and occupational policies.

149   Lane, Ann J. THE BROWNSVILLE AFFAIR: NATIONAL CRISIS AND BLACK REACTION. Port Washington, N.Y.: Kennikat, 1971. 184 p.

Account of the Brownsville, Texas, raid (August 1906) and the reaction of the black community to President Roosevelt's order dishonorably discharging the black soldiers involved.

150   Larson, Arthur D., comp. CIVIL-MILITARY RELATIONS AND MILITARISM: A CLASSIFIED BIBLIOGRAPHY COVERING THE UNITED STATES AND OTHER NATIONS OF THE WORLD WITH INTRODUCTORY NOTES. Bibliographical Series no. 9. Manhattan: Kansas

State University Press, 1971. 113 p.

A broad bibliography but contains many entries on American military affairs.

151 Leach, Jack F. CONSCRIPTION IN THE UNITED STATES: HISTORICAL BACKGROUND. Rutland, Vt.: C.E. Tuttle, 1952. 501 p.

Covers period 1789-1865. Focuses on the Civil War period, but much background material on the revolutionary war period and the War of 1812.

152 Lerche, Charles O. "The Professional Officer and Foreign Policy." U.S. NAVAL INSTITUTE PROCEEDINGS 90 (1964): 24-29.

Argues that although traditionally the Defense and State Departments have been widely separate, physically and politically, today they share equally in making foreign policy.

153 Levontrosser, William F. CONGRESS AND THE CITIZEN-SOLDIER. Columbus: Ohio State University Press, 1967. 267 p.

Political scientist analyzes the nature of Congress's role in making reserve policy after World War II.

154 Lotchin, Roger W. "The City and the Sword: San Francisco and the Rise of the Metropolitan-Military Complex, 1919-1941." JOURNAL OF AMERICAN HISTORY 65 (1979): 997-1020.

Discusses the relationship and significance of the military in the growth of an urban area such as San Francisco and shows how the military shaped not only the city's development but its attitudes.

155 Lovell, John. "A Political Warrior or Soldier-Statesman: A Commentary." ARMED FORCES AND SOCIETY 4 (1977): 119-25.

Argues that Slater (see entry 169) misses the mark a bit. What is required is that both the military and civilians involved in the policy process understand the limitations of military solutions to vexing international problems.

156 Lyons, Gene M. "The New Civil Military Relations." AMERICAN POLITICAL SCIENCE REVIEW 55 (1961): 53-63.

Believes that traditional concept of civilian control has little significance for contemporary national security problems. The civilian has been militarized and the military has been civilianized.

157   May, Ernest R. "The Development of Political-Military Consultation
       in the United States." POLITICAL SCIENCE QUARTERLY 20 (1957):
       161-80.

    Discusses the slow but steady development of political-mili-
    tary consultation from early in the twentieth century to the
    post-World War II period, arguing that fifty years growth
    and experiment lay behind the creation of the National Se-
    curity Council in 1947.

158   Millis, Walter; Mansfield, Harvey; and Stein, Harold. ARMS AND
       THE STATE: CIVIL MILITARY ELEMENTS IN NATIONAL POLICY.
       New York: Twentieth Century Fund, 1958. 436 p.

    Survey of American civil military relations after 1930. Stresses
    the theme of the confluence of civil and military factors in
    national policy. Chapter on the Truman-MacArthur affair is
    very useful.

159   Molander, Earl A. "Historical Antecedents of Military-Industrial Crit-
       icisms." MILITARY AFFAIRS 40 (1976): 59-63.

    Discusses the origins of the criticism of the military-industrial
    complex throughout American history which laid the ideologi-
    cal basis for the criticism of the 1960s.

160   Morison, Samuel E., et al. DISSENT IN THREE AMERICAN WARS.
       Cambridge, Mass.: Harvard University Press, 1970. 104 p.

    Morison, and Harvard colleagues, Frederich Merk and Frank
    Freidel, discuss popular American dissent during the War of
    1812, Mexican War, and Spanish-American War.

161   Moskos, Charles C., ed. PUBLIC OPINION AND THE MILITARY
       ESTABLISHMENT. Beverly Hills, Calif.: Sage, 1971. 294 p.

    Collection of sociological essays on public attitudes toward
    present American military. Generally predicts a more socially
    isolated military establishment.

162   Nelson, Keith L. "'Warfare State': History of a Concept." PACIFIC
       HISTORICAL REVIEW 40 (1971): 127-43.

    Argues that "Warfare State" as a concept has a long and
    varied history. The idea that rulers, soldiers, and merchants
    could and would start wars dates to the early twentieth cen-
    tury.

163   Pursell, Carrole W., ed. THE MILITARY-INDUSTRIAL COMPLEX.
       New York: Harper, 1972. 342 p.

Collection of essays and readings that cast light on whether or not there is a military-industrial complex.

164   Sapin, Burton M., and Snyder, Richard C. THE ROLE OF THE MILITARY IN AMERICAN FOREIGN POLICY. Doubleday Short Series in Political Science. Garden City, N.Y.: Doubleday, 1954. 84 p.

A good introduction to the topic for the period after World War II.

165   Sarkesian, Sam C., ed. THE MILITARY INDUSTRIAL COMPLEX: A REASSESSMENT. Beverly Hills, Calif.: Sage, 1974. 340 p.

Papers emanate from a Ford Foundation sponsored conference. Uneven in quality. Mostly by political scientists and military sociologists.

166   Schiller, Herbert I., and Phillips, Joseph D., eds. SUPERSTATE: READINGS IN THE MILITARY-INDUSTRIAL COMPLEX. Urbana: University of Illinois Press, 1970. 353 p.

Articles on the social, economic, political, and psychological aspects of the military-industrial complex. Concludes the military-industrial is present and powerful.

167   Schlessel, Lillian, ed. CONSCIENCE IN AMERICA: A DOCUMENTARY HISTORY OF CONSCIENTIOUS OBJECTION IN AMERICA, 1757-1967. New York: Dutton, 1969. 444 p.

Documents presented chronologically in six sections, each section containing an introductory essay. Documents range from John Woolman to Martin Luther King, Jr.

168   Schonberger, Howard. "The General and the Presidency: Douglas MacArthur and the Election of 1948." WISCONSIN MAGAZINE OF HISTORY 57 (1974): 201-19.

Although MacArthur denied it, author concludes that the general was open for the presidential nomination in 1948 but his efforts went awry.

169   Slater, Jerome. "Apolitical Warrior or Soldier-Statesman: The Military and Foreign Policy Process in Post-Vietnam Era." ARMED FORCES AND SOCIETY 4 (1977): 101-15.

Argues that the drift toward more military participation in nonmilitary policy is potentially dangerous to American civil-military relations.

170   Smith, Louis. AMERICAN DEMOCRACY AND MILITARY POWER: A
       STUDY OF CIVIL CONTROL OF MILITARY POWER IN THE UNITED
       STATES. Chicago: University of Chicago Press, 1951. Reprint.
       New York: Arno, 1979. 370 p.

       A comprehensive insitutional study of American civil-military
       relations with a slightly promilitary bias. Emphasizes consti-
       tutional and administrative devices designed to maintain civil
       control of the military.

171   Social Science Research Council. Committee on Civil-Military Rela-
       tions Research. CIVIL-MILITARY RELATIONS: AN ANNOTATED
       BIBLIOGRAPHY, 1940–1952. New York: Columbia University Press,
       1954. 140 p.

172   Stein, Harold, ed. AMERICAN CIVIL MILITARY DECISIONS: A
       BOOK OF CASE STUDIES. Tuscaloosa: University of Alabama Press,
       1963. 705 p.

       Cases studied include the Far Eastern Crisis of 1931-32, the
       M-Day Plan in World War II, and the controversy over the
       B-36 bomber.

173   Tapson, Alfred J. "The Sutler and the Soldier." MILITARY AFFAIRS
       21 (1957): 175-81.

       Account of the relationship between a civilian entrepreneur
       selling goods to the military and the American soldier, 1775-
       1893, but mainly emphasizes the Civil War period.

174   White, Howard. EXECUTIVE INFLUENCE IN DETERMINING MILI-
       TARY POLICY IN THE UNITED STATES. Urbana: University of Illi-
       nois Press, 1925. Reprint. New York: Arno, 1979. 292 p.

       Still a highly useful, well researched study which explores
       the role of the president and his relationship with Congress
       in the shaping of military policy. Covers the period from
       just after the Revolution to World War I.

175   Wright, Monte, and Pazek, Lawrence J., eds. SOLDIERS AND
       STATESMEN: PROCEEDINGS OF THE 4TH MILITARY HISTORY SYM-
       POSIUM UNITED STATES AIR FORCE ACADEMY. October, 1970.
       Washington, D.C.: U.S. Office of Air Force History, 1973. 211 p.

       A collection of essays by prominent military and diplomatic
       historians focusing on civil-military relations at the policy-
       making level.

D. THE MILITARY ESTABLISHMENT

176   Addington, Larry H. "The U.S. Coastal Artillery and the Problem of
        Artillery Organization, 1907-1954." MILITARY AFFAIRS 40 (1976):
        1-6.

        Story of the intraservice struggle after Congress reorganized
        the artillery in 1907.

177   Ambrose, Stephen. DUTY, HONOR, COUNTRY: A HISTORY OF
        WEST POINT. Baltimore: Johns Hopkins University Press, 1966.
        357 p.

        Most recent and most scholarly history of the military acad-
        emy.

178   _____. UPTON AND THE ARMY. Baton Rouge: Louisiana State
        University Press, 1964. 190 p.

        Study of the officer who laid the foundation for America's
        modern professional military establishment.

179   _____, ed. "West Point in the Fifties: The Letters of Henry A.
        duPont." CIVIL WAR HISTORY 10 (1964): 291-308.

        A selected collection of informative and interesting letters by
        a member of the famous duPont family who attended the mili-
        tary academy in the mid-1850s.

180   American Military Institute. "The Reserves of the Armed Forces: A
        Historical Symposium." MILITARY AFFAIRS 17 (1953): 1-36.

        Collection of papers at an American Military Institute sym-
        posium. Contains articles on the reserves of all branches of
        the armed forces and a general survey of reserve policy since
        1945, plus a comment by John K. Mahon.

181   Ansell, Samuel. "Legal and Historical Aspects of the Militia." YALE
        LAW REVIEW 26 (1917): 474-80.

182   Baskir, Lawrence M., and Strauss, William A. CHANCE AND CIR-
        CUMSTANCE: THE DRAFT, THE WAR AND THE VIETNAM GENERA-
        TION. New York: Knopf, 1978. 320 p.

        An account of the system that provided the manpower for the
        Vietnam War. Argue that the draft greatly affected a whole
        generation of young people, even those who did not fight.

183   Bergey, Ellwood. WHY SOLDIERS DESERT FROM THE UNITED STATES
        ARMY. Philadelphia: Fell, 1903. 157 p.

A devastating, though unsubstantiated, indictment of the old army's inhumane treatment of enlisted men, including several first hand accounts of enlisted life in the infamous Jefferson Barracks, Missouri, in the 1880s.

184   Bigelow, Donald. WILLIAM CONANT CHURCH AND THE ARMY AND NAVY JOURNAL. New York: Columbia University Press, 1952. 266 p.

A study of the editor and America's most influential military professional journal in the pre-World War II period. Covers also Church's early life and his activities as a Civil War correspondent.

185   Bishop, Joseph W. JUSTICE UNDER FIRE: A STUDY OF MILITARY LAW. New York: Charterhouse, 1974. 315 p.

Sympathetic analysis of the system of military justice. Written in a light, somewhat casual style.

186   Boynton, Edward C. HISTORY OF WEST POINT, AND ITS MILITARY IMPORTANCE DURING THE AMERICAN REVOLUTION: AND THE ORIGIN AND PROGRESS OF THE UNITED STATES MILITARY ACADEMY. New York: Van Nostrand, 1871. 416 p.

An early history of the military academy. Dated but still useful for anecdotes.

187   Brayton, Abbott A. "American Reserve Policies Since W.W. II." MILITARY AFFAIRS 36 (1972): 139-47.

Surveys American reserve policies since 1900 and then focuses on post-World War II policies. Concludes that present reserve policy is the result of compromises among several competing interests.

188   Brinckerhoff, Sidney B. "The Army's Search For a Repeating Rifle, 1873-1903." MILITARY AFFAIRS 32 (1968): 20-30.

Traces the search for a standard issue rifle in the late nineteenth century which ended with the adoption of the Krag and then the Springfield, both of European origin.

189   Cantor, Louis. "Elihu Root and the National Guard: Friend or Foe?" MILITARY AFFAIRS 33 (1969): 361-72.

Many writers have criticized Root for neglecting the guard. Argues that Root ingenuously found a working compromise between the Guard's supporters and its detractors.

190   Coffman, Edward M., and Herrly, Peter F. "The American Regular

Army Officer Between Two World Wars: A Collective Biography."
ARMED FORCES AND SOCIETY 4 (1977): 55-74.

Projects thesis that typical officer during this period was forty
years old, veteran of World War I, a West Point or civilian
college graduate, and a southerner.

191   Colby, Elbridge. "Elihu Root and the National Guard." MILITARY
AFFAIRS 23 (1959): 28-34.

Deals with Secretary of War Root's attempt to pacify the National Guard while introducing professional military reforms.

192   Cosmas, Graham A. "Military Reform After the Spanish-American
War: The Army Reorganization Fight of 1898-1899." MILITARY AF-
FAIRS 35 (1971): 12-18.

Argues that the debate over army reform immediately after
the Spanish-American War raised most of the critical issues
of command and organization that Root later attempted to
resolve.

193   Cullum, George W. BIOGRAPHICAL REGISTER OF THE OFFICERS
AND GRADUATES OF THE UNITED STATES MILITARY ACADEMY.
9 vols. New York: Van Nostrand, 1868-1956.

Useful as a source for basic biographical career information
on graduates of the military academy.

194   Dupuy, R. Ernest. THE NATIONAL GUARD: A COMPACT HISTORY.
New York: Hawthorn, 1971. 194 p.

Brief, popular account.

195   _____. SYLVANUS THAYER, FATHER OF TECHNOLOGY IN THE
UNITED STATES. West Point, N.Y.: Association of Graduates, U.S.
Military Academy, 1958. 24 p.

Brief and somewhat incomplete. The only available account
of the father of the military academy at West Point.

196   _____. WHERE THEY HAVE TROD: THE WEST POINT TRADITION
IN AMERICAN LIFE. New York: Stoher, 1940. 424 p.

Popular account now supplanted by Ambrose's study (see entry 177).

197   Ellis, Joseph, and Moore, Robert. SCHOOL FOR SOLDIERS: WEST
POINT AND THE PROFESSION OF ARMS. New York: Oxford University Press, 1974. 291 p.

Analysis of the military academy by two former teachers at

West Point. Conclude that the academy has serious deficiencies.

198   Finn, James. CONSCIENCE AND COMMAND: JUSTICE AND DISCIPLINE IN THE MILITARY. New York: Random, 1971. 300 p.

Argues that soldiers deserve and should receive the same legal and constitutional rights as any other citizen, but do not.

199   Fish, Williston. MEMORIES OF WEST POINT, 1877-1881. New York: Batavia, 1957. 135 p.

A useful recollection of the author's experience as a cadet at the military academy in the post-Civil War period.

200   Fletcher, Marvin. THE BLACK SOLDIER AND OFFICER IN THE UNITED STATES ARMY, 1891-1917. Columbia: University of Missouri Press, 1974. 205 p.

Argues racism in the military before 1890 was discouraged because black soldiers were needed on the frontier. When this need ceased to exist after 1891, racism increased.

201   Flipper, Henry O. THE COLORED CADET AT WEST POINT. New York: Homer Lee, 1878. 322 p.

Autobiography of the trials and tribulations of the first black graduate from West Point. Flipper was finally court-martialed out of the army.

202   Foner, Jack D. BLACKS AND THE MILITARY IN AMERICAN HISTORY: A NEW PERSPECTIVE. New York: Praeger, 1974. 278 p.

A survey that reveals a constant pattern of discrimination against black soldiers. Presents a broad overview of blacks in the American military. Based on many sources but not well documented.

203   _____. THE UNITED STATES SOLDIER BETWEEN THE TWO WARS: ARMY LIFE AND REFORMS 1865-1898. New York: Humanities, 1970. 229 p.

Social history of the common soldier, 1865-1898 with emphasis on food, clothing, military justice, and punishment. Special chapters on Indians and Negroes seem to be an afterthought.

204   Forman, Sidney. WEST POINT: A HISTORY OF THE UNITED STATES MILITARY ACADEMY. New York: Columbia University Press, 1950. 255 p.

A very brief account of a complex and complicated subject. Ambrose's (see entry 177) is a better study.

205 _____. "Why the United States Military Academy Was Established in 1802." MILITARY AFFAIRS 29 (1965): 16-29.

Concludes that the military academy was established to meet the needs of an expanding military policy and was adapted to the conditions of American military and political life.

206 Galloway, K. Bruce, and Johnson, Robert B. WEST POINT: AMERICA'S POWER FRATERNITY. New York: Simon and Schuster, 1973. 448 p.

A muckraking account of the military academy but some points made are worth considering.

207 Generous, William T., Jr. SWORDS AND SCALES: THE DEVELOPMENT OF THE UNIFORM CODE OF MILITARY JUSTICE. Post Washington, N.Y.: Kennikat, 1973. 250 p.

Emphasis is on the difficulties of keeping military criminal justice up to date with corresponding changes in civilian law.

208 Greene, Robert E. BLACK DEFENDERS OF AMERICA, 1775-1973. Chicago: Johnson, 1974. 416 p.

A pictorial account that depicts black military personnel from the revolutionary war to the present. A useful reference book for the general public.

209 Hammond, Paul Y. ORGANIZING FOR DEFENSE: THE AMERICAN MILITARY ESTABLISHMENT IN THE TWENTIETH CENTURY. Princeton, N.J.: Princeton University Press, 1961. 403 p.

A thoughtful study of American military affairs in the twentieth century, focusing on the period after World War II.

210 Hampton, H. Duane. HOW THE U.S. CAVALRY SAVED OUR NATIONAL PARKS. Bloomington: Indiana University Press, 1971. 246 p.

Discusses how U.S. Cavalry worked to restore national parks after depredations under civilian administration in the 1870s and 1880s.

211 Heitman, Francis B. HISTORICAL REGISTER AND DICTIONARY OF THE UNITED STATES ARMY. Washington, D.C.: Government Printing Office, 1914. 685 p.

Useful source for biographical data on American officers.

212   Hewes, James E., Jr. FROM ROOT TO McNAMARA: ARMY OR-
       GANIZATION AND ADMINISTRATION, 1900-1963. Washington,
       D.C.: Government Printing Office, 1975. 452 p.

       Survey of the organizational and administrative development
       of the War Department and Department of Army. Focuses on
       the issue of control over men, money, and other resources
       required to raise and equip the U.S. Army.

213   _____. "The United States General Staff, 1900-1917." MILITARY
       AFFAIRS 38 (1974): 67-72.

       Argues that the Root organizational reforms and subsequent
       ones in the War Department reflected similar changes in in-
       dustry and faced similar opposition.

214   Hill, Jim Dan. THE MINUTE MAN IN PEACE AND WAR: A HIS-
       TORY OF THE NATIONAL GUARD. Harrisburg, Pa.: Stackpole,
       1964. 585 p.

       Popular, perhaps overly-sympathetic, account. Author looks
       at the National Guard as a national rather than a state insti-
       tution.

215   Hittle, James D. THE MILITARY STAFF. Harrisburg, Pa.: Military
       Service, 1949. 286 p.

       A historical study of the development of General Staffs, in-
       cluding the American use of a military staff, 1775-1949.

216   Huston, James A. THE SINEWS OF WAR: ARMY LOGISTICS, 1775-
       1953. Washington, D.C.: Government Printing Office, 1966.
       789 p.

       A comprehensive account of the army's experience in develop-
       ing an effective logistical system from the revolutionary war
       through the Korean War. Focuses on the means and methods
       utilized by the army to supply its forces and reasons for
       changes.

217   Ingersoll, Lurton D. A HISTORY OF THE WAR DEPARTMENT OF THE
       UNITED STATES. Washington, D.C.: Mohun, 1880. 613 p.

       A dated but still useful account.

218   Janowitz, Morris. THE PROFESSIONAL SOLDIER: A SOCIAL AND
       POLITICAL STUDY. New York: Free Press, 1960. 464 p.

In-depth sociological-historical analysis of the American military establishment in the twentieth century, based on documentary evidence, questionnaires, and interviews.

219   Just, Ward. MILITARY MEN. New York: Knopf, 1970. 256 p.

Sketches of recent soldiers from privates to generals. Provides illuminating and useful portraits of the modern U.S. Army.

220   Karsten, Peter. "The American Democratic Citizen Soldier: Triumph or Disaster." MILITARY AFFAIRS 30 (1965): 34-40.

Critical of those who argue that Korean War was the only one that produced defector POWs. Concludes that, historically, the citizen soldiers have never been a model but neither has America been a model military state.

221   Kennett, Lee, and Anderson, James C. THE GUN IN AMERICA: THE ORIGINS OF A NATIONAL DILEMMA. Westpost, Conn.: Greenwood, 1975. 339 p.

Useful historical survey of the politics of gun control and the meaning of guns in American society.

222   Korb, Lawrence J., ed. THE SYSTEM OF EDUCATING MILITARY OFFICERS IN THE U.S. Pittsburgh: International Studies Association, 1976. 210 p.

A collection of essays by social scientists on American military schools system.

223   Lewy, Guenter. "Superior Orders, Nuclear Warfare and the Dictates of Conscience: The Dilemma of Obedience in the Atomic Age." AMERICAN POLITICAL SCIENCE REVIEW 55 (1961): 3-25.

Argues that the dilemma of military obedience is magnified and more critical in the Nuclear Age when an individual officer may be asked to push a button that could destroy the world.

224   Little, Roger W., ed. HANDBOOK OF MILITARY INSTITUTIONS. Beverly Hills, Calif.: Sage, 1971. 607 p.

Essays by social scientists analyzing military institution from the point of view of organizational theory. Useful material on American military institutions.

225   London, Lena. "The Militia Fine, 1830-1860." MILITARY AFFAIRS 15 (1951): 133-44.

Determines that the militia fine was an ineffective method of coercing men into militia service.

226   Lyons, Gene M., and Masland, John.   "The Origins of the ROTC."
MILITARY AFFAIRS 23 (1956): 1-12.

Traces American military reserve policy, 1862-1956, focusing on the growth and development of the Reserve Officers Training Corps (ROTC) after World War I.

227   Lyons, Gene M., and Morton, Louis. SCHOOLS FOR STRATEGY:
EDUCATION AND RESEARCH IN NATIONAL SECURITY AFFAIRS.
New York: Praeger, 1965. 356 p.

Stresses how governmental groups influence national security affairs in the military educational establishments. Concludes that armed forces have met the educational challenge of the post-World War II era.

228   Margulies, Herbert F. "The Articles of War, 1920: The History of a
Forgotten Reform." MILITARY AFFAIRS 43 (1979): 85-89.

Argues that the Articles of War, 1920, passed as part of the Army Reorganization Act, liberalized the code of military justice and should be seen as a continuation of progressive reform.

229   Masland, John W., and Radway, Laurence I. SOLDIERS AND SCHOL-
ARS: MILITARY EDUCATION AND NATIONAL POLICY. Princeton,
N.J.: Princeton University Press, 1957. 530 p.

Examines the whole array of military education institutions, focusing on the three war colleges--Army War College, Naval War College, and Air War College. Focuses on the kind of education that provides officers with preparation for careers that involve formulating national policy.

230   Meiwold, Robert D. "The Army Post Schools: A Report From the
Bureaucratic Wars." MILITARY AFFAIRS 39 (1975): 8-11.

Uses post-school controversy as a case study of the army's managerial theory of organization in the nineteenth century.

231   Michie, Peter. LIFE AND LETTERS OF GENERAL EMORY UPTON.
New York: Appleton, 1885. Reprint. New York: Arno, 1979.
511 p.

Covers the struggle of Upton to establish professionalism in the American Army. Although Ambrose (see entry 178) is more interpretive, still an important source for understanding Upton's thought.

232   Millett, Allan R. THE GENERAL: ROBERT L. BULLARD AND OF-
      FICERSHIP IN THE UNITED STATES ARMY, 1881-1925. Westport,
      Conn.: Greenwood, 1975. 499 p.

      Analyzes Bullard's career as a case study in officership, with
      emphasis on pre-World War I and war period.

233   Morrison, James L. "Educating Civil War Generals: West Point,
      1833-1861." MILITARY AFFAIRS 38 (1974): 108-11.

      Contradicts the view that the military academy's fundamental
      pre-Civil War mission was to prepare cadets for combat.
      Argues that curriculum at the academy was not professional.

234   Morton, Louis. "The Long Road to Unity of Command." MILITARY
      REVIEW 39 (1960): 3-12.

      Discusses the period 1905-1941 as a prelude to unification of
      1950s.

235   Nelson, Otto. NATIONAL SECURITY AND THE GENERAL STAFF.
      Washington, D.C.: Infantry Journal Press, 1946. 608 p.

      Useful study of the development of the American General
      Staff system in the first decades of the twentieth century.

236   Neninger, Timothy K. THE LEAVENWORTH SCHOOLS AND THE
      OLD ARMY: EDUCATION, PROFESSIONALISM, AND THE OFFICER
      CORPS OF THE UNITED STATES ARMY, 1881-1918. Westport,
      Conn.: Greenwood, 1978. 173 p.

      Traces the school at Fort Leavenworth from the creation of
      Infantry and Cavalry School in 1881 to the Line and Staff
      College for mid-career officers. Argues that the school pro-
      duced competant operational officers who served the nation
      well in World War I.

237   Nyberg, Kenneth, and Snyder, William. "Program Structure and
      Career Socialization in the ROTC: A Bibliographic Note." MILI-
      TARY AFFAIRS 40 (1976): 179-81.

      Survey of the recent literature on ROTC indicating recent
      trends. Suggest areas for research.

238   Pappas, George S. 'PRUDENS FUTURI': THE UNITED STATES ARMY
      WAR COLLEGE, 1901-1957. Carlisle Barracks, Pa.: U.S. Army War
      College, 1967. 337 p.

      Useful history of the War College from its origins to the mid-
      1960s.

239   Powe, Mark B. THE EMERGENCE OF THE WAR DEPARTMENT IN-
       TELLIGENCE AGENCY, 1885-1918. Manhattan: Kansas State Uni-
       versity Press, 1975. 146 p.

       Surveys the evolution of the Military Information Division of
       the War Department.

240   Radine, Lawrence B. THE TAMING OF THE TROOPS: SOCIAL
       CONTROL IN THE UNITED STATES ARMY. Westport, Conn.: Green-
       wood, 1976. 277 p.

       Examines the army's efforts to control deviant behavior.
       Critical of these methods.

241   Ransom, Edward. "The Endicott Board of 1885-1886 and the Coast
       Defenses." MILITARY AFFAIRS 31 (1967): 74-84.

       Traces how Congress, even though concerned with coastal de-
       fense, failed to implement a study made in the 1880s and
       also failed to improve American artillery.

242   Reeves, Ira L. MILITARY EDUCATION IN THE UNITED STATES.
       New York: Free Press, 1914. 431 p.

       Early history of American military education.

243   Riker, William. SOLDIERS OF THE STATES: THE ROLE OF THE
       NATIONAL GUARD IN AMERICAN DEMOCRACY. Washington,
       D.C.: Public Affairs, 1957. Reprint. New York: Arno, 1979.
       129 p.

       A useful study of the Militia-National Guard as a state in-
       stitution from a meaningful historical perspective. Sees mili-
       tia as a response of federalism.

244   Risch, Erna. QUARTERMASTER SUPPORT OF THE ARMY, 1775-1939.
       Washington, D.C.: Government Printing Office, 1962. 796 p.

       Comprehensive history of the American Quartermaster Corps.

245   Rodenbaugh, Theophilus, ed. THE ARMY OF THE UNITED STATES:
       HISTORICAL SKETCHES OF STAFF AND LINE WITH PORTRAITS OF
       GENERALS-IN-CHIEF. New York: Maynard, Merrill, 1896. 741 p.

       Originally printed as "Historical Sketches of the United States
       Army" in the JOURNAL OF THE MILITARY SERVICE INSTI-
       TUTION OF THE UNITED STATES. Vols. 11-17, 1890-95.

246   Schoff, Morris. THE SPIRIT OF OLD WEST POINT. New York:
       Houghton-Mifflin, 1907. 289 p.

Revealing memoirs of the author's experiences at the military academy, 1858-62.

247   Scott, James B. "The Militia." Senate Document no. 695. 64th Cong., 2d sess., 1917.

Useful factual brief history of the militia.

248   Skelton, William B. "The Commanding-General and the Problem of Command in the United States Army, 1821-1841." MILITARY AFFAIRS 34 (1970): 117-22.

Discusses the debate over the nature of the commanding general system in the pre-Civil War period. Argues that because the debate never settled the matter, the result was tension and ambiguity later on in the twentieth century.

249   _____. "Professionalization of the U.S. Officer Corps During the Age of Jackson." ARMED FORCES AND SOCIETY 1 (1975): 445-71.

Determines that military professionalization coincided with other professional developments in Jacksonian society.

250   Smith, Paul. "Militia of the United States from 1846 to 1860." INDIANA MAGAZINE OF HISTORY 15 (1919): 20-47.

Describes the militia in its declining years as an institution sadly lacking in organization and discipline.

251   Stillman, Richard J. INTEGRATION OF THE NEGRO IN THE U.S. ARMED FORCES. New York: Praeger, 1968. 167 p.

Surveys past military racial policies focusing on post-World War II era, and the continuing strides toward integration of the armed forces.

252   Stone, Richard G. A BRITTLE SWORD: THE KENTUCKY MILITIA, 1776-1912. Lexington: University of Kentucky Press, 1978. 120 p.

Important state study that traces and interprets Kentucky's experience with the citizen soldier militia system from the Revolution to the nationalization of the militia in 1912.

253   Todd, Frederick. "Our National Guard: An Introduction to the History." MILITARY AFFAIRS 5 (1941): 73-86.

Even as an introduction, somewhat superficial. Useful on differences between the common militia and the volunteer militia.

254   Ulmer, S. Sidney. MILITARY JUSTICE AND THE RIGHT TO COUN-
SEL. Lexington: University of Kentucky Press, 1970. 114 p.

> Suggests that citizen soldiers in the twentieth century have
> given impetus to military rights because they have brought
> pressure on Congress for reform. Mostly an introduction to
> the subject but contains some analysis.

255   Vaughan, William P. "West Point and the First Negro Cadet." MIL-
ITARY AFFAIRS 35 (1971): 100-102.

> Story of the first Negro cadet (James W. Smith) to enter West
> Point Military Academy. Smith did not graduate but his room-
> mate, Henry Flipper, did.

256   Wade, Arthur P. "Roads to the Top: An Analysis of General-Officer
Selection in the United States Army, 1789-1898." MILITARY AFFAIRS
40 (1976): 157-63.

> Finds that prior to 1865 general officers chosen for political
> reasons; but from 1865 to 1898, Civil War experience was
> more important.

257   Windrow, Martin, and Embleton, Gerry. MILITARY DRESS OF NORTH
AMERICA, 1665-1970. New York: Scribner, 1973. 159 p.

> Describes appearance of the fighters of North America through
> one hundred illustrations and commentary.

258   Wolf, Charlotte. GARRISON COMMUNITY: A STUDY OF AN
OVERSEAS AMERICAN COLONY. Westport, Conn.: Greenwood,
1977. 324 p.

> A sociological study which concludes that American military
> forces overseas are poor exporters of good will.

259   Yarmolinsky, Adam. THE MILITARY ESTABLISHMENT: ITS IMPACT
ON AMERICAN SOCIETY. New York: Harper, 1971. 434 p.

> A broadly conceived assessment of the American military's
> role in post-World War II society. The study is thorough,
> calmly presented, and without polemics.

E. MILITARY HISTORIOGRAPHY

260   Agnew, James B. "USAMHRC: The Mother Lode For Military History." MILITARY AFFAIRS 39 (1975): 146-48.

> Brief history and description of present holdings of the United
> States Army Military History Research Collection at Carlisle
> Barracks, Pennsylvania.

261   Blumenson, Martin. "Can Official History Be Honest History?" MIL-
       ITARY AFFAIRS 26 (1963): 96–109.

       Author's answer is yes, official military history can be more
       than self-serving.

262   _____. "Why Military History?" ARMY 25 (1975): 33–36.

       Why military history? Argues it is a necessary ingredient for
       military statecraft.

263   Cole, Hugh M. "Writing Contemporary Military History." MILITARY
       AFFAIRS 12 (1948): 162–67.

264   Conger, A.L. "The Functions of Military History." MISSISSIPPI VAL-
       LEY HISTORICAL REVIEW 3 (1916): 161–71.

       Discusses the problems of writing military history. Accepts
       military history as serving didactic purposes.

265   Conn, Stetson. "The Army's World War II History and Related Publi-
       cations." In OFFICIAL HISTORIES, edited by Robin Higham, pp. 553–
       64. Manhattan: Kansas State University Library, 1970.

       A discussion of the writing of the Department of Army's World
       War II history series by one of the original participants.

266   _____. "The Pursuit of Military History." MILITARY AFFAIRS 30
       (1966): 1–8.

       Discusses military history as a meaningful scholarly endeavor.

267   Cooling, B. Franklin. "Technology and the Frontiers of Military His-
       tory." MILITARY AFFAIRS 39 (1975): 206–8.

       Argues that military history and history of technology have
       always been intimately connected and now must be rediscov-
       ered.

268   Ekirch, Arthur A. "Military History: A Civilian Caveat." MILITARY
       AFFAIRS 21 (1957): 49–54.

       Supports the civilianization of military history. Argues that
       trained historians should be analyzing and explaining this im-
       portant field.

269   Feld, Maury. "The Writing of Military History." MILITARY AFFAIRS
       22 (1958): 38–39.

       Argues for organizational analysis in the writing of military
       history.

270   Gordon, Martin K. "American Military Studies." AMERICAN STUD-
       IES INTERNATIONAL 15 (1976): 3-16.

       A recent critical survey of the literature of American military
       history. Covers mostly general works.

271   Greenfield, Kent. THE HISTORIAN AND THE ARMY. New Bruns-
       wick, N.J.: Rutgers University Press, 1954. 93 p.

       A collection of essays by the general editor of the U.S. Army
       in World War II series. Discusses some of the findings and
       conclusions of this scholarship and provides some insights of
       his own.

272   Higginbotham, Don. "American Historians and the Military History of
       the American Revolution." AMERICAN HISTORICAL REVIEW 70
       (1964): 18-34.

       Surveys historical interpretations of military affairs in the
       American Revolution. Analyzes what he determines are three
       distinct periods of historical writing on the American Revolu-
       tion.

273   Karsten, Peter. "Demilitarizing Military History: Servants of Power
       or Agents of Understanding?" MILITARY AFFAIRS 36 (1972): 88-92.

       Questions whether it is possible to write detached objective
       official history. Believes historians become the captives of
       the institutions they are serving.

274   Kleber, Brooks E. "History and Military Education: The U.S Army."
       MILITARY AFFAIRS 42 (1978): 136-41.

       Survey of the place of history within the Army officer's edu-
       cation at all educational schools from the Military Academy
       to the Branch service schools. History as a subject has had
       its ups and downs in these schools but doing very well today.

275   Lane, Jack C. "American Military Past: The Need for New Ap-
       proaches." MILITARY AFFAIRS 41 (1977): 109-13.

       Surveys major literature and then suggests new approaches
       through period studies and by viewing America's military past
       in terms of localism and the rise of nationalism.

276   MacDonald, Charles B. "Official History and the War in Vietnam."
       MILITARY AFFAIRS 32 (1968): 2-11.

       Discusses the work planned for an official history of the role
       of the army in Vietnam. Argues it will be difficult to write,
       but made easier by the earlier official history of World War
       II.

277   McLellan, David, and Reuss, John. "Foreign and Military Policies."
        In THE TRUMAN PERIOD AS A RESEARCH FIELD, edited by Richard
        Kirkendall. Columbia: University of Missouri Press, 1967.

        Discuss research opportunities in military history in the Truman
        era.

278   Mahon, John K. "Teaching and Research on Military History in the
        United States." HISTORIAN 27 (1965): 170–84.

279   Millett, Allan R. "American Military History: Over the Top." In
        THE STATE OF AMERICAN HISTORY, edited by Herbert J. Bass,
        pp. 157–82. Chicago: Quadrangle, 1970.

        One of the first surveys of American military history litera-
        ture. Enthusiastic concerning progress made to 1970.

280   _____. "American Military History: Struggling Through the Wire."
        INTERNATIONAL COMMISSION FOR MILITARY HISTORY ACTA, no.
        2, 1975, pp. 173–80.

        Author's second review of American military history literature
        critical of military historians for failing to establish a mean-
        ingful historiographical tradition.

281   _____. "The Study of American Military History in the United States."
        MILITARY AFFAIRS 41 (1977): 58–61.

        Analyzes the progress made in military historical scholarship
        since World War II. Gives cautious praise to that progress.

282   Millett, Allan R., and Cooling, B. Franklin, comps. DOCTORAL DIS-
        SERTATIONS IN MILITARY AFFAIRS. Manhattan: Kansas State University
        Press, 1972. 153 p.

        Divided into: "Studies in World Military History"; "Military
        Affairs of the U.S."; and "Studies of War and the Military."
        Supplements printed in MILITARY AFFAIRS in the following
        volumes: Vol. 37 (1973): 62–68; Vol. 38 (1974): 12–16;
        Vol. 39 (1975): 29–48; Vol. 40 (1976): 32–45; Vol. 41
        (1977): 21–25; Vol. 42 (1978): 37–54.

283   Millis, Walter. MILITARY HISTORY. Service Center for Teachers of
        History Publication no. 39. Washington, D.C.: American Historical
        Association, 1961. 18 p.

        Argues that technological innovations in nuclear weapons has
        reduced the usefulness of military history and created a need
        for a new approach.

284 Morton, Louis. "Historia Mentem Armet: Lessons of the Past."
     WORLD POLITICS 22 (1960): 155-64.

     Critical of the military history-as-lesson-school of writing.

285 _____. "Historian and the Study of War." MISSISSIPPI VALLEY
     HISTORICAL REVIEW 49 (1962): 599-613.

     Discusses the state of military history to 1962 and makes sug-
     gestions (pleads) for a greater effort by scholars in the field.

286 _____. "Sources For the History of World War II." WORLD POLI-
     TICS 13 (1961): 435-53.

     An early survey of World War II historical records, focusing
     almost exclusively on primary sources.

287 _____. WRITINGS ON WORLD WAR II. Service Center for Teachers
     of History Publication no. 66. Washington, D.C.: American Histori-
     cal Association, 1967. 54 p.

     Much similar to author's article in WORLD POLITICS (above),
     but including more secondary sources.

288 Nelson, Paul D. "British Conduct of the American Revolutionary War:
     A Review of Interpretations." JOURNAL OF AMERICAN HISTORY
     65 (1978): 623-53.

     Explores historical literature that argues that the British lost
     the war rather than that the Americans won it. Concludes
     that this scholarship is correct in its interpretations.

289 Possony, Stefan, and Smith, Dale. "The Utility of Military History."
     MILITARY AFFAIRS 22 (1958): 216-18.

     Defends the military's writing of military history.

290 Robinett, Paul, ed. GUIDE TO THE STUDY AND WRITINGS OF
     AMERICAN MILITARY HISTORY. Washington, D.C.: Office of the
     Chief of Military History, U.S. Army, 1954. 231 p.

     A dated but still useful bibliography. Arranged according to
     wars fought.

291 Ropp, Theodore. "Military History and the Social Sciences." MILI-
     TARY AFFAIRS 30 (1966): 8-13.

     Discusses how historians could make better use of findings by
     social scientists. Argues for an interdisciplinary approach to
     writing military history and suggests ways of employing social
     science findings.

292   Sandler, Stanley. "History and the Military." MILITARY REVIEW
       52 (1972): 26-31.

       Argues that history is not an oracle brimming with lessons,
       but it can give perspective and therefore is helpful, perhaps
       even necessary, to military study.

293   Scheips, Paul J. "Military History and Peace Research." MILITARY
       AFFAIRS 36 (1972): 92-96.

       Suggests that military historians must move from a narrow con-
       cept of lessons learned to a consideration of armed forces as
       agents of violence. Thus, military history is peace research
       by another name.

294   Weigley, Russell. "A Historian Looks at the Army." MILITARY RE-
       VIEW 52 (1972): 25-36.

       Argues that the military can find much in military history to
       guide them and give them solace, and that despite many
       times of troubles, the army has survived.

295   Wilson, Tyson. "The Case For Military History and Research." MIL-
       ITARY AFFAIRS 21 (1957): 54-60.

       An early argument for the place of military history in the
       academic and scholarly worlds.

296   Woodward, C. Vann. THE AGE OF REINTERPRETATION. Service
       Center for Teachers of History Publication no. 35. Washington, D.C.:
       American Historical Association, 1961.

       In view of the historic changes in weapons, tactics, and strat-
       egy after World War II, calls for reinterpretation.

297   Yarnell, H.E. "The Utility of Military History." MILITARY AFFAIRS
       8 (1944): 1-6.

       Discusses lessons students can learn from military history.

298   Young, Kenneth R. "The Stilwell Controversy: A Bibliographical Re-
       view." MILITARY AFFAIRS 39 (1975): 66-68.

       Examines Stilwell's military career in Asia and discusses the
       literary debate concerning that career.

299   Zobrist, Benedict K. "Resources of Presidential Libraries for the His-
       tory of Post World War II American Government in Germany and Ja-
       pan." MILITARY AFFAIRS 42 (1978): 17-19.

       This essay and the one following survey the holdings in all

Presidential Libraries from Franklin Roosevelt to John F.
Kennedy.

300   _____. "Resources of Presidential Libraries for the History of the Second World War." MILITARY AFFAIRS 39 (1975): 82–85.

Chapter 2
ORIGINS OF THE AMERICAN
MILITARY EXPERIENCE (1607-1783)

A. THE COLONIAL MILITIA AND COLONIAL WARS

301   Baker-Crothers, Hayes. VIRGINIA AND THE FRENCH AND INDIAN WAR. Chicago: University of Chicago Press, 1928. 179 p.

Focuses on Virginia's concern over the fur trade during the war.

302   Beers, Henry P. "The Papers of the British Commanders-in-Chief in North America, 1754-1783." MILITARY AFFAIRS 13 (1949): 79-94.

Describes and locates the manuscripts of each of the British commanders involved in the American Revolutionary War.

303   Bird, Harrison. BATTLE FOR A CONTINENT. New York: Oxford University Press, 1965. 376 p.

Narrative of the French and Indian War. Focuses on individual action in battle, rather than planning and strategy.

304   Boucher, Ronald L. "The Colonial Militia as a Social Institution: Salem, Massachusetts, 1764-1775." MILITARY AFFAIRS 37 (1973): 125-29.

Argues that as colonies became more militarily secure, the militia became increasingly social.

305   Buffington, Arthur H. "The Puritan View of War." COLONIAL SOCIETY OF MASSACHUSETTS PUBLICATIONS 27 (1930): 67-86.

Discusses the Puritan attitude toward war and describes the colonial New England military system.

306   Burns, John F. CONTROVERSIES BETWEEN ROYAL GOVERNORS AND THEIR ASSEMBLIES IN THE NORTH AMERICAN COLONIES.

Boston: Wright-Patter, 1923. 447 p.

Much material on the relationship between military affairs and colonial policy.

307   Caldwell, Norman W. "The Southern Frontier During King George's War." JOURNAL OF SOUTHERN HISTORY 7 (1941): 37-54.

Concentrates on the rivalry of the British and the French in the southern region in King George's War, 1744-48, and particularly on the role of the Indians.

308   Carter, Clarence E. "The Significance of the Military Office in America, 1763-1775." AMERICAN HISTORICAL REVIEW 28 (1923): 475-88.

Argues that, although it was established for defensive purposes, this administrative office took on more significance when conflict arose between England and the colonies.

309   Church, Benjamin. DIARY OF KING PHILIP'S WAR, 1675-1676. New York: Pequot, 1975. 226 p.

Invaluable primary source by an eyewitness of one of the most significant red and white conflicts in North America. Discusses Church's adaption of European tactics to wilderness warfare.

310   Clendenen, Clarence. "A Little Known Period of American Military History." MILITARY AFFAIRS 19 (1955): 37-38.

Like Morton (see entry 348) argues that American military started not with the Revolution but in the colonial period.

311   Cuneo, John R. ROGERS OF THE RANGERS. New York: Oxford University Press, 1959. 308 p.

A sympathetic biography marred by the absence of a discussion of Rogers' original tactics.

312   DeForest, Louis E., ed. LOUISBOURG JOURNALS, 1745. New York: The Society of Colonial Wars in the State of New York, 1932. 253 p.

A valuable collection of soldier narratives.

313   Dickerson, O.M., comp. BOSTON UNDER MILITARY RULE. Boston: Chapman, Grimes, 1936. 137 p.

Articles from the New York JOURNAL and Boston EVENING POST, 1768-69, dealing with martial law in Boston during the prerevolutionary crisis.

314   Drake, Samuel A. THE BORDER WARS OF NEW ENGLAND. New York: Scribner, 1897. 305 p.

Covers King William's War and Queen Anne's War.

315   Flexner, James T. MOHAWK BARONET: SIR WILLIAM JOHNSON OF NEW YORK. New York: Harper, 1957. 400 p.

Much material on Johnson's experiences in fighting the French and their Indian allies.

316   Freeman, Douglas S. GEORGE WASHINGTON. 3 vols. New York: Scribner, 1938.

Volume 1 covers Washington's early experiences as a colonial officer in the British Army.

317   French, Allen. "Arms and Military Training of Our Colonizing Ancestors." MASSACHUSETTS HISTORICAL SOCIETY PROCEEDINGS 47 (1945): 3-21.

Summarizes the colonists' English military background.

318   Furlong, Patrick. "Civilian-Military Conflict and the Restoration of the Royal Province of Georgia, 1778-1782." JOURNAL OF SOUTHERN HISTORY 38 (1972): 415-42.

Account of Archibald Campbell's efforts not only to fight rebels but also provide civil administration to the conquered areas of Georgia, 1780-82.

319   Galvin, John R. THE MINUTEMEN: A COMPACT HISTORY OF THE DEFENDERS OF THE AMERICAN COLONIES, 1645-1775. New York: Hawthorn, 1967. 288 p.

Detailed, descriptive account of the Massachusetts militia as a successful American military organi~ation.

320   Gipson, Lawrence. THE BRITISH EMPIRE BEFORE THE AMERICAN REVOLUTION. 12 vols. New York: Knopf, 1936-65.

Similar to Parkman's massive undertaking (see entry 355), but able to take advantage of more sources and a broader perspective. Much material on military affairs.

321   Greene, Jack P. "The South Carolina Quartering Dispute, 1757-1758." SOUTH CAROLINA HISTORICAL MAGAZINE 60 (1959): 193-204.

Discusses how South Carolina colony successfully resisted the quartering efforts of the British Army.

322   Hamilton, Charles, ed. BRADDOCK'S DEFEAT. Norman: University of Oklahoma Press, 1959. 133 p.

Collection of narratives from contemporary observers of the Battle of the Monongahela.

323   Hamilton, Edward P. "Colonial Warfare in North America." PROCEEDINGS OF THE MASSACHUSETTS HISTORICAL SOCIETY 80 (1969): 3-15.

324   _____. THE FRENCH AND INDIAN WARS: THE STORY OF BATTLES AND FORTS IN THE WILDERNESS. Garden City, N.Y.: Doubleday, 1962. 318 p.

Sets forth thesis that the French and Indian War was the precursor of total wars of the nineteenth and twentieth centuries.

325   Harkness, Albert. "Americanism and Jenkins' Ear." MISSISSIPPI VALLEY HISTORICAL REVIEW 37 (1950): 61-90.

Argues the War of Jenkins' Ear stirred latent feelings of distrust between the colonists and England.

326   Hart, F.R. "Struggle for Control of America." JOURNAL OF AMERICAN HISTORY 2 (1908): 315-31.

Covers War of Jenkins' Ear.

327   Hibbert, Christopher. WOLFE AT QUEBEC. Cleveland: World, 1959. 194 p.

Popular account but contains some sound analysis.

328   Jameson, Hugh. "Subsistence For Middle States Militia, 1775-1781." MILITARY AFFAIRS 30 (1966): 121-34.

Argues that, although the colonies resisted using the militia as regular soldiers, revolutionary conditions forced them to change.

329   Ketcham, Robert L. "Conscience, War, and Politics in Pennsylvania, 1755-1757." WILLIAM AND MARY QUARTERLY 20 (1963): 416-39.

Argues that conscientious resistance by Franklin and the Quakers in the 1750s gave them the experience to resist effectively when the time came twenty years later.

330   Knollenberg, Bernhard. "General Amherst and Germ Warfare." MISSISSIPPI VALLEY HISTORICAL REVIEW 41 (1955): 489-94.

Though some historians have argued that the British tried to start a smallpox epidemic among Indians, author denies the evidence is there.

331 Laning, John T. "The American Colonies in the Preliminaries of the War of Jenkins' Ear." GEORGIA HISTORICAL QUARTERLY 11 (1927): 129-55.

Discusses the American role in the outbreak of the war between Britain and Spain over control of trade in the Americas.

332 _____. "American Participation in the War of Jenkins' Ear." GEORGIA HISTORICAL QUARTERLY 11 (1927): 191-215.

Discusses the colonists' role in the war between England and Spain. Concludes that the American role was extensive and critical.

333 Leach, Douglas E. FLINTLOCK AND TOMAHAWK: NEW ENGLAND IN KING PHILIP'S WAR. New York: Macmillan, 1958. 304 p.

Most recent and most comprehensive account of King Philip's Indian War.

334 _____. "The Military System of Plymouth Colony." NEW ENGLAND QUARTERLY 24 (1951): 342-64.

Discusses the origins, development, and decay of the Plymouth militia system, 1620-85. Views it as a laboratory for studying the New England militia.

335 _____. THE NORTHERN COLONIAL FRONTIER, 1607-1763. New York: Holt, 1966. 266 p.

Several chapters deal with colonial wars against France.

336 _____. "The Question of French Involvement in King Philip's War." COLONIAL SOCIETY OF MASSACHUSETTS PUBLICATION 38 (1959): 414-21.

337 Lincoln, Charles H., ed. NARRATIVES OF THE INDIAN WARS, 1675-1699. New York: Scribner, 1913. 316 p.

Collection of six reprints of old chronicles on early New England wars with the Indians. Contains useful introduction and critical textual annotations.

338 Loescher, Burt G. HISTORY OF ROGER'S RANGERS. 3 vols. San Francisco: N.P., 1946.

Definitive study critical of Roger's effectiveness.

339 Long, John C. LORD JEFFREY AMHERST, A SOLDIER OF THE KING. New York: Macmillan, 1933. 373 p.

Utilizing correspondence made available in the 1930s, raises Amherst's reputation as a colonial officer of the Crown. Interpretation is sometimes casual and impressionistic.

340 McCardell, Lee. ILL-STARRED GENERAL: BRADDOCK OF THE COLDSTREAM GUARDS. Pittsburgh: University of Pittsburgh Press, 1958. 335 p.

A sympathetic biography of a much maligned general who died in the Indian ambush near Fort Duquesne in 1775.

341 McCormac, Eugene I. COLONIAL OPPOSITION TO IMPERIAL AUTHORITY DURING THE FRENCH AND INDIAN WAR. Berkeley: University of California Press, 1911. 96 p.

Dated but still the major work on this topic.

342 Mahon, John K. "Anglo-American Methods of Indian Warfare, 1676–1794." MISSISSIPPI VALLEY HISTORICAL REVIEW 45 (1958): 254–75.

Argues that trained regular soldiers were more effective than unorganized frontiersmen in breaking the power of the Indians.

343 Marcus, Richard A. "The Connecticut Valley: A Problem in Inter-Colonial Defense." MILITARY AFFAIRS 33 (1969): 230–41.

Discusses how intercolonial jealousies and particularism made it difficult for the British to develop an effective defense policy.

344 Mead, Spencer P. "The First American Soldiers." THE JOURNAL OF AMERICAN HISTORY 1 (1907): 123–28.

Discusses the organization of the Minutemen.

345 Mook, Telfer H. "Training Day in New England." NEW ENGLAND QUARTERLY 11 (1938): 675–97.

Shows how militia training day was as much a social as a military affair.

346 Morgan, Gwenda. "Virginia and the French and Indian War: A Case Study of the War's Effects on Imperial Relations." VIRGINIA MAGAZINE OF HISTORY AND BIOGRAPHY 81 (1973): 23–48.

Argues that rather than blunting the sensitivity of the colonies to British domination, the French and Indian War created many frustrations in Virginia and increased dissatisfaction.

347   Morton, Louis. "The End of Formalized Warfare." AMERICAN HERITAGE 6 (1955): 12-19.

Deals with the impact and influence of Indian warfare on early colonial military tactics, which changed from the more rigid ways to the more individual methods.

348   _____. "The Origins of American Military Policy." MILITARY AFFAIRS 22 (1958): 75-82.

An introduction to military policy of the colonial period. Argues that American military tradition was firmly established in the colonial period.

349   Nichols, F.T. "The Organization of Braddock's Army." WILLIAM AND MARY QUARTERLY 4 (1947): 127-30.

Discusses methods of recruiting colonials into the British Army.

350   Osgood, Herbert L. THE AMERICAN COLONIES IN THE SEVENTEENTH CENTURY. 3 vols. New York: Macmillan, 1904-7.

Chapter 12, Vol. 2 and chapter 15, Vol. 2 deal with colonial defense system in New England and South.

351   Paret, Peter. "Colonial Experience and European Military Reform at the End of the Eighteenth Century." BULLETIN OF THE INSTITUTE OF HISTORY 37 (1964): 47-59.

Sees eighteenth century warfare as less inflexible than usually pictured, reflecting some colonial experiences of British officers.

352   Pargellis, Stanley. "Braddock's Defeat." AMERICAN HISTORICAL REVIEW 41 (1936): 253-69.

Argues that the causes of Braddock's defeat lay in the quality of leadership—Braddock's refusal to follow fundamental tactics—rather than the quality of the men.

353   _____. LORD LOUDOUN IN NORTH AMERICA. New Haven, Conn.: Yale University Press, 1933. 399 p.

More than a study of the British commander-in-chief (1756-57). Also a monographic study of the French and Indian War.

354   _____, ed. MILITARY AFFAIRS IN NORTH AMERICA, 1748-1765: SELECTED DOCUMENTS FROM THE CUMBERLAND PAPERS IN WINDSOR CASTLE. New York: Appleton, 1936. 514 p.

Standard work for sources on American colonial wars.

355   Parkman, Francis. FRANCE AND ENGLAND IN NORTH AMERICA. 9 vols. Boston: Little, Brown, 1865-93.

This massive undertaking still remains the classic and one of the most readable accounts of colonial wars. Stirring and dramatic narrative.

356   _____. MONTCALM AND WOLFE. 3 vols. Boston: Little, Brown, 1894-97.

From the multivolume series covering the French and Indian Wars.

357   Peckham, Howard H. THE COLONIAL WARS, 1689-1762. Chicago: University of Chicago Press, 1964. 240 p.

A recent one-volume account of the British-French struggle. Chronicles the struggle for empire in America.

358   _____. "Speculation on Colonial Wars." WILLIAM AND MARY QUARTERLY 17 (1960): 463-72.

Discusses the variety of military organizations usually referred to under the common term "militia."

359   Quarles, Benjamin. "The Colonial Militia and Negro Manpower." MISSISSIPPI VALLEY HISTORICAL REVIEW 45 (1958): 643-52.

Account of the exclusion of Negroes from the ranks of the colonial militia, even in nonslave-holding areas of the north. Yet in times of peril, some men enlisted.

360   Radabaugh, Jack S. "The Militia of Colonial Massachusetts." MILITARY AFFAIRS 18 (1945): 1-18.

Argues that the militia was established in colonial Massachusetts because it was the most convenient military organization. Once established, it became an avenue to political success.

361   Rogers, J. Alan. "Colonial Opposition to the Quartering of Troops During The French and Indian War." MILITARY AFFAIRS 34 (1970): 7-10.

Argues that the British made a serious mistake when they left the quartering of troops to the British Army, for colonists saw this as violating the tradition of military subservience to civilian society.

362 _____. EMPIRE AND LIBERTY: AMERICAN RESISTANCE TO BRIT-
ISH AUTHORITY, 1755-1763. Berkeley and Los Angeles: University
of California Press, 1974. 205 p.

> Thesis is that the causes of the Revolution lay in the Ameri-
> can attempt to maintain an independent existence in the ever-
> expanding British empire.

363 Scisco, Louis. "Evolution of the Colonial Militia in Maryland."
MARYLAND HISTORICAL MAGAZINE 35 (1940): 166-77.

> Useful as an example of the traditional reliance of the col-
> onies on the militia for defense.

364 Sharp, Morrison. "Leadership and Democracy in the Early New England System of Defense." AMERICAN HISTORICAL REVIEW 50
(1945): 244-60.

> Argues that, although it was conceived in aristocratic tradi-
> tions of England, the New England militia was given new
> vigor under the democratic conditions of the frontier.

365 Shea, William L. "Virginia At War, 1644-1646." MILITARY AF-
FAIRS 41 (1977): 142-47.

> Account of Virginia militia against Indian hostilities. Shows
> how militia was capable of defending the colony.

366 Shy, John W. "A New Look at the Colonial Militia." WILLIAM
AND MARY QUARTERLY 20 (1963): 175-85.

> Discusses the variety of colonial militias. Thesis is that the
> colonial militia was not a static institution as usually pre-
> sented. It was a complicated institution that varied from
> colony to colony and changed over a period of time.

367 Sosin, Jack. "Louisbourg and the Peace of Aix-la-Chapelle, 1748."
WILLIAM AND MARY QUARTERLY 14 (1957): 516-35.

> Discusses how the peace treaty in 1748 ending King George's
> War angered New Englanders when they learned that the re-
> cently captured Louisbourg had been returned to France.

368 Stacey, C.P. QUEBEC, 1759: THE SIEGE AND THE BATTLE. New
York: St. Martin's, 1959. 210 p.

> Well-researched, carefully documented account of the Battle
> of Quebec with much military analysis leading to new con-
> clusions.

369 Thayer, Theodore. "The Army Contractors for the Niagara Campaign, 1755-1756." WILLIAM AND MARY QUARTERLY 14 (1957): 31-46.

Argues that army contractors were not as corrupt and incompetent as generally believed. At least in the Niagara campaign they performed admirably.

370 Van Every, Dale. FORTH TO THE WILDERNESS: THE FIRST AMERICAN FRONTIER, 1754-1774. New York: Morrow, 1961. 369 p.

Vivid popular account of battles during the French and Indian War.

371 Wade, Herbert. A BRIEF HISTORY OF THE COLONIAL WARS IN AMERICA FROM 1607 TO 1775. New York: Society of Colonial Wars in the State of New York, 1948. 120 p.

Brief synopsis of the colonial wars, adequate for a quick reference and introduction.

372 Waller, George M. "New York's Role in Queen Anne's War, 1702-1713." NEW YORK HISTORY 33 (1952): 40-53.

373 _____. SAMUEL VETCH: COLONIAL ENTERPRISER. Chapel Hill: University of North Carolina Press, 1960. 311 p.

Considerable material on Queen Anne's War.

374 Washburn, Wilcomb E. THE GOVERNOR AND THE REBEL: A HISTORY OF BACON'S REBELLION IN VIRGINIA. Chapel Hill: University of North Carolina Press, 1957. 248 p.

Discusses Bacon's rebellion as a failure of the militia to deal with the Indians.

375 Wilkinson, Norman B. "The Pennsylvania Rifle." AMERICAN HERITAGE 7 (1950): 3-5, 64-66.

Discusses the impact of the rifle on colonial warfare.

376 Wood, Gordon. THE CREATION OF THE AMERICAN REPUBLIC 1776-1787. Chapel Hill: University of North Carolina Press, 1969. 653 p.

Contains material on colonial antimilitary thought.

B. WAR FOR AMERICAN INDEPENDENCE

377 Adams, Randolph G. "A View of Cornwallis' Surrender at Yorktown."

AMERICAN HISTORICAL REVIEW 37 (1931): 25-49.

Recounts story of the Battle of Yorktown by surveying the correspondence between Cornwallis and Clinton, among others.

378   Adams, Randolph G., and Peckham, Howard. LEXINGTON TO FALLEN TIMBERS, 1775-1774. Ann Arbor: University of Michigan Press, 1942. 41 p.

Traces history of the Continental Army and its successor after the Revolution through original maps and letters.

379   Alden, John R. THE AMERICAN REVOLUTION, 1775-1783. New American Nation series. New York: Harpers, 1954. 294 p.

Authoritative synthesis of recent historical scholarship. Covers the Revolution in all its aspects, and argues that it was justifiable.

380   _____. GENERAL CHARLES LEE: TRAITOR OR PATRIOT? Baton Rouge: Louisiana State University Press, 1951. 369 p.

Account of Lee at Monmouth where he was convicted and disgraced by a court-martial. Criticizes the young officers responsible for Lee's predicament.

381   _____. GENERAL GAGE IN AMERICA: BEING PRINCIPALLY HIS ROLE IN THE AMERICAN REVOLUTION. Baton Rouge: Louisiana State University Press, 1948. 313 p.

Traces Gage's career in the colonies, how he held a low opinion of the colonials, and was recalled because of his outspokenness.

382   _____. THE SOUTH IN THE REVOLUTION, 1763-1789. Baton Rouge: Louisiana State University Press, 1957. 442 p.

Discusses the role of the South in the Revolution, the internal changes afterward, and the part taken by the South in forming the federal union. Useful on the military campaigns in the South.

383   Alexander, Arthur. "Desertion and Its Punishment in Revolutionary Virginia." WILLIAM AND MARY QUARTERLY 3 (1946): 383-97.

Argues that Virginia responded to massive desertion by passing severe punishment laws, but had little capability of enforcing them.

384   _____. "Exemptions From Military Service in the Old Dominion

During the War of Revolution." VIRGINIA MAGAZINE OF HISTORY AND BIOGRAPHY 53 (1945): 163-71.

Surveys the various exemptions allowed by Virginia and concludes that they were quite extensive.

385 _____. "A Footnote on Deserters From Virginia Forces During the American Revolution." VIRGINIA MAGAZINE OF HISTORY AND BIOGRAPHY 55 (1947): 137-46.

Argues that, though quite a few deserters were foreign born, the average deserter was an American.

386 _____. "How Maryland Tried to Raise Her Continental Quotas." MARYLAND HISTORICAL MAGAZINE 13 (1947): 193-95.

An example of the attempt to enforce compulsory service.

387 _____. "Service by Substitute in the Militia of Lancaster and Northhampton Counties During the War of the Revolution." MILITARY AFFAIRS 9 (1945): 278-82.

Surveys the conscription system in two counties in Pennsylvania and concludes that, like Virginia, exemptions were quite extensive.

388 Applegate, Howard L. "The Medical Administrators of the American Revolutionary Army." MILITARY AFFAIRS 25 (1961): 1-10.

Story of the origins, work, and development of the first medical department.

389 Augur, Helen. THE SECRET WAR OF INDEPENDENCE. New York: Duell, Sloan, Pearce, 1955. 381 p.

Story of Benjamin Franklin's successful effort to establish contraband trade between the colonies and France, Holland, and Spain, 1775-82.

390 Barnhort, John D. "A New Evaluation of Henry Hamilton and George Rogers Clark." MISSISSIPPI VALLEY HISTORICAL REVIEW 37 (1951): 643-52.

Argues that Clark and his exploits are better understood by studying his opponent, Hamilton, and by understanding Indian warfare during this period.

391 Barrow, Thomas C. "The American Revolution as a Colonial War for Independence." WILLIAM AND MARY QUARTERLY 25 (1968): 452-64.

Feels that attempts to put the American Revolution in the mold of European revolutions are misleading. America's was a "colonial war for liberation."

392   Bass, Robert D. GAMECOCK: THE LIFE AND CAMPAIGNS OF GENERAL THOMAS SUMTER. New York: Holt, 1961. 288 p.

Account of an unorthodox commander of a South Carolina militia force. Readable, with interest for the general reader.

393   _____. SWAMP FOX: THE LIFE AND CAMPAIGNS OF GENERAL FRANCIS MARION. New York: Holt, 1959. 275 p.

Deals with the partisan war in South Carolina, with Marion's camp, his marches and skirmishes, but fails to give the value of Marion to the Revolution.

394   Berg, Fred A. ENCYCLOPEDIA OF CONTINENTAL ARMY UNITS. Harrisburg, Pa.: Stackpole, 1972. 160 p.

Reviews briefly every regiment, battalion, and independent corps of the Continental Army.

395   Berger, Carl. BROADSIDES AND BAYONETS: THE PROPAGANDA WAR OF THE AMERICAN REVOLUTION. Philadelphia: University of Pennsylvania Press, 1961. 256 p.

A study of both British and American wartime efforts to propagandize Americans who were vulnerable.

396   Bernath, Stuart L. "George Washington and the Genesis of American Military Discipline." MID-AMERICA 69 (1967): 83-100.

A comprehensive analysis of Washington's approach to military discipline. Concludes Washington was successful during the revolutionary war in establishing effective discipline.

397   Bill, Alfred H. THE CAMPAIGN OF PRINCETON, 1776-1777. Princeton, N.J.: Princeton University Press, 1948. 145 p.

Brief but detailed account of the Trenton-Princeton campaigns. Argues that battle aroused the colonists anew and upset the British conviction that they could win by overrunning New Jersey.

398   _____. VALLEY FORGE: THE MAKING OF AN ARMY. New York: Harper, 1952. 259 p.

Account of the Continental Army under the personal direction of Washington, 1777-78. Tends to be sympathetic to Washington and unsympathetic to his critics.

399   Billias, George A., ed. GEORGE WASHINGTON'S GENERALS.
        New York: Morrow, 1964. 327 p.

        Essays on the military careers of Washington's generals, in-
        cluding Lee, Gates, Greene, Arnold Knox, and Wayne,
        among others. Clear well-written summaries.

400   _____, ed. GEORGE WASHINGTON'S OPPONENTS: BRITISH
        GENERALS AND ADMIRALS IN THE AMERICAN REVOLUTION. New
        York: Morrow, 1969. 362 p.

        Essays by authorities on a dozen British military leaders dur-
        ing the revolutionary war.

401   Bliven, Bruce. THE BATTLE FOR MANHATTAN. New York: Holt,
        1956. 128 p.

402   _____. UNDER THE GUNS: NEW YORK: 1775-1776. New York:
        Harper, 1972. 397 p.

        Popular account of New York on the eve of the Revolution.
        Believes New Yorkers were enthusiastic about independence.

403   Bolton, Charles. THE PRIVATE SOLDIER UNDER WASHINGTON.
        New York: Scribner, 1902. 258 p.

        A dated but nevertheless valuable study of the common revo-
        lutionary soldier.

404   Bowman, Allen. THE MORALE OF THE AMERICAN REVOLUTIONARY
        ARMY. Washington, D.C.: American Council on Public Affairs,
        1943. 160 p.

        Covers the general problem of morale, particularly the crises
        of December 1775.

405   Boyd, Thomas. LIGHT-HORSE HARRY LEE. New York: Scribner,
        1931. 359 p.

        Biography of the extraordinary career of a member of a famous
        Virginia family. Focuses on Lee's exploits in revolutionary
        war, for which he was ultimately court-martialed.

406   Boylan, Brian R. BENEDICT ARNOLD: THE DARK EAGLE. New
        York: Norton, 1973. 266 p.

        Traces the sequence of events that led to the Arnold defec-
        tion. Accepts Arnold's explanation that he did so to hasten
        the end of a bad war.

407   Bray, Robert C., and Bushnell, Paul E., eds. DIARY OF A COM-
       MON SOLDIER IN THE AMERICAN REVOLUTION, 1775-1783: AN
       ANNOTATED EDITION OF THE MILITARY JOURNAL OF JEREMIAH
       GREEMAN. De Kalb: University of Northern Illinois Press, 1978.
       333 p.

       Diary of a 17-year-old who served with Benedict Arnold and
       was twice captured and exchanged.

408   Butterfield, Lyman H. "Psychological Warfare in 1776: The Jeffer-
       son-Franklin Plan to Cause Hessian Desertions." PROCEEDINGS OF
       THE AMERICAN PHILOSOPHICAL SOCIETY 94 (1940): 233-41.

       Discusses the efforts to convert German mercenaries to the
       rebel cause. Concludes the effort was successful, because
       large numbers did desert.

409   Callahan, North. GEORGE WASHINGTON: SOLDIER AND MAN.
       New York: Morrow, 1972. 296 p.

       Readable, popular account that focuses on the eight years
       Washington commanded the Continental Army.

410   _____. HENRY KNOX: GEORGE WASHINGTON'S GENERAL.
       New York: Rinehart, 1958. 404 p.

       Account of the bookseller who became Washington's artillery
       commander and later the first Secretary of War. Biography
       falters when dealing with Knox's military roles.

411   _____. ROYAL RAIDERS: THE TORIES OF THE AMERICAN REVO-
       LUTION. Indianapolis: Bobbs-Merrill, 1963. 288 p.

       A general popular account of Tories during the Revolution.
       Mostly anecdotal.

412   Carter, Clarence E., ed. THE CORRESPONDENCE OF GENERAL
       THOMAS GAGE, 1763-1775. 2 vols. New Haven, Conn.: Yale
       University Press, 1931-33.

       Valuable correspondence of the British commander at the out-
       break of the Revolution. Contains much information on pre-
       revolutionary conditions.

413   Chidsey, Donald B. THE LOYALISTS: THE STORY OF THOSE AMER-
       ICANS WHO FOUGHT AGAINST INDEPENDENCE. New York:
       Crown, 1973. 213 p.

       Shows Loyalists as men of integrity who suffered personal
       sacrifices for their beliefs.

414 _____. THE TIDE TURNS: AN INFORMAL HISTORY OF THE CAM-
PAIGN OF 1776 IN THE AMERICAN REVOLUTION. New York:
Crown, 1966. 182 p.

Account of the battle of Long Island and New Jersey in the
winter of 1776. Mostly a popular, though interesting, narrative.

415 _____. VICTORY AT YORKTOWN. New York: Crown, 1962.
190 p.

Story begins with Arnold's betrayal at West Point, continues
with Washington's maneuvering and ends with Cronwallis's surrender. Popular, exciting account.

416 _____. THE WAR IN THE NORTH: AN INFORMAL HISTORY OF
THE AMERICAN REVOLUTION IN AND NEAR CANADA. New York:
Crown, 1967. 214 p.

Popular account of the capture of Ticonderoga by Allen and
Arnold and their attack on Canada.

417 Clark, Jane. "Responsibility for the Failure of the Burgoyne Campaign." AMERICAN HISTORICAL REVIEW 35 (1930): 542-59.

Argues most of the responsibility lay with General Howe.

418 Cometti, Elizabeth. "Morals and the American Revolution: Efforts to
Curb Luxury, Dissipation and Extravagances." SOUTH ATLANTIC
QUARTERLY 66 (1947): 62-71.

419 Commager, Henry S., and Morris, Robert B., eds. THE SPIRIT OF
SEVENTY-SIX: THE STORY OF THE AMERICAN REVOLUTION AS
TOLD BY PARTICIPANTS. 2 vols. Indianapolis: Bobbs-Merrill, 1958.

Mostly narratives of politicians and statesmen, but contains
many accounts by military participants.

420 Cumming, William P., and Rankin, Hugh. THE FATE OF A NATION:
THE AMERICAN REVOLUTION THROUGH CONTEMPORARY EYES.
New York: Phaidon, 1975. 352 p.

Successfully combines narrative with contemporary documents.

421 Cunliffe, Marcus. GEORGE WASHINGTON: MAN AND MONU-
MENT. Boston: Little, Brown, 1958. 234 p.

Argues that historians and others have turned Washington into
a monumental myth, a legend. Tries to demythify Washington in this unorthodox biography.

422   Dandridge, Danske. AMERICAN PRISONERS OF THE REVOLUTION. Charlottesville, Va.: Michie, 1911. 504 p.

A definitive narrative with a list of over eight thousand prisoners.

423   Davidson, Philip. PROPAGANDA AND THE AMERICAN REVOLUTION, 1763-1783. Chapel Hill: University of North Carolina Press, 1941. 460 p.

History of American propaganda before and during the Revolution. Covers such documents as pamphlets, broadsides, almanacs. Shows the decisive role of ideas in the Revolution.

424   Davis, Burke. THE CAMPAIGN THAT WON AMERICA: THE STORY OF YORKTOWN. New York: Dial Press, 1970. 319 p.

Popular account of the American victory at Yorktown. Sees Clinton as the goat and Cornwallis as a puppet of the English government.

425   _____. THE COWPENS-GUILFORD COURTHOUSE CAMPAIGN. Philadelphia: Lippincott, 1962. 208 p.

Argues that Nathanael Greene's campaign was critical to the rest of the revolutionary war.

426   _____. GEORGE WASHINGTON AND THE AMERICAN REVOLUTION. New York: Random, 1975. 497 p.

Popular narrative with focus on eyewitness accounts.

427   Dean, Sydney W. FIGHTING DAN OF THE LONG RIFLES. Philadelphia: Macrae-Smith, 1942. 320 p.

Account of Gen. Daniel Morgan's life focusing on his part in Braddock's defeat, the march to Quebec with Arnold, and experience through the Revolution.

428   Dorson, Richard M., ed. AMERICAN REBELS: NARRATIVES OF THE PATRIOTS. New York: Pantheon, 1953. 347 p.

Collection of contemporary popular narratives by participants spliced together by author to make an absorbing narrative. Covers period from 1777 to Yorktown.

429   Drake, Francis S. THE LIFE AND CORRESPONDENCE OF MAJOR-GENERAL HENRY KNOX IN THE AMERICAN REVOLUTIONARY ARMY. Boston: Drake, 1873. 160 p.

Contains useful letters concerning Knox's military experience.

430   Dupuy, R. Ernest, and Dupuy, Trevor N. THE COMPACT HISTORY
OF THE REVOLUTIONARY WAR. New York: Hawthorn, 1963.
510 p.

Mostly descriptive, popular account.

431   Dupuy, Trevor N., and Hammerman, Gay M. THE MILITARY HIS-
TORY OF REVOLUTIONARY WAR LAND BATTLES. New York:
Watts, 1970. 142 p.

Very brief descriptions of military tactics, maneuvers, and
results of revolutionary war battles.

432   Echeverra, Durand, and Murphy, Orville T. "The American Revolutionary Army: A French Estimate in 1777." MILITARY AFFAIRS 27
(1963): 1-7, 153-63.

A personal account by a young French officer who travelled
to America to observe the American insurgents revolting
against British rule.

433   Edwards, William W. "Morgan and His Riflemen." WILLIAM AND
MARY QUARTERLY 23 (1914): 73-106.

Narrative of Morgan's frontier force--"Knights of the Wilderness" in buckskins and carrying Indian axes--and its service
with Washington's Continental Army.

434   Elting, John. THE BATTLES OF SARATOGA. Monmouth Beach,
N.J.: Frenau, 1977. 96 p.

Brief account blames inept London ministry and incompetence
of Burgoyne for the British defeat. Basically an operational
history.

435   Epstein, Beryl, and Epstein, Samuel. FRANCIS MARION: SWAMP
FOX OF THE REVOLUTION. New York: Messner, 1956. 192 p.

436   Fisher, Sydney. THE STRUGGLE FOR AMERICAN INDEPENDENCE.
2 vols. Philadelphia: Lippincott, 1908.

Scholarly work still useful, though dated. Highly critical of
the American effort.

437   Fitzpatrick, John C. THE SPIRIT OF REVOLUTION. Boston: Houghton-Mifflin, 1924. 300 p.

Much information and interesting observations on the private
revolutionary soldier.

438 _____ , ed. THE WRITINGS OF GEORGE WASHINGTON FROM THE ORIGINAL MANUSCRIPT SOURCES, 1745-1781. 39 vols. Washington, D.C.: Government Printing Office, 1931-44.

Volumes 5-20 cover the revolutionary war. An indispensable primary source.

439 Fleming, Thomas J. BEAT THE LAST DRUM: THE SEIGE OF YORK-TOWN, 1781. New York: St. Martin's, 1963. 375 p.

Tells story of the last revolutionary battle by combining quotations from the diaries and letters of participants with his own text. Appraises Washington favorably, but criticizes Cornwallis and Clinton.

440 Flexner, James T. GEORGE WASHINGTON IN THE AMERICAN REVOLUTION. Boston: Little, Brown, 1968. 599 p.

Covers in detail the administration of Washington's main army.

441 _____ . TRAITOR AND THE SPY: BENEDICT ARNOLD AND JOHN ANDRE. New York: Harcourt, Brace, 1953. 431 p.

Dual biography which actually covers the fatal relationship between three characters: Arnold, Andre and Arnold's second wife, Peggy Shippen. Little original interpretation and few new details but excitingly written.

442 Ford, Worthington C., et al., eds. JOURNALS OF THE CONTINENTAL CONGRESS. 34 vols. Washington, D.C.: Government Printing Office, 1934-37.

Basic primary source for military affairs during this era.

443 Freeman, Douglas. GEORGE WASHINGTON. 7 vols. New York: Scribner, 1948-57.

Definitive study of Washington as officer and commander. Volume 3 emphasizes origins of the Continental Army. Volumes 4 and 5 deal with revolutionary campaigns.

444 French, Allen. THE DAY OF CONCORD AND LEXINGTON: THE NINETEENTH OF APRIL, 1775. Boston: Little, Brown, 1925. 295 p.

Detailed study of a single day of battle. Focuses on the military events that transpired after the skirmish at Concord and Lexington.

445 _____ . THE FIRST YEAR OF THE REVOLUTION. Boston: Houghton-Mifflin, 1934. 795 p.

Focuses on the creation of the Continental Army.

446 _____. GENERAL GAGE'S INFORMERS: NEW MATERIALS ON LEXINGTON AND CONCORD. Ann Arbor: University of Michigan Press, 1932. Reprint. New York: Greenwood, 1968. 207 p.

Tries to answer the question of what was the secret information that caused Gage to strike at Concord.

447 _____. THE SIEGE OF BOSTON. New York: Macmillan, 1911. 450 p.

A well-developed narrative of the siege of the city of Boston by Washington's army. Dated, but still valuable.

448 _____. THE TAKING OF TICONDEROGA IN 1775: THE BRITISH STORY: A STUDY OF CAPTORS AND CAPTIVES. Cambridge, Mass.: Harvard University Press, 1928. 90 p.

Thesis that Arnold was present and in command during the capture of Fort Ticonderoga. Believes Ethan Allen must share glory of capture.

449 Frothingham, Thomas G. WASHINGTON, COMMANDER IN CHIEF. New York: Houghton-Mifflin, 1930. 405 p.

Effort at appraising the part played by Washington as military chief of the American Revolution.

450 Gerlach, Don R. PHILIP SCHUYLER AND THE AMERICAN REVOLUTION IN NEW YORK. Lincoln: University of Nebraska Press, 1964. 358 p.

Deals with Schuyler as a politician but also as a revolutionary general. Focuses on Schuyler's dismissal before the battle of Saratoga.

451 Gerson, Noel B. LIGHT-HORSE HARRY: A BIOGRAPHY OF WASHINGTON'S GREAT CAVALRYMAN, GENERAL HENRY LEE. Garden City, N.Y.: Doubleday, 1966. 257 p.

Useful short biography of an exciting general with focus on military operations in which Lee was a participant.

452 Gottschalk, Louis R. LAFAYETTE AND THE CLOSE OF THE AMERICAN REVOLUTION. Chicago: University of Chicago Press, 1942. 458 p.

A standard account of the Yorktown campaign and Cornwallis's surrender.

453 _____. LAFAYETTE JOINS THE AMERICAN ARMY. Chicago: University of Chicago Press, 1937. 364 p.

A standard account of the early years of the revolutionary war.

454 Greene, Francis V. THE REVOLUTIONARY WAR AND THE MILITARY POLICY OF THE UNITED STATES. New York: Scribner, 1911. 350 p.

Discusses the influence of revolutionary war campaigns on future American military policy. Dated but still useful.

455 Gruber, Ira D. THE HOWE BROTHERS AND THE AMERICAN REVOLUTION. New York: Atheneum, 1972. 396 p.

Account of how the Howe brothers, sent by the English government to end the revolt, lost the colonies instead.

456 Hall, Robert C. "The Beginnings of American Military Medicine." ANNALS OF MEDICAL HISTORY 4 (1942): 122-31.

457 Haskett, Richard C. "Prosecuting the Revolution." AMERICAN HISTORICAL REVIEW 59 (1954): 578-87.

Discusses the legal struggle between patriots and loyalists that went on behind the military lines. Focuses on the attorney generals of the states.

458 Hatch, Louis C. THE ADMINISTRATION OF THE AMERICAN REVOLUTIONARY ARMY. New York: Longmans, 1904. 229 p.

Dated but still the best on the subject. Discusses the evolution of the Continental Army and explores its relationship with the Continental Congress. Valuable chapter on the appointment and promotion of officers.

459 Heitman, Francis B. HISTORICAL REGISTER OF OFFICERS OF THE CONTINENTAL ARMY. Washington, D.C.: Rare Book, 1914. 410 p.

Extremely useful primary source. Contains over fourteen thousand names of Continental Army officers.

460 Higginbotham, Don. DANIEL MORGAN: REVOLUTIONARY RIFLEMAN. Chapel Hill: University of North Carolina Press, 1961. 239 p.

Authoritative biography of a colorful revolutionary war general whose sharpshooting riflemen played a critical role in the battles of Quebec, Saratoga, and Cowpens. Scholarly and well documented.

461 _____. THE WAR OF AMERICAN INDEPENDENCE: MILITARY AT-
TITUDES, POLICIES, AND PRACTICE, 1763-1789. New York: Macmillan, 1971. 509 p.

Analyzes the war from the broad perspective that armies reflect the societies they serve and that war produces a significant effect on society.

462 _____, ed. RECONSIDERATIONS ON THE REVOLUTIONARY WAR:
SELECTED ESSAYS. Westport, Conn.: Greenwood, 1978. 217 p.

Essays by prominent scholars covering such topics as logistics
and supplies, strategy, civil-military relations, and the war
in historical perspective. Thus goes beyond campaigns and
considers the long range effects of the war.

463 Hudleston, Francis J. GENTLEMAN JOHNNY BURGOYNE: MIS-
ADVENTURES OF AN ENGLISH GENERAL IN THE REVOLUTION.
Indianapolis: Bobbs-Merrill, 1927. 367 p.

Covers Burgoyne's experience in the battle of Bunker Hill,
the Saratoga campaign, and contains material on Cambridge
and the convention troops.

464 Jackson, Luther P. "Virginia Negro Soldiers and Seamen in the American Revolution." JOURNAL OF NEGRO HISTORY 27 (1942): 247-
87.

Traces the large contingent of blacks who served in the revolutionary services. Contains a list of names.

465 James, James A. THE LIFE OF GEORGE ROGERS CLARK. Chicago:
University of Chicago Press, 1928. 534 p.

Scholarly, comprehensive study of Clark's military experience
in the Northwest. Dated but still useful.

466 Johnston, Henry P. THE YORKTOWN CAMPAIGN AND THE SUR-
RENDER OF CORNWALLIS, 1781. New York: Harper, 1881. Reprint. New York: DaCapo, 1971. 206 p.

Remains one of the standard accounts of the campaign. Based
primarily on Washington's journal.

467 Jollison, Charles A. ETHAN ALLEN: FRONTIER REBEL. Syracuse,
N.Y.: Syracuse University Press, 1969. 360 p.

Lively narrative of the leader of Green Mountain boys. Author paints Allen as a boisterous, larger-than-life figure.
Lacks analysis.

468   Kaplan, Sydney. THE BLACK PRESENCE IN THE ERA OF THE AMER-
        ICAN REVOLUTION, 1770-1800. New York: Graphic Society,
        1977. 211 p.

        Short biographies of blacks who were involved in the Revolu-
        tion. Contains illustrations from an exhibition in the Na-
        tional Art Gallery.

469   _____. "Rank and Status Among Massachusetts Continental Officers."
        AMERICAN HISTORICAL REVIEW 56 (1950): 318-26.

        Argues that equalitarian tendencies in officer corps of the
        Massachusetts line of the Continental Army help explain the
        Newburgh Conspiracy.

470   Ketchum, Richard. THE BATTLE FOR BUNKER HILL. Garden City,
        N.Y.: Doubleday, 1962. 232 p.

        Based on sound scholarship, and places battle in its proper
        historical perspective. Deals with its causes, its develop-
        ment, who was responsible, and its effects.

471   _____. THE WINTER SOLDIERS. Garden City, N.Y.: Doubleday,
        1973. 435 p.

        Covers the first year of the revolutionary war. Focuses on
        military operations and methods of fighting.

472   Knollenberg, Bernard. "Bunker Hill Re-viewed: A Study of the Con-
        flict of Historical Evidence." PROCEEDINGS OF MASSACHUSETTS
        HISTORICAL SOCIETY 71 (1960): 84-100.

473   _____. WASHINGTON AND THE REVOLUTION, A REAPPRAISAL:
        GATES, CONWAY, AND THE CONTINENTAL CONGRESS. New
        York: Macmillan, 1940. 269 p.

        Suggests that historians' reverence for Washington has obscured
        the extensive political in-fighting in the Continental Army.

474   Knopf, Richard C., ed. ANTHONY WAYNE: A NAME IN ARMS.
        Pittsburgh: University of Pittsburgh Press, 1960. 568 p.

        A collection of the Wayne-Knox-Pickering-McHenry corre-
        spondence.

475   Lancaster, Bruce. FROM LEXINGTON TO LIBERTY: THE STORY OF
        THE AMERICAN REVOLUTION. Garden City, N.Y.: Doubleday,
        1955. 470 p.

        Popular, narrative of the Revolution from its origins to Wash-
        ington's farewell to the Continental Army.

476   Lawrence, Alexander A. STORM OVER SAVANNAH: THE STORY OF COUNT d'ESTAING AND THE SIEGE OF THE TOWN IN 1779. Athens: University of Georgia Press, 1951. 220 p.

Account of the unsuccessful Franco-American seige of Savannah in 1779, told in detail and with scholarly accuracy.

477   Lee, Charles. THE LEE PAPERS, 1754-1811. 4 vols. New York: New York Historical Society, 1872-75.

Important primary source on revolutionary and early American history.

478   Lee, Henry. CAMPAIGN OF 1781 IN THE CAROLINAS. 1824. Reprint. Chicago: Quadrangle, 1962. 511 p.

Reprint of memoirs. One of the most valuable personal accounts of a participant in the revolutionary war.

479   Lengyel, Cornell I. BENEDICT ARNOLD: THE ANATOMY OF TREASON. New York: Doubleday, 1960. 237 p.

Account of Arnold's uncertain and sometimes ambiguous behavior in the American Army and his defection to the British in 1788. Also covers his unhappy experiences in England after the war.

480   Lossing, Benson J. THE LIFE AND TIMES OF PHILIP SCHUYLER. 2 vols. New York: Sheldon, 1873. Reprint. New York: DaCapo, 1973.

481   Lundin, Leonard. COCKPIT OF THE REVOLUTION: THE WAR FOR INDEPENDENCE IN NEW JERSEY. Princeton, N.J.: Princeton University Press, 1940. 463 p.

Useful survey of military operations in New Jersey. Presents the Revolution in microcosm.

482   Mackesy, Piers. THE WAR FOR AMERICA, 1775-1783. Cambridge, Mass.: Harvard University Press, 1964. 565 p.

Discusses the war strategy from the point of view of the British government, thus places the war in its global context. Useful for its coverage of military affairs.

483   Maurer, Maurer. "Military Justice Under Washington." MILITARY AFFAIRS 28 (1964): 8-16.

Problems Washington faced in maintaining discipline in a war for freedom.

484   Metzger, Charles. THE PRISONER IN THE AMERICAN REVOLUTION.
       Chicago: Loyola University Press, 1971.

       Discusses treatment of prisoners, their management, their
       feeding, complaints, and redresses. Argues British treated
       American prisoners as prisoners of war rather than as rebels.

485   Miller, John C. ALEXANDER HAMILTON: PORTRAIT IN PARADOX.
       New York: Harper, 1959. 659 p.

       Contains much useful information on Hamilton's military serv-
       ice.

486   _____. TRIUMPH OF FREEDOM, 1775-1783. Boston: Little, Brown,
       1948. 718 p.

       Account of the American revolutionary period, written in
       clear, smooth style but undocumented and lacks authenticity.

487   Mitchell, Broadus. THE PRICE OF INDEPENDENCE: A REALISTIC
       VIEW OF THE AMERICAN REVOLUTION. New York: Oxford Uni-
       versity Press, 1974. 374 p.

       Essays on the seamier side of the war including mutinies, dis-
       eases, and horrors of prisons.

488   Mitchell, Joseph B. DISCIPLINE AND BAYONETS: THE ARMIES
       AND LEADERS IN THE WAR OF THE AMERICAN REVOLUTION.
       New York: Putnam, 1967. 223 p.

       An analysis of the way in which both British and American
       commanders approached the problems of war. Focuses on the
       individual concepts of strategy.

489   Montross, Lynn. RAG, TAG, AND BOBTAIL: THE STORY OF THE
       CONTINENTAL ARMY. New York: Harper, 1952. 519 p.

       Popular account of America's first armed force. Discusses
       army administration and supply, but still a history of battles
       and campaigns.

490   _____. THE RELUCTANT REBELS: THE STORY OF THE CONTINEN-
       TAL CONGRESS, 1774-1789. New York: Harper, 1950. 467 p.

       Account of the organization of and membership in the Conti-
       nental Congress and how it responded to war. Much material
       on military affairs.

491   Moore, Frank, ed. DIARY OF THE AMERICAN REVOLUTION FROM
       NEWSPAPERS AND ORIGINAL DOCUMENTS. 2 vols. New York:
       Scribner, 1960. 605 p.

A basic source for research in the revolutionary period. Contains a broad range of documentary material.

492   Murdock, Harold. THE NINETEENTH OF APRIL, 1775. Boston: Houghton-Mifflin, 1923. 134 p.

Readable account of the unusual day when three major battles occurred: Lexington, Concord, and Charleston.

493   Murphy, Orville T. "The Revolutionary Army and the Concept of 'Leve en Masse.'" MILITARY AFFAIRS 23 (1959): 13-20.

Discusses French nation-in-arms concept as reflected in the American revolutionary army.

494   Nell, William C. THE COLORED PATRIOTS OF THE AMERICAN REVOLUTION. Boston: Walcott, 1855. Reprint. New York: Arno Press, 1968. 275 p.

Early attempt to establish the role of the blacks in the American Revolution. Sketches several preminent black leaders and describes conditions of their participation.

495   Nelson, Paul D. GENERAL HORATIO GATES: A BIOGRAPHY. Baton Rouge: Louisiana State University Press, 1976. 319 p.

Biography of one of Washington's military commanders whose abilities were sometimes negated by his inability to get along with his colleagues.

496   _____. "Horatio Gates in the Southern Department, 1780: Serious Errors and a Costly Defeat." NORTH CAROLINA HISTORICAL REVIEW 50 (1973): 256-72.

Discusses why Gates, a successful commander at Saratoga, made serious errors of judgment and of leadership in the South.

497   _____. "Legacy of Controversy: Gates, Schuyler, and Arnold at Saratoga, 1777." MILITARY AFFAIRS 37 (1973): 41-47.

Argues Gates must be given credit for the outcome of the Saratoga campaign.

498   Nickerson, Hoffman. TURNING POINT OF THE REVOLUTION: BURGOYNE IN AMERICA. New York: Houghton-Mifflin, 1928. 500 p.

Presents Burgoyne's campaign as the decisive or turning point of the Revolution because it brought France into the war.

499   Palmer, Dave R. THE WAY OF THE FOX: AMERICAN STRATEGY
        IN THE WAR FOR AMERICA, 1775-1783. Westport, Conn.: Green-
        wood, 1975. 229 p.

        Develops thesis that Washington employed an effective strat-
        egy in his military direction of the American Revolution.

500   Palmer, John. GENERAL VON STEUBEN. New Haven, Conn.:
        Yale University Press, 1937. Reprint. Port Washington, N.Y.:
        Kennikat, 1966. 434 p.

        Deals forthrightly with Von Steuben's strengths and weaknesses
        and his contribution to the American victory.

501   Panagopoulous, E.D. "Hamilton's Notes in His Pay Book of the New
        York State Artillery Company." AMERICAN HISTORICAL REVIEW
        62 (1957): 310-25.

        A study of Hamilton's ideas and reading habits during the war
        as expressed in the blank pages of the pay book he kept.

502   Pancake, John. "American Militia in the War of Independence."
        HISTORY TODAY 22 (1972): 793-98.

        Argues that the British, at their own peril, miscalculated the
        worth of the colonial citizen soldier, comparing him to their
        own ineffective militiamen.

503   Patterson, Samuel W. HORATIO GATES: DEFENDER OF AMERICAN
        LIBERTIES. New York: Columbia University Press, 1941. 466 p.

        Sympathetic, almost partisan, account of one of the most
        controversial revolutionary war generals. Focuses on the
        Conway cabal.

504   _____. KNIGHT ERRANT OF LIBERTY: THE TRIUMPH AND TRAG-
        EDY OF GENERAL CHARLES LEE. New York: Lantern, 1958. 287 p.

        Useful biography of one of the revolution's most original mil-
        itary thinkers. Lee advocated partisan warfare against the
        British.

505   Peckham, Howard H. THE TOLL OF INDEPENDENCE: ENGAGE-
        MENTS AND BATTLE CASUALTIES OF THE AMERICAN REVOLUTION.
        Chicago: University of Chicago Press, 1974. 176 p.

        Lists 1,331 engagements with brief summaries of what occurred
        and an estimate of the casualties.

506   _____. THE WAR FOR INDEPENDENCE: A MILITARY HISTORY.

Chicago: University of Chicago Press, 1958. 226 p.

Concentrates on how and why the American victory in the revolutionary war was accomplished.

507   Peckham, Howard H., and Brown, Lloyd, eds. REVOLUTIONARY WAR JOURNALS OF HENRY DEARBORN, 1775-1783. Chicago: Caxton Club, 1939. 264 p.

Account by a keen, unemotional participant in the revolutionary war.

508   Pettengill, Ray W., trans. LETTERS FROM AMERICA, 1776-1779. New York: Houghton, 1924. 281 p.

Letters of Brunswick and Hessian officers serving with the British Army during the Revolution. Chief value lies in the depiction of American life during the war.

509   Preston, John H. A GENTLEMAN REBEL: THE EXPLOITS OF ANTHONY WAYNE. New York: Rinehart, 1930. 370 p.

Presents Wayne as an old-fashioned swashbuckling hero, without bothering with historical complexities.

510   Quaife, M.M. "The Ohio Campaigns of 1782." MISSISSIPPI VALLEY HISTORICAL REVIEW 17 (1931): 515-29.

Describes the bloody conflict that took place west of the Alleghenies between the victory at Yorktown and the Paris Peace Treaty.

511   Quarles, Benjamin. THE NEGRO IN THE AMERICAN REVOLUTION. Chapel Hill: University of North Carolina Press, 1961. 231 p.

A solidly researched account of a little-known topic. Author makes a convincing case for the Negro's contribution.

512   Rankin, Hugh F., ed. THE AMERICAN REVOLUTION. New York: Putnam, 1964. 382 p.

Collection of contemporary accounts--diaries, journals, letters--by participants and strung together by author.

513   _____. "Cowpens: Prelude to Yorktown." NORTH CAROLINA HISTORICAL REVIEW 31 (1954): 336-69.

Discusses how after Gates's defeat at Camden, Morgan's victory at Cowpens was critical in bringing about the British defeat at Yorktown.

514 _____. FRANCIS MARION: THE SWAMP FOX. New York:
Crowell, 1973. 346 p.

Account of Marion's military activities in South Carolina.
Focuses on the period 1780-81, when Marion turned a half-
trained, ill-equipped militia into a potent guerrilla fighting
force.

515 _____. THE NORTH CAROLINA CONTINENTALS. Chapel Hill:
University of North Carolina Press, 1971. 428 p.

Traces the experience of the North Carolina Continental Line
as it fought under Washington and later in the Southern Department.

516 Reed, John. CAMPAIGN TO VALLEY FORGE, JULY 1, 1777 -
DECEMBER 19, 1777. Philadelphia: University of Pennsylvania Press,
1965. 448 p.

Rich in detail, written from primary sources, but marred by
editorializing instead of analysis.

517 Rice, Howard, and Brown, Anne. THE AMERICAN CAMPAIGNS OF
ROCHAMBEAU'S ARMY. 2 vols. Princeton, N.J.: Princeton University Press, 1972.

Uses journals, maps, and sketches to recreate the French
Army's participation in the American revolutionary war.

518 Roberts, Kenneth L., ed. MARCH TO QUEBEC: JOURNALS OF THE
MEMBERS OF ARNOLD'S EXPEDITION. Garden City, N.Y.: Doubleday, 1938. 657 p.

Journals present a realistic picture of the expedition to Quebec in 1775.

519 Rossie, Jonathan G. THE POLITICS OF COMMAND IN THE AMERI-
CAN REVOLUTION. Syracuse, N.Y.: Syracuse University Press,
1975. 252 p.

Focuses on the "causes of discord" among Washington's lieutenants and their friends in Congress during the campaigns of
1775-78.

520 Saffell, William T.R. RECORDS OF THE REVOLUTIONARY WAR.
New York: Pudney, Russell, 1858. 554 p.

Roster with service record of fifteen thousand revolutionary
soldiers and officers.

521   Scheer, George F., and Rankin, Hugh F. REBELS AND REDCOATS.
       Cleveland: World, 1957. 572 p.

       Narrates the story of the Revolution through diaries, journals,
       and letters of participants.

522   Sherwin, Oscar. BENEDICT ARNOLD: PATRIOT AND TRAITOR.
       New York: Century, 1931. 395 p.

       Though does not condone treason, presents a sympathetic ac-
       count, giving full treatment of Arnold's services to his coun-
       try.

523   Showman, Richard K., et al. THE PAPERS OF NATHANAEL GREENE,
       DECEMBER 1766-DECEMBER 1776. Chapel Hill: University of North
       Carolina Press, 1976. 411 p.

       Greene's papers are second in importance only to Washing-
       ton's. This is the first volume.

524   Shy, John. A PEOPLE NUMEROUS AND ARMED: REFLECTIONS
       ON THE STRUGGLE FOR AMERICAN INDEPENDENCE. New York:
       Oxford University Press, 1976. 304 p.

       Ten scholarly essays on aspects of the Revolution by a re-
       spected military historian.

525   _____. TOWARD LEXINGTON: THE ROLE OF THE BRITISH ARMY
       IN THE COMING OF THE AMERICAN REVOLUTION. Princeton,
       N.J.: Princeton University Press, 1965. 463 p.

       Argues that the British Army failed to perform effectively be-
       cause it was a European machine unequipped to deal with
       frontier wars and urban disorders.

526   Smelser, Marshall. THE WINNING OF INDEPENDENCE. Chicago:
       Quadrangle, 1972. 427 p.

       Covers no new ground, but written in a lively narrative style.
       Believes British blunders less significant than American strengths
       in the outcome of the war.

527   Smith, Jonathan. "How Massachusetts Raised Her Troops in the Revo-
       lution." PROCEEDINGS OF THE MASSACHUSETTS HISTORICAL SO-
       CIETY 55 (1923): 345-70.

528   Smith, Page. A NEW AGE BEGINS: A PEOPLE'S HISTORY OF THE
       AMERICAN REVOLUTION. 2 vols. New York: McGraw-Hill, 1976.

       Scholarly and concerned with moral judgments, but not bi-
       ased. Majestic history.

529   Smith, Paul H. LOYALISTS AND REDCOATS: A STUDY OF BRITISH
        REVOLUTIONARY POLICY. Chapel Hill: University of North Caro-
        lina Press, 1964. 199 p.

        Argues that the British first ignored the Loyalists and then
        placed too much reliance on them too late.

530   Spaulding, Oliver. "The Military Studies of George Washington."
        AMERICAN HISTORICAL REVIEW 29 (1924): 675-80.

        By investigating Washington's military reading, author attempts
        to evaluate his generalship. Concludes Washington read widely
        and in depth.

531   Stephenson, Orlando W. "The Supply of Gunpowder in 1776." AMER-
        ICAN HISTORICAL REVIEW 30 (1925): 271-81.

        Recounts how the colonists' success in importing large supplies
        of gunpowder played a large part in their final victory over
        England.

532   Swiggett, Howard. WAR OUT OF NIAGARA: WALTER BUTLER AND
        THE TORY RANGERS. New York: Columbia University Press, 1933.
        309 p.

        Account of the fighting in northern New York with an attempt
        to rehabilitate the reputation of Walter Butler.

533   Thayer, Theodore G. THE MAKING OF A SCAPEGOAT: WASH-
        INGTON AND LEE AT MONMOUTH. Port Washington, N.Y.:
        Kennikat, 1976. 124 p.

        An account of the controversy between Lee and Washington
        and how subsequent historians have debated the issue even
        further. Favors Lee.

534   _____. NATHANAEL GREENE: STRATEGIST OF THE AMERICAN
        REVOLUTION. New York: Twayne, 1960. 500 p.

        Covers Greene's early life and business activity in Rhode Is-
        land but concentrates on his service in the revolutionary war
        and his life afterward as a planter in South Carolina and
        Georgia.

535   Treacy, M.F. PRELUDE TO YORKTOWN: THE SOUTHERN CAM-
        PAIGN OF NATHANAEL GREENE, 1780-1781. Chapel Hill: Uni-
        versity of North Carolina Press, 1963. 261 p.

        Readable, scholarly study of Greene's winter campaign, 1780-
        81, focusing on the men who fought with him.

536   Trussell, John B. BIRTHPLACE OF AN ARMY: A STUDY OF THE VALLEY FORGE ENCAMPMENT. Harrisburg: Pennsylvania Historical and Museum Commission, 1976. 145 p.

Synthesizes recent scholarship and focuses on the physical environment in which suffering and death occurred.

537   _____. THE PENNSYLVANIA LINE: REGIMENTAL ORGANIZATION AND OPERATIONS, 1776-1783. Harrisburg: Pennsylvania Historical and Museum Collection, 1977. 368 p.

Attempt to look deeper into the American Revolutionary Army by focusing on the organization and operations of the Pennsylvania Continental regiments. Much useful, detailed information for students of the revolutionary army.

538   Valentine, Alan. LORD STIRLING. New York: Oxford University Press, 1969. 299 p.

Attempt to rehabilitate the reputation of an American revolutionary general who heretofore has received low marks from American historians.

539   Van Doren, Carl C. MUTINY IN JANUARY. New York: Viking, 1949. 450 p.

Discusses a minor crisis in the Continental Army: the mutiny of several regiments in the Pennsylvania Line, 1780-81. A definitive, if somewhat plodding, account.

540   _____. THE SECRET HISTORY OF THE AMERICAN REVOLUTION. New York: Viking, 1941. 534 p.

An account of the conspiracies of Benedict Arnold and others drawn from secret service files of the British headquarters.

541   Van Tyne, Claude H. THE WAR OF INDEPENDENCE: AMERICAN PHASE. New York: Houghton-Mifflin, 1929. 518 p.

Written from both British and American sources, with an effort at presenting a balanced account.

542   Waldo, Albigence. "Valley Forge: 1777-78: Diary of a Surgeon of the Continental Line." PENNSYLVANIA MAGAZINE OF HISTORY AND BIOGRAPHY 31 (1897): 299-323.

Most often quoted personal account of Valley Forge.

543   Wallace, Willard M. APPEAL TO ARMS: A MILITARY HISTORY OF THE AMERICAN REVOLUTION. New York: Harper, 1951. 308 p.

Popular history of the war.

544 _____. TRAITOROUS HERO: THE LIFE AND FORTUNES OF BEN-
EDICT ARNOLD. New York: Harper, 1954. 394 p.

Expertly treats Arnold as a military figure. Concludes that
Arnold was the Revolution's most outstanding field officer.

545 Ward, Christopher. THE WAR OF THE REVOLUTION. 2 vols. New
York: Macmillan, 1952.

Reliable guide to the most important events of the Revolution.
Focuses mostly on land hostilities.

546 Weigley, Russell. THE PARTISAN WAR: THE SOUTH CAROLINA
CAMPAIGN OF 1780-1782. Columbia: University of South Carolina
Press, 1970.

Story of unconventional warfare in South Carolina during the
Revolution. The British could do everything but defeat the
partisans.

547 Weller, Joe. "The Irregular War in the South." MILITARY AFFAIRS
24 (1960): 124-36.

Discusses the revolutionary conflict in the South as an international and internal political war.

548 Whittlemore, Charles P. A GENERAL OF THE REVOLUTION: JOHN
SULLIVAN OF NEW HAMPSHIRE. New York: Columbia University
Press, 1961. 317 p.

Account of neglected revolutionary war general, one of Washington's most active officers. Career began with Battle of
Bunker Hill and ended in New York with Clinton.

549 Wildes, Harry E. ANTHONY WAYNE: TROUBLE SHOOTER OF THE
REVOLUTION. New York: Harcourt, Brace, 1941. Reprint. Westport, Conn.: Greenwood, 1976. 514 p.

Well-researched, and contains a rich store of information not
only on Wayne, but also on the Revolution.

550 _____. VALLEY FORGE. New York: Macmillan, 1938. 337 p.

Detailed account of the winter spent by the Continental Army
at Valley Forge, with much local history and legend.

551 Wright, Esmond. WASHINGTON AND THE AMERICAN REVOLU-
TION. London: English Universities Press, 1957. 192 p.

British writer presents a critical estimate of Washington as a symbol. Useful for eighteenth century background to the Revolutionary War.

552   Wright, John W. "The Rifle in the American Revolution." AMERICAN HISTORICAL REVIEW 29 (1924): 293-99.

Argues that the musket was much superior to the rifle because of the latter's laborious loading process and its sensitiveness to weather conditions.

553   _____. "Some Notes on the Continental Army." WILLIAM AND MARY QUARTERLY 11 (1931): 81-105, 185-209.

Contains much information on military tactics, military literature, and the organization of the Continental Army.

554   York, Neil L. "Clandestine Aid and the American Revolutionary War: A Re-Examination." MILITARY AFFAIRS 43 (1979): 26-30.

Discusses the process of acquiring foreign aid in the early months of the Revolution. Argues it was necessarily clandestine but also essential to the American cause.

555   Young, Henry J. "Treason and Its Punishment in Revolutionary Pennsylvania." PENNSYLVANIA MAGAZINE OF HISTORY 90 (1966): 287-313.

Discusses various methods of punishing Tories who remained opposed to the Revolution, from judicial prosecution to execution.

556   Zucker, A.E. GENERAL DE KALB: LAFAYETTE'S MENTOR. Chapel Hill: University of North Carolina Press, 1966. 251 p.

First serious account of Bavaria-born general appointed by the Continental Congress to serve in the American Army during the Revolution.

Chapter 3

THE MILITARY IN THE NEW REPUBLIC (1783-1815)

A. FEDERALIST AND REPUBLICAN MILITARY POLICY

557   Adams, Randolph G. "The Harmar Expedition of 1790." OHIO
STATE ARCHAEOLOGICAL AND HISTORICAL QUARTERLY 50 (1941):
60-62.

Briefly discusses the first of three attempts to break the Indian power in the Maumee Valley.

558   Bakeless, John. LEWIS AND CLARK, PARTNERS IN DISCOVERY.
New York: Morrow, 1947. 498 p.

Combined biography of Lewis and Clark but focuses on the
expedition ordered by Jefferson. Very readable story of a
dramatic event.

559   Bandel, Eugene. FRONTIER LIFE IN THE ARMY, 1854-1861.   Glen-
dale, Calif.:   Clark, 1932.   330 p.

Account of a young soldier of German birth who served on
the western frontier just prior to the Civil War. Describes
in detail the topography, the frontier soldier's life, and Indian life.

560   Beers, Henry P. THE WESTERN MILITARY FRONTIER, 1815-1846.
Philadelphia: University of Pennsylvania Press, 1935.   227 p.

Account of the U.S. Army as a peace-time institution helping
to develop the frontier.

561   Benton, William. "Pennsylvania Revolutionary Officers and the Federal
Constitution." PENNSYLVANIA HISTORY 31 (1964):   419-35.

Finds a strong correlation between revolutionary officers' experience in the war and their attitudes toward the constitution.

562   Brown, Alan. "The Role of the Army in Western Settlement: Josiah Harmar's Command, 1785-1790." PENNSYLVANIA MAGAZINE OF HISTORY AND BIOGRAPHY 93 (1969): 161-78.

Discusses the public work provided by the small American Army in the settlement of the West after 1785.

563   Croffut, E.A., ed. FIFTY YEARS IN CAMP AND FIELD: DIARY OF ETHAN ALLEN HITCHCOCK. New York: Putnam, 1900. 350 p.

Diary covers almost all of Hitchcock's active and controversial career.

564   Davies, Wallace. "Society of Cincinnati in New England." WILLIAM AND MARY QUARTERLY 5 (1948): 2-25.

Discusses how opposition to the organization of Cincinnati arose in New England and, when it aligned itself with the Federalists, how it began to decline.

565   Donahoe, Bernard, and Smelser, Marshall. "The Congressional Power to Raise Armies: The Constitutional and Ratifying Conventions." REVIEW OF POLITICS 32 (1971): 202-21.

566   Elliott, Charles W. WINFIELD SCOTT: THE SOLDIER AND THE MAN. New York: Macmillan, 1937. 817 p.

Chapters 24-27 discuss Scott's role in creating a peace-time professional military force.

567   Falk, Sidney L. "Artillery for Land Service: The Development of a System." MILITARY AFFAIRS 28 (1964): 97-110.

Story of how the army went about creating an artillery system, focusing on the efforts of Captain Alfred Mordecai and the official publication of ARTILLERY FOR U.S. LAND SERVICE.

568   Forman, Sidney. "Thomas Jefferson on Universal Military Training." MILITARY AFFAIRS 11 (1947): 177-89.

Argues that Jefferson was inclined to support universal military training for the militia as a means of avoiding a standing army.

569   _____. "Why the United States Military Academy was Established in 1802." MILITARY AFFAIRS 29 (1965): 16-28.

Narrative story of the process of establishing the academy at West Point, focusing on those individuals--particularly Hamilton--who were involved in its creation.

570   Gaines, William A., Jr. "The Forgotten Army: Recruiting For a
      National Emergency." VIRGINIA MAGAZINE OF HISTORY 56
      (1948): 267-79.

      Account covering the recruitment of the Provisional Army,
      particularly in Virginia, during the crisis with France after
      the XYZ affair.

571   Guthman, William H. MARCH TO MASSACRE: A HISTORY OF
      THE FIRST SEVEN YEARS OF THE UNITED STATES ARMY, 1784-1791.
      New York: McGraw, 1975. 275 p.

      For the general reader. First part of the book deals with
      recruiting, discipline, and training. The second part with
      Indian expeditions in America's vast frontier during the first
      years of nationhood.

572   Hagan, William T. "General Henry Atkinson and the Militia." MIL-
      ITARY AFFAIRS 23 (1959): 194-97.

      Describes Atkinson's handling of the militia raised to subdue
      the Indians in Mississippi in 1832.

573   Hay, Thomas K. "Some Reflections on the Career of General James
      Wilkinson." MISSISSIPPI VALLEY HISTORICAL REVIEW 21 (1935):
      471-94.

      Discusses Wilkinson's stormy career of intrigues and schemes,
      and concludes that he was a reflection of his times.

574   Jacobs, James R. THE BEGINNING OF THE UNITED STATES ARMY,
      1783-1812. Princeton, N.J.: Princeton University Press, 1947.
      419 p.

      A detailed history of the U.S. Army from the end of the
      Revolution to the Mexican War with emphasis on the role of
      the army in protecting the western frontier.

575   _____. THE TARNISHED WARRIOR: MAJ. GEN. JAMES WILKIN-
      SON. New York: Macmillan, 1938. 380 p.

      An account of the revolutionary officer, doctor, merchant,
      politician but most of all an adventurer and a scoundrel.
      Also useful on military in the first decades after independ-
      ence.

576   Kaplan, Sidney. "Pay, Pension, and Power: Economic Grievances
      of Massachusetts Officers of the Revolution." BOSTON PUBLIC LI-
      BRARY QUARTERLY 3 (1951): 15-34, 127-42.

577 _____. "Veteran Officers and Politics in Massachusetts, 1783–1787."
WILLIAM AND MARY QUARTERLY 9 (1952): 29–57.

Discusses how veterans of the Continental Army served in the
force that subdued Shay's Rebellion and afterward reaped political rewards.

578 Kerby, Robert L. "The Militia System and the State Military in the
War of 1812." INDIANA MAGAZINE OF HISTORY 73 (1977):
102–24.

Argues that failure of the militia system in the War of 1812
lay not with the system itself but with factors extraneous to
the system.

579 Knopf, Richard C. "Crime and Punishment in the American Legion,
1792–1793." BULLETIN OF THE HISTORICAL AND PHILOSOPHICAL
SOCIETY OF OHIO 14 (1956): 232–38.

Discusses institutional aspects of the early American army
called "Legion of the United States."

580 Kohn, Richard. EAGLE AND SWORD: THE FEDERALISTS AND THE
CREATION OF THE MILITARY ESTABLISHMENT IN AMERICA, 1783–
1802. New York: Free Press, 1975. 443 p.

Analyzes the significant role military affairs played in the
Federalist–Republican political struggle. Sympathetic to Federalist military policy.

581 _____. "The Inside History of the Newburgh Conspiracy: America
and the Coup d'Etat." WILLIAM AND MARY QUARTERLY 27 (1970):
189–220.

Argues that although one was plotted, a coup d'etat was not
likely or even possible, but states that Newburgh incident
did threaten to establish a pattern for the young republic's
civil–military relations.

582 _____. "Washington Administration's Decision to Crush the Whiskey
Rebellion." JOURNAL OF AMERICAN HISTORY 59 (1976): 567–84.

Discusses the Washington administration's problem in deciding
not only to use force but what kind of force. Thinks administration united on the first but uncertain on the latter.

583 Lofgren, Charles A. "Compulsory Military Service Under the Constitution: The Original Understanding." WILLIAM AND MARY QUAR-
TERLY 33 (1976): 61–88.

Concludes that founders and early Americans did accept the

concept of compulsory service, though they did conceive of it in terms of state militias.

584   Mahon, John K. THE AMERICAN MILITIA: DECADE OF DECISION, 1789-1800. Gainesville: University of Florida Press, 1960.

Emphasizes the strong relationship between the militia and state attitudes and conditions.

585   _____. "Pennsylvania and the Beginnings of the Regular Army." PENNSYLVANIA HISTORY 21 (1954): 33-44.

586   Meek, Basil. "General Harmar's Expedition." OHIO STATE AR-CHAEOLOGICAL AND HISTORICAL QUARTERLY 20 (1911): 74-108.

Traces the story of the Harmar expedition against the Indians shortly after the formation of the nation.

587   Motte, Jacob Rhett. JOURNEY INTO WILDERNESS; AN ARMY SUR-GEON'S ACCOUNT OF LIFE IN CAMP AND FIELD DURING THE CREEK AND SEMINOLE WARS, 1836-1838. Gainesville: University of Florida Press, 1953. 326 p.

Vividly describes the intense physical discomforts of the campaigns against the Seminoles in the swampy wildernesses of Florida.

588   Nelson, Paul D. "Horatio Gates at Newburgh, 1783: A Misunder-stood Role." WILLIAM AND MARY QUARTERLY 29 (1972): 143-51.

Refutes Kohn's assertion (see entry 581) that Gates was treason-ous. Asserts that Gates and his followers were simply attempting to pressure Congress for justice.

589   _____. "Military Roads for War and Peace, 1791-1836." MILITARY AFFAIRS 19 (1955): 1-15.

Discusses army's participation in internal improvements in the early national period through the building of military roads.

590   Nichols, Roger L. "The Army and the Indians 1800-1830--A Reap-praisal: The Missouri Valley Example." PACIFIC HISTORICAL RE-VIEW 41 (1972): 151-68.

Argues incompetence and bungling characterized the army experience in the Missouri Valley.

591   _____. "Army Contributions to River Transportation, 1818-1825." MILITARY AFFAIRS 33 (1969): 242-49.

Discusses the army's efforts to create safe navigation on the Missouri River (1818-25) as an example of the army's peaceful contributions in the nineteenth century.

592 Peckham, Howard H. "Josiah Harmar and His Indian Expedition." OHIO STATE ARCHAEOLOGICAL AND HISTORICAL QUARTERLY 55 (1946): 227-41.

Depicts Harmar as a dedicated loyal officer, even though his first expedition failed in its purpose.

593 Pelzer, Louis. HENRY DODGE. Iowa City: State Historical Society of Iowa, 1911. 266 p.

Biography of the commander of America's first cavalry regiment.

594 Prucha, Francis P., ed. ARMY LIFE ON THE WESTERN FRONTIER: SELECTIONS FROM OFFICIAL REPORTS MADE BETWEEN 1826 AND 1845. Norman: University of Oklahoma Press, 1958. 187 p.

Selection from official reports of Inspector General George Croghan dealing with the drab boring conditions of army life on the western frontier.

595 Quaife, M.M. "General Hull and His Critics." OHIO STATE ARCHAEOLOGICAL AND HISTORICAL QUARTERLY 47 (1938): 168-82.

Argues that Hull's failures should be more correctly laid at the door of the government and society for giving him such a miserable army.

596 Silver, James W. EDMUND PENDLETON GAINES: FRONTIER GENERAL. Baton Rouge: Louisiana State University Press, 1949. 291 p.

Study of Gaines's long military career, focusing on his experience with the army and its role on the frontier.

597 Skeen, C. Edward. "The Newburgh Conspiracy Reconsidered." WILLIAM AND MARY QUARTERLY 31 (1974): 273-98.

Attempts to refute Kohn's contention (see entry 581) that a plot did exist. Kohn replies to the charges on pages 290-98.

598 Smith, Carlton B. "Congressional Attitudes Toward Military Preparedness During the Monroe Administration." MILITARY AFFAIRS 40 (1976): 22-25.

Discusses the conflict between the Monroe administration (which wanted an enlarged defense program) and an economy-minded Congress.

599   Steiner, Bernard C. THE LIFE AND CORRESPONDENCE OF JAMES
       McHENRY. Cleveland: Burrows, 1907. Reprint. New York: Arno,
       1979. 640 p.

       Biography of Washington's staff surgeon who later served as
       secretary of War under Washington and Adams. Includes
       substantial amount of McHenry's correspondence.

600   Syrett, Harold C., et al. THE PAPERS OF ALEXANDER HAMILTON.
       Vols. 22 and 23. New York: Columbia University Press, 1975.

       Volumes concern the period when Hamilton commanded the
       army to the quasiwar with France. Useful on Federalist mil-
       itary policy.

601   Tucker, Glenn. MAD ANTHONY WAYNE AND THE NEW NATION:
       THE STORY OF WASHINGTON'S FRONT LINE GENERAL. Harris-
       burg, Pa.: Stackpole, 1973. 287 p.

       Covers Wayne's career as one of Washington's lieutenants,
       but focuses on his campaigns in the Old Northwest after the
       Revolution.

602   Tucker, Glen. TECUMSEH: VISION OF GLORY. Indianapolis:
       Bobbs-Merrill, 1956. Reprint. New York: Russell, 1973. 399 p.

       Long, detailed narrative of the Indian warrior chief who tried
       unsuccessfully to hold back the white man's westward advance.

603   Vivian, Jean H. "Military Land Bounties During the Revolutionary
       and Confederation Periods." MARYLAND HISTORICAL MAGAZINE
       61 (1966): 231-56.

       Discusses the land officers of the Confederation Congress, the
       efforts of the soldiers to acquire the land, and congress's pol-
       icies.

604   Ward, Harry M. THE DEPARTMENT OF WAR, 1781-1795. Pittsburgh:
       University of Pittsburgh Press, 1962. 287 p.

       Well-documented narrative on the administration of the early
       War Department.

605   Watson, Richard L. "Congressional Attitudes Toward Military Prepared-
       ness, 1829-1835." MISSISSIPPI VALLEY HISTORICAL REVIEW 34
       (1948): 611-36.

       Discusses what author sees as constant congressional bickering
       on military appropriations but nothing was done. Congressmen
       were satisfied to rely on the ineffective militia.

606   Wesley, Edgar B. GUARDING THE FRONTIER: A STUDY OF FRON-
       TIER DEFENSE FROM 1815-1825. Minneapolis: University of Minne-
       sota Press, 1935. Reprint. Westport, Conn.: Greenwood, 1970.
       217 p.

       A study of Jeffersonian Republican military policy.

607   White, Leonard D. THE FEDERALISTS: A STUDY IN ADMINISTRA-
       TIVE HISTORY 1789-1801. New York: Macmillan, 1948. 538 p.

       Chapters 12 and 29 deal with military policy of the Federa-
       lists.

608   _____. THE JEFFERSONIANS: A STUDY IN ADMINISTRATIVE
       HISTORY, 1801-1829. New York: Macmillan, 1951. 572 p.

       Chapters 17, 18, and 34 discuss growth of military profession-
       alism.

B. THE WAR OF 1812

609   Adams, Henry. THE WAR OF 1812. Edited by H.A. DeWeerd.
       Washington, D.C.: Infantry Journal Press, 1944. 377 p.

       Excerpts from Adams's nine-volume history of the United
       States, 1801-17, dealing chiefly with military affairs. Still
       one of the best general histories of the war.

610   Adams, Reed M.B. "New Orleans and the War of 1812." LOUISI-
       ANA HISTORICAL QUARTERLY 16 (1933): 221-34, 479-503, 681-
       703; 17 (1934): 169-82, 349-63, 502-23.

       In five separate articles, discusses the strategic importance of
       New Orleans, focusing on the battle to take the city in the
       War of 1812.

611   Armstrong, John. NOTICES OF THE WAR OF 1812. 2 vols. New
       York: Wiley and Putnam, 1840.

       Views of an eyewitness of the campaigns on the Canadian
       border.

612   Beirne, Frances. THE WAR OF 1812. New York: Dutton, 1949.
       410 p.

       Dated account, mostly useful in historiography.

613   Bird, Harrison. WAR FOR THE WEST, 1790-1813. New York: Ox-
       ford University Press, 1971. 277 p.

Study of the war on the Canadian-American border, focusing on the land campaign of the War of 1812.

614 Bond, Beverly W., Jr. "William Henry Harrison in the War of 1812." MISSISSIPPI VALLEY HISTORICAL REVIEW 13 (1927): 499-516.

Account based on primary sources and aimed at estimating the quality of Harrison's military skills and the outcome of his campaign in the War of 1812.

615 Brannan, John, comp. OFFICIAL LETTERS OF THE MILITARY AND NAVAL OFFICERS OF THE UNITED STATES DURING THE WAR WITH GREAT BRITAIN IN THE YEARS 1812, 13, 14 AND 15. Washington, D.C.: Gideon, 1823. 510 p.

616 Brant, Irving. JAMES MADISON. 6 vols. Indianapolis: Bobbs-Merrill, 1961.

Volume 4, chapters 9-27 specifically deal with Madison's experience as commander-in-chief during the War of 1812. Corrects distortions, but very pro-Madison.

617 Brooks, Charles B. THE SIEGE OF NEW ORLEANS. Seattle: University of Washington Press, 1961. 334 p.

Straightforward, nonanalytical account of the campaign, presenting both the British and American point of view.

618 Brown, Roger H. THE REPUBLIC IN PERIL: 1812. New York: Columbia University Press, 1964. 238 p.

Shows how Republicanism and concern for the republic led to war with Great Britain.

619 Brown, Wilburt S. THE AMPHIBIOUS CAMPAIGN FOR WEST FLORIDA AND LOUISIANA, 1814-1815: A CRITICAL REVIEW OF STRATEGY AND TACTICS AT NEW ORLEANS. Tuscaloosa: University of Alabama Press, 1969. 233 p.

Describes Battle of New Orleans as "classic" amphibious warfare.

620 Caffrey, Kate. THE TWILIGHT'S LAST GLEAMING: BRITAIN VS. AMERICA, 1812-1815. New York: Stein and Day, 1977. 340 p.

War of 1812 from the British point of view by a British writer.

621 Carter, Samuel. BLAZE OF GLORY: THE FIGHT FOR NEW ORLEANS, 1814-1815. New York: St. Martin's, 1971. 351 p.

Popular account with useful discussion of the free black militia and information on the conditions in the city at the time.

622   Cassell, Frank A. "Baltimore in 1813: A Study of Urban Defense in the War of 1812." MILITARY AFFAIRS 33 (1969): 349-61.

Account of how the Baltimore citizens expended much time and money to make their city secure against a British attack. Argues that this was responsible for the repulse of the British in 1814.

623   Chidsey, Donald B. THE BATTLE OF NEW ORLEANS: AN INFORMAL HISTORY OF THE WAR THAT NOBODY WANTED, 1812. New York: Crown, 1961. 212 p.

Popular account combining the style of a historical novel with a journalistic approach to military operations.

624   Coles, Harry L. THE WAR OF 1812. Chicago: University of Chicago Press, 1965. 298 p.

Both analysis of strategy and tactics and a summary of recent scholarship on the causes and consequences of the war.

625   Cruikshank, Ernest A. "The Employment of Indians in the War of 1812." ANNUAL REPORT, AMERICAN HISTORICAL ASSOCIATION, 1895, pp. 367-98.

Discusses how the British took advantage of the Northwest Indians' grievances against Americans to enlist them in the struggle against the United States.

626   _____, ed. THE DOCUMENTARY HISTORY OF THE CAMPAIGN UPON THE NIAGARA FRONTIER, 1812-14. 9 vols. Niagara: Lundy's Lane Historical Society, 1896-1908.

Dated but contains a wide variety of source materials.

627   _____. DOCUMENTS RELATING TO THE INVASION OF CANADA AND THE SURRENDER OF DETROIT, 1812. Ottawa: Government Printing Bureau, 1912. Reprint. New York: Arno, 1979. 258 p.

Valuable documents on the northern theatre of the War of 1812. Over one hundred and sixty documents, covering conditions confronting General Hull when his invasion of Canada culminated in disaster at Detroit.

628   Edgar, James E. "The Army Medical Department in the War of 1812." MILITARY SURGEON 60 (1927): 301-13.

629   Egan, Clifford L. "The Origins of the War of 1812: Three Decades
       of Historical Writing." MILITARY AFFAIRS 38 (1974): 72-75.

       Useful survey of the historical literature written in the past
       thirty years.

630   Fisher, Robert L. "The Western Prologue to the War of 1812." MIS-
       SOURI HISTORICAL REVIEW 30 (1936): 267-81.

       Argues that British fur companies put great pressure on the
       British government to stay in the Northwest, thus precipitating
       problems with the new American government. These troubles
       emerge as causes of the War of 1812.

631   Gilpin, Alec R. THE WAR OF 1812 IN THE OLD NORTHWEST.
       East Lansing: Michigan State University Press, 1958. 286 p.

       A regional study, meticulously detailed and documented,
       concerning the war as it occurred in the old Northwest.

632   Goodman, Warren H. "Origins of the War of 1812: A Survey of
       Changing Interpretations." MISSISSIPPI VALLEY HISTORICAL REVIEW
       28 (1941): 171-86.

       Reviews historical literature on the War of 1812 to 1941.

633   Gouldburn, Henry. "A British View of the War of 1812 and the
       Peace Negotiations." MISSISSIPPI VALLEY HISTORICAL REVIEW 45
       (1958): 481-87.

       Discusses autobiography of a British official who did not see
       the War of 1812 as important as Americans have seen it.

634   Green, James A. WILLIAM HENRY HARRISON: HIS LIFE AND
       TIMES. Richmond, Va.: Garrett and Massie, 1941. 536 p.

       Massive work, with prodigious detail, concerned with making
       Harrison a soldier of substance who played a significant role
       in saving the Old Northwest from the British during the War
       of 1812.

635   Gribben, William. THE CHURCHES MILITANT: THE WAR OF 1812
       AND AMERICAN RELIGION. New Haven, Conn.: Yale University
       Press, 1973. 210 p.

       Argues that church position on War of 1812 reflected public
       opinion.

636   Hare, John. "Military Punishment in the War of 1812." MILITARY
       AFFAIRS 4 (1940): 225-39.

637   Harrison, William H. WILLIAM HENRY HARRISON, AND THE WAR
       OF 1812. Columbus, Ohio: Anthony Wayne Parkway Board, 1957.
       105 p.

       Documents concerning Harrison's military activities.

638   Hawthorne, Nathaniel, ed. YARN OF A YANKEE PRIVATEER. In-
       troduction by Clifford Smith. New York: Funk, 1926. 308 p.

       First-hand narrative (found in Hawthorne's papers) of a priva-
       teer who was captured by the British.

639   Haynes, Robert V. "The Southwest and War of 1812." LOUISIANA
       HISTORY 5 (1964): 41-51.

       Describes the factors that influenced the people of the South-
       west to strongly favor a war fought to protect maritime inter-
       ests.

640   Horsman, Reginald. THE CAUSES OF THE WAR OF 1812. Philadel-
       phia: University of Pennsylvania Press, 1962. 345 p.

       Focuses on British and American policies and diplomacy that
       led to war.

641   _____. THE WAR OF 1812. New York: Knopf, 1969. 286 p.

       Discusses all aspects (economic, political, strategical) of the
       war and emphasizes difficulties of waging war with state mili-
       tias.

642   Hull, William. MEMOIR OF THE CAMPAIGN OF THE NORTHWEST-
       ERN ARMY OF THE UNITED STATES. Boston: True and Greene,
       1824. 229 p.

       Personal recollections of a leading commander of American
       forces in the Northwest during the War of 1812. Covers the
       surrender of Detroit.

643   Jacobs, James P., and Tucker, Glenn. THE WAR OF 1812: A
       COMPACT HISTORY. New York: Hawthorn, 1969. 224 p.

       For those interested in a reliable brief account.

644   James, Marquis. ANDREW JACKSON: THE BORDER CAPTAIN. In-
       dianapolis: Bobbs-Merrill, 1937. 627 p.

       Interesting narrative account of the southern campaigns, with
       Jackson at the center. Chapters 9-20 cover Jackson's par-
       ticipation in the War of 1812.

645   Kimball, Jeffrey. "The Battle of Chippewa: Infantry Tactics in the War of 1812." MILITARY AFFAIRS 31 (1967): 169-86.

Discusses European rather than native influences on American tactics. Argues American achieved their first victory over British regulars when a well-drilled American regiment employed European tactics at the Battle of Chippewa.

646   Knopf, Richard, comp. WILLIAM HENRY HARRISON AND THE WAR OF 1812. Columbus: Ohio State Museum, 1957. 233 p.

Documents relating to Harrison's activities in the War of 1812 in the Old Northwest.

647   Lambert, Robert S. "The Conduct of the Militia at Tippecanoe: Elihu Stout's Controversy With Colonel John P. Boyd." INDIANA MAGAZINE OF HISTORY 51 (1955): 237-50.

Documents concerning the controversy waged by an editor and an army officer over the relative merits of the militia in the battle.

648   Lloyd, Alan. THE SCORCHING OF WASHINGTON: THE WAR OF 1812. Washington, D.C.: Luce, 1975. 216 p.

A light, informal account by an Englishman. Covers the British attack on the Capitol.

649   Lord, Walter. THE DAWN'S EARLY LIGHT. New York: Norton, 1972. 384 p.

Popular account of the War of 1812 with graphic descriptions of the capture and burning of Washington.

650   _____. "Humiliation and Triumph." AMERICAN HERITAGE 23 (1972): 91-93.

Narrative of fall of Washington during the War of 1812.

651   Lossing, Benson J. THE PICTORIAL FIELD-BOOK OF THE WAR OF 1812. 3 vols. New York: Harper, 1867.

Dated, but still useful book of illustrations and sketches of people and battles.

652   Mahon, John K. "British Command Decisions Relative to the Battle of New Orleans." LOUISIANA HISTORY 6 (1965): 53-76.

653   _____. "British Strategy and Southern Indians: War of 1812." FLORIDA HISTORICAL QUARTERLY 44 (1966): 285-302.

Argues that British attempt to use Indians as allies in the
South was not as successful as in the Northwest.

654   _____. THE WAR OF 1812. Gainesville: University of Florida
Press, 1972. 476 p.

Study of land and water military operations with an emphasis
on command, decisions, strategy, and tactics.

655   Mason, Philip, ed. AFTER TIPPECANOE: SOME ASPECTS OF THE
WAR OF 1812. East Lansing: Michigan State University Press, 1963.
106 p.

Three lectures by authorities on the War of 1812, dealing
with specialized topics. Includes essays by G.F.G. Stanley,
C.P. Stanley, and Reginald Horsman.

656   Muller, Charles. THE DARKEST DAY, 1814: THE WASHINGTON-
BALTIMORE CAMPAIGN. Philadelphia: Lippincott, 1963. 232 p.

Account of the ignominious defeat of the American Army at
Bladensburg and the subsequent capture and burning of Washington.

657   Pratt, Julius W. EXPANSIONISTS OF 1812. New York: Macmillan,
1925. 309 p.

Emphasizes demands for expansion as the predominant cause
of outbreak of the War of 1812. Also deals with military
operations in the Floridas.

658   _____. "Fur Trade Strategy and the American Left Flank in the War
of 1812." AMERICAN HISTORICAL REVIEW 40 (1935): 246-73.

Argues a separate war was going on the western frontier con-
ducted by the British, the fur traders, and the Indians trying
to reconquer the Missouri Valley.

659   Quaife, Milo M. "A Diary of the War of 1812." MISSISSIPPI VAL-
LEY HISTORICAL REVIEW 1 (1914): 272-78.

Diary of a scout in the Detroit campaign in 1812.

660   _____, ed. WAR ON THE DETROIT: CHRONICLES OF THOMAS
DE BOUCHERVILLE. Chicago: Lakeside, 1940.

Important primary source by a soldier who served with Gen.
William Hull in the Great Lakes region during the War of
1812.

661   Reilly, Robin. THE BRITISH AT THE GATES: THE NEW ORLEANS CAMPAIGN IN THE WAR OF 1812. New York: Putnam, 1974. 379 p.

Corrects some myths, but does not alter general picture of the war and campaign presented by older accounts.

662   Robinson, Ralph. "Controversy Over the Command at Baltimore in the War of 1812." MARYLAND HISTORICAL MAGAZINE 39 (1944): 177-98.

Narrative of the conflict over command between Gen. Samuel Smith and Gen. William Winder.

663   Rowland, Eron O. ANDREW JACKSON'S CAMPAIGN AGAINST THE BRITISH: THE MISSISSIPPI TERRITORY IN THE WAR OF 1812. New York: Macmillan, 1926. 424 p.

A dated descriptive account of military operations in the Mississippi territory, 1813-15 with an emphasis on Jackson's coast campaigns culminating with the Battle of New Orleans.

664   Sapio, Victor. PENNSYLVANIA AND THE WAR OF 1812. Lexington: University of Kentucky Press, 1970. 206 p.

Author concludes that Pennsylvanians patriotically supported the war effort.

665   Shaw, Peter. "The War of 1812 Could Not Take Place: Henry Adams' History." YALE REVIEW 62 (1973): 544-56.

Author argues that in accepting Adams's work as a classic, historians have missed his passionate morality and the intensely personal biases of his history.

666   Smelser, Marshall. "Tecumseh, Harrison and the War of 1812." INDIANA MAGAZINE OF HISTORY 65 (1969): 25-44.

Sees the struggle in the Indiana territory as a conflict between two able natural leaders--Tecumseh and Gen. Harrison.

667   Stacy, C.P. "An American Plan for a Canadian Campaign: Secretary James Monroe to Major Jacob Brown, February, 1815." AMERICAN HISTORICAL REVIEW 46 (1941): 348-58.

Discusses Monroe's capabilities as a strategist while Secretary of War. Gives Monroe high marks.

668   Stanley, George. "The Indians in the War of 1812." CANADIAN HISTORICAL REVIEW 31 (1950): 145-65.

Military in the New Republic

Discusses how both Americans and the British sought the aid
of Indian tribes. Concludes the British were far more successful.

669   Swanson, Neil H. THE PERILOUS FIGHT. New York: Farrar, 1945.
555 p.

Detailed account of the fighting and events in the Baltimore
and Washington area in 1814.

670   Tucker, Glenn. POLTROONS AND PATRIOTS, A POPULAR AC-
COUNT OF THE WAR OF 1812. 2 vols. Indianapolis: Bobbs-Merrill, 1954.

A journalistic, generally exciting account of the war focusing
on the major events, and the people and motives behind them.

671   White, Patrick. A NATION ON TRIAL: AMERICA AND THE WAR
OF 1812. New York: Wiley, 1965. 177 p.

Examines issues which led to conflict between the United
States and Great Britain in 1812, with emphasis on unsuccessful attempts to resolve those issues.

Chapter 4

THE MILITARY IN THE ERA OF NATIONALISM
AND WESTWARD EXPANSION (1815-1877)

A. THE MILITARY AND CONTINENTAL EXPANSION

672   Adams, George R. "Caloosahatchee Massacre: Its Significance in
the Second Seminole War." FLORIDA HISTORICAL QUARTERLY 48
(1970): 368-80.

Argues that the massacre was one of the most significant engagements because it helped prolong the war.

673   Beers, Henry P. THE WESTERN MILITARY FRONTIER, 1815-1846.
Philadelphia: University of Pennsylvania Press, 1935. 227 p.

A study of military posts designed to protect white settlements
against Indian attacks.

674   Boyd, Mark F. "Florida Aflame: Background and Onset of the Seminole War, 1835." FLORIDA HISTORICAL QUARTERLY 30 (1951):
3-115.

A kind of outline narrative of the war. Somewhat superficial.

675   Brittle, George C. "First Campaign of the Second Seminole War."
FLORIDA HISTORICAL QUARTERLY 46 (1967): 39-45.

Discusses how the militia attempted but failed miserably to
deal with the Indians, necessitating the calling of federal
troops.

676   Caldwell, Norman W. "The Enlisted Soldier at the Frontier Post,
1790-1814." MID-AMERICA 37 (1955): 195-204.

Discusses many aspects of how it was to be an enlisted soldier
on the pre-Civil War frontier. Deals with discipline, eating
and drinking habits, and living quarters.

677   _____. "The Frontier Army Officer, 1794-1814." MID-AMERICA
37 (1955): 101-28.

Discusses the experiences of the frontier officer in the pre-
Civil War period, covering everything from the officer's ward-
robe, eating and drinking habits, to medical facilities.

678   Clarke, Dwight L. STEPHEN WATTS KEARNY: SOLDIER OF THE
WEST. Norman: University of Oklahoma Press, 1961. 448 p.

Covers Kearny's early life in New Jersey, his studies at Columbia, but focuses on his service in the army from the War
of 1812 to his death.

679   Cleaves, Freeman. OLD TIPPECANOE: WILLIAM HENRY HARRISON
AND HIS TIME. New York: Scribner, 1939. 422 p.

Based on manuscript sources, rich in detail and finely captures
Harrison's personality.

680   Dillon, Richard. MERIWETHER LEWIS, A BIOGRAPHY. New York:
Coward-McCann, 1965. 364 p.

Focuses on the famous Lewis and Clark expedition, told from
the point of view of Lewis. Uses frequent quotations from
the day-to-day journal.

681   Downes, Randolph C. COUNCIL FIRES ON THE UPPER OHIO. Pittsburgh: University of Pittsburgh Press, 1940. 367 p.

Narrative of the Upper Ohio Indians' struggle with the white
man, 1775-95, for control of the region. Written from the
point of view of the Indians.

682   Downey, Fairfax. INDIAN WARS OF THE UNITED STATES ARMY.
1776-1865. Garden City, N.Y.: Doubleday, 1963. 248 p.

Popular account of U.S. Army engagements with the Indians
starting with colonial period.

683   Eby, Cecil. "THAT DISGRACEFUL AFFAIR": THE BLACK HAWK WAR.
New York: Norton, 1973. 354 p.

Account of the war caused by American removal policy. Useful on American and Indian tactics.

684   Foreman, Grant. ADVANCING THE FRONTIER 1830-1860. Norman:
University of Oklahoma Press, 1933. 363 p.

Portion of the study focuses on the North American Indians
and the frontier army, and covers Indian Wars, 1815-75.

685   Fremont, John C. MEMOIRS OF MY LIFE. Chicago: Belford,
       Clarke, 1887. 655 p.

       Much of the material on Fremont's exploration experiences,
       but also covers his role in the Mexican War.

686   Goetzmann, William H. ARMY EXPLORATION IN THE AMERICAN
       WEST, 1803-1863. New Haven, Conn.: Yale University Press, 1959.
       509 p.

       Analyzes and evaluates role of army in exploring the Trans-
       Mississippi West. Most useful study on the subject.

687   Goodwin, Cardinal L. "A Larger View of the Yellowstone Expedition,
       1819-1820." MISSISSIPPI VALLEY HISTORICAL REVIEW 4 (1917):
       299-313.

       Discusses the scientific and military aims of the army expedi-
       tion sent by Secretary of War Calhoun.

688   Hill, Forest G. ROADS, RAILWAYS AND WATERWAYS: THE ARMY
       ENGINEERS AND EARLY TRANSPORTATION. Norman: University of
       Oklahoma Press, 1957. 248 p.

       History of the role of the army engineers in the opening of
       the west from 1812 to the Civil War.

689   Hine, Robert, and Lattinville, Savoie, eds. SOLDIER OF THE WEST:
       LETTERS OF THEODORE TALBOT. Norman: University of Oklahoma
       Press, 1972. 210 p.

       Letters center on Talbot's experiences in California, Mexico,
       and Oregon, 1845-53 where he served as an explorer and sol-
       dier, partially in the service of John C. Fremont.

690   Hollon, W. Eugene. THE LOST PATHFINDER: ZEBULON MONT-
       GOMERY PIKE. Norman: University of Oklahoma Press, 1949.
       240 p.

       Account of the experiences of an officer-explorer who died
       in one of the first battles in the War of 1812.

691   Holt, W. Stull. THE OFFICE OF THE CHIEF OF ENGINEERS OF
       THE ARMY, ITS NON-MILITARY HISTORY, ACTIVITIES AND OR-
       GANIZATION. Baltimore: Johns Hopkins University Press, 1923.
       166 p.

       Covers the nonmilitary activities of the army engineers in
       the pre-Civil War period, focusing on its organization and
       its problems.

692   Horsman, Reginald. "American Indian Policy in the Old Northwest, 1783-1812." WILLIAM AND MARY QUARTERLY 18 (1961): 35-53.

Discusses how Americans seized the land from the Indians and then justified it on the high moral purpose that they were helping the Indians.

693   Jackson, Donald. LETTERS OF THE LEWIS AND CLARK EXPEDITION WITH RELATED DOCUMENTS, 1783-1854. Urbana: University of Illinois Press, 1962. 728 p.

A collection of 428 letters, memoranda, and other documents covering the expedition and the months following its return.

694   Jackson, William T. WAGON ROADS WEST. Berkeley and Los Angeles: University of California Press, 1952. 422 p.

Story of the federal road surveys and construction in the trans-Mississippi West during the period 1846-69, emphasizing the work done by the army engineers.

695   Lambert, Joseph I. "The Black Hawk War: A Military Analysis." JOURNAL OF THE ILLINOIS STATE HISTORICAL SOCIETY 32 (1939): 442-73.

Discussion of the causes and consequences of the war against the Black Hawk group of the Sac Indians in the 1820s.

696   Leckie, William H. THE MILITARY CONQUEST OF THE SOUTHERN PLAINS. Norman: University of Oklahoma Press, 1963. 269 p.

Story of the army's struggle with the Comanches, Kiowas, and Southern Cheyennes.

697   Mahon, John K. HISTORY OF THE SECOND SEMINOLE WAR, 1839-1842. Gainesville: University of Florida Press, 1967. 387 p.

A study of American struggle with the Seminole Indians, focusing on the conflict of personalities in both the army and Seminole camps.

698   _____, ed. REMINISCENCES OF THE SECOND SEMINOLE WAR. Gainesville: University of Florida Press, 1966. 115 p.

Memories of John Bemrose, a young Englishman who served in the army, 1831-36. Describes life in the ranks during the Second Seminole War.

699   Nichols, Roger L. GENERAL HENRY ATKINSON: A WESTERN MILITARY CAREER. Norman: University of Oklahoma Press, 1965. 243 p.

Biography of a man deeply involved in Mississippi Valley
military activities, 1819-42. Covers also the role of the
army in western expansion.

700   Oliva, Leo E. "The Army and the Indian." MILITARY AFFAIRS 38
       (1974): 117-19.

       Surveys the recent historical literature on the army's struggle
       with the Indians.

701   _____. SOLDIERS ON THE SANTA FE TRAIL. Norman: University
       of Oklahoma Press, 1967. 226 p.

       A kind of total military history of one of America's most
       colorful overland trade routes, from the first escort in 1829
       to the arrival of the railroad in 1880.

702   Osgood, Ernest S. THE FIELD NOTES OF CAPTAIN WILLIAM CLARK,
       1803-1805. New Haven, Conn.: Yale University Press, 1964.
       335 p.

703   Owsley, Frank L., Jr. "Jackson's Capture of Pensacola." ALABAMA
       REVIEW 19 (1966): 175-85.

704   Patrick, Rembert W. ARISTOCRAT IN UNIFORM: GENERAL DUN-
       CAN L. CLINCH. Gainesville: University of Florida Press, 1963.
       226 p.

       First part deals with Indian fighting on the Florida frontier
       following the War of 1812 and the last part deals with Com-
       mander Clinch's experiences in Florida.

705   Porter, Kenneth W. "Negroes and the Seminole War, 1835-1842."
       JOURNAL OF SOUTHERN HISTORY 30 (1964): 427-50.

       Discusses how Negroes who had run away to the Seminoles
       fought with the Indians against the army in the Second Sem-
       inole War.

706   Prucha, Francis P. BROADAX AND BAYONET: THE ROLE OF THE
       UNITED STATES ARMY IN THE DEVELOPMENT OF THE NORTHWEST,
       1815-1860. Madison: State Historical Society of Wisconsin, 1953.
       263 p.

       An account not only of the military campaigns in the West,
       but also the army's contribution to the economic and cultural
       development of the West.

707   _____. THE SWORD OF THE REPUBLIC: THE UNITED STATES

ARMY ON THE FRONTIER, 1783-1846. New York: Macmillan, 1969. 442 p.

Traces the development of the U.S. Army through six decades, showing the army as an instrument of westward expansion. Extensive use of state and regional published sources.

708   Skelton, William B. "Army Officers' Attitudes Toward Indians, 1830-1860." PACIFIC NORTHWEST QUARTERLY, 1976, pp. 113-24.

709   Sprague, John T. THE ORIGIN, PROGRESS AND CONCLUSION OF THE FLORIDA WAR. 1848. Reprint. Introduction by John Mahon. Gainesville: University of Florida Press, 1964. 557 p.

Covers the Seminole War. By an early observer.

710   Sunderman, James F., ed. JOURNEY INTO WILDERNESS. Gainesville: University of Florida Press, 1963. 326 p.

An account of surgeon Jacob Motte's experience in the Seminole War, 1836-38.

711   Symons, T.W. "The Army and the Exploration of the West." JOURNAL OF THE MILITARY SERVICE INSTITUTION OF THE UNITED STATES 4 (1883): 205-49.

712   Taylor, Mendell L. "The Western Services of Stephen Watts Kearney, 1815-1848." NEW MEXICO HISTORICAL REVIEW 21 (1946): 171-84.

713   Thwaites, Reuben G. "The Black Hawk War." WISCONSIN HISTORICAL COLLECTIONS 12 (1892): 217-65.

714   _____, ed. ORIGINAL JOURNALS OF THE LEWIS AND CLARK EXPEDITION. 8 vols. New York: Dodd, Mead, 1904-5.

Essential to research on the army and western settlement.

715   Utley, Robert M. FRONTIERSMEN IN BLUE: THE UNITED STATES ARMY AND THE INDIAN, 1848-1865. New York: Macmillan, 1967. 384 p.

A synthetic and analytical account of America's frontier army prior to the Civil War.

716   Wallace, Edward S. THE GREAT RECONNAISSANCE: SOLDIERS, ARTISTS AND SCIENTISTS ON THE FRONTIER. Boston: Little, Brown, 1955. 288 p.

An informal account of the men who explored, surveyed, and

mapped America's frontier prior to the Civil War.

717   Wesley, Edgar B. GUARDING THE FRONTIER: A STUDY OF THE
       FRONTIER DEFENSE FROM 1815 TO 1825. Minneapolis: University
       of Minnesota Press, 1935. 217 p.

       Discusses American defense policy on the early frontier.
       Scholarly, well-developed study of military defense.

718   Wright, J. Leitch, Jr. "A Note on the First Seminole War as Seen
       by the Indians, Negroes, and Their British Advisers." JOURNAL OF
       SOUTHERN HISTORY 34 (1968): 565-75.

       Discusses how diplomatic documents reveal American expan-
       sionist urges as one of the major causes of the First Semi-
       nole War.

B. THE MEXICAN WAR

719   Anderson, Robert. AN ARTILLERY OFFICER IN THE MEXICAN WAR,
       1846-1847. New York: Putnam, 1911. 339 p.

       Letters of the future commander of Fort Sumter in 1861. He
       was a captain in Scott's army.

720   Backus, Electus. "A Brief Sketch of the Battle of Monterey." HIS-
       TORICAL MAGAZINE 10 (1866): 207-13.

       A useful description by a participant in the battle.

721   Bailey, Thomas. "Diary of the Mexican War." INDIANA MAGA-
       ZINE OF HISTORY 14 (1918): 134-47.

       Written by a participant in the Fifth Indiana Regiment.

722   Bauer, K. Jack. THE MEXICAN WAR: 1846-1848. New York:
       Macmillan, 1974. 454 p.

       Emphasizes influence of guerrilla warfare on the fringes of
       the two armies and also the difficulties of fighting an unpop-
       ular war.

723   _____. SURFBOATS AND HORSE MARINES: U.S. NAVAL OPERA-
       TIONS IN THE MEXICAN WAR, 1846-1848. Annapolis, Md.: U.S.
       Naval Institute, 1969. 291 p.

       Account of naval operations in the Gulf of Mexico and in
       the Pacific. Indicates how Navy supplied part of the land
       forces.

724   Bill, Alfred H.   REHEARSAL FOR CONFLICT: THE WAR WITH MEX-
       ICO, 1846-1848.   New York: Knopf, 1947.   342 p.

       Emphasis on the politics of war making during the Polk ad-
       ministration.

725   Brack, Gene M.   "Mexican Opinion, American Racism and the War
       of 1846."   WESTERN HISTORICAL QUARTERLY 1 (1970): 161-74.

       Finds widespread anti-American attitude among Mexicans who
       were demanding war with United States.

726   Brooks, Nathan C.   A COMPLETE HISTORY OF THE MEXICAN WAR.
       1849.   Reprint.   Glorieta, N.M.:   Rio Grande, 1969.   558 p.

       Reprint of an earlier standard work focusing on the war as
       planned by American expansionists.

727   Carleton, James H.   THE BATTLE OF BUENA VISTA.   New York:
       Harper, 1848.   238 p.

       An officer during the encounter uses his own observations
       plus those of other observers.   Still considered best description
       of the battle.

728   Castaneda, Carlos E.   "Relations of General Scott with Santa Anna."
       HISPANIC-AMERICAN HISTORICAL REVIEW 29 (1949): 455-73.

       Narrative of the reasons why Scott kept his army from taking
       Mexico City when it was defenseless after August 19, 1847.

729   Chamberlain, Samuel E.   MY CONFESSIONS: RECOLLECTIONS OF
       A ROGUE.   New York: Harper, 1956.   301 p.

       Incredibly, this first-hand account first discovered in 1955.
       Dramatic description of camp life in the army during the
       Mexican War.

730   Collins, John R.   "Mexican War: A Study in Fragmentation."   JOUR-
       NAL OF THE WEST 11 (1972): 225-34.

731   Connor, Seymour V.   "Attitudes and Opinions About the Mexican War,
       1846-1970."   JOURNAL OF THE WEST 11 (1972): 361-66.

732   Connor, Seymour V., and Faulk, Odie B.   NORTH AMERICA DIVIDED:
       THE MEXICAN WAR, 1846-1848.   New York: Oxford University
       Press, 1971.   300 p.

       Emphasize political maneuvering in Washington and military
       campaigns.   Complements Justin Smith's work (see entry 784).

733   Crimmins, Martin L. "First Stage of the Mexican War: Initial Oper-
        ations of the Army in 1846." ARMY ORDANANCE 15 (1935): 222-
        25.

734   Croffut, W.H., ed. FIFTY YEARS IN CAMP AND FIELD: DIARY
        OF ETHAN A. HITCHCOCK. New York: Putnam, 1909. 514 p.

        Significant because Hitchcock held an important position on
        Scott's staff.

735   Davis, Wallace E. "The Mexican War Veterans as an Organized
        Group." MISSISSIPPI VALLEY HISTORICAL REVIEW 35 (1948): 221-
        38.

        Discusses the activity of a veterans' pressure group, the Na-
        tional Association of Mexican War Veterans. It followed the
        same pattern as other veteran groups.

736   DeVoto, Bernard. "Anabasis in Buckskin: An Exploit of Our War with
        Mexico." HARPER'S 180 (1940): 400-410.

        Popular account of the exploits of Alexander Doniphan and
        the Missouri Mounted Volunteers in the Southwest during the
        Mexican War.

737   Dillon, Lester R. "American Artillery in the Mexican War, 1846-
        1847." MILITARY HISTORY IN THE TEXAS SOUTHWEST 11 (1973):
        7-29, 109-27.

738   Donnavan, Corydon. ADVENTURES IN MEXICO. Boston: Holbrook,
        1848. 112 p.

        Extremely popular book by a man who claimed he was cap-
        tured and sold into slavery by Mexican guerrillas.

739   Downey, Fairfax. "The Flying Batteries." ARMY 7 (1957): 60-64,
        66-72.

        Discusses artillery action during the Mexican War.

740   Dufour, Charles L. THE MEXICAN WAR: A COMPACT HISTORY.
        New York: Hawthorn, 1968. 304 p.

        Narrative of the Mexican conflict based almost entirely on
        printed records. Clearly written but unoriginal.

741   Duncan, Charles T. "Fremont in California: Hero or Montebank?"
        NEBRASKA HISTORY 29 (1948): 33-54.

        Critical analysis of Nevins' (see entry 767) and DeVoto's in-
        terpretations (see entry 736).

742   Duncan, Louis C. "A Medical History of General Zachary Taylor's
       Army of Occupation in Texas and Mexico, 1845-1847." MILITARY
       SURGEON 48 (1921): 76-104.

743   Eglin, H.W.T. "General Scott's Landing at Vera Cruz." COAST
       ARTILLERY JOURNAL 48 (1928): 244-47.

744   Elliott, Charles W. WINFIELD SCOTT: THE SOLDIER AND THE
       MAN. New York: Macmillan, 1937. Reprint. New York: Arno,
       1979. 817 p.

       Author argues that Scott's decorous personality and his exces-
       sive loguaciousness have obscured his real military abilities.
       Based on manuscript and printed sources and covers Scott's
       service in the War of 1812, Indian Wars as well as the Mex-
       ican War.

745   Ellsworth, Clayton S. "The American Churches and the Mexican War."
       AMERICAN HISTORICAL REVIEW 45 (1940): 301-26.

       Discusses the problems the churches faced during the war with
       conflicting demands: patriotism versus pacifism, and pacifism
       versus anti-Catholicism.

746   Furber, George C. THE TWELVE MONTHS VOLUNTEER: JOURNAL
       OF A PRIVATE IN THE CAMPAIGN IN MEXICO, 1846-1847. Cin-
       cinnati: James, 1848. 624 p.

       By a veteran of Scott's army who discusses camp life and cam-
       paigns.

747   Giddings, Luther. SKETCHES OF THE CAMPAIGN IN NORTHERN
       MEXICO BY AN OFFICER OF THE FIRST OHIO VOLUNTEERS. New
       York: Putnam, 1853. 336 p.

       Useful personal account by a participant.

748   Haferkorn, Henry E. THE WAR WITH MEXICO, 1846-1848: A SE-
       LECT BIBLIOGRAPHY. 1914. Reprint. New York: Argonaut, 1965.
       93 p.

       Covers causes, works on campaigns, and political consequences
       with annotations.

749   Hamilton, Holman. ZACHARY TAYLOR: SOLDIER OF THE REPUBLIC.
       Indianapolis: Bobbs-Merrill, 1941. 335 p.

       Generally considered the most useful biography of "Old Rough
       and Ready."

750 Henry, Robert S. THE STORY OF THE MEXICAN WAR. Indianapolis: Bobbs-Merrill, 1950. 424 p.

Dated, but still considered by many to be the best single volume account of the war.

751 Henry, William S. CAMPAIGN SKETCHES OF THE WAR WITH MEX-ICO. New York: Harper, 1847. 331 p.

A diary by a major with Taylor's army at Monterrey.

752 Hinckley, Ted C. "American Anti-Catholicism During the Mexican War." PACIFIC HISTORICAL REVIEW 31 (1962): 121-38.

Finds little evidence for widespread anti-Catholicism during the war.

753 Jacobs, James. "Our First Expeditionary Force Across the Sea." INFANTRY JOURNAL 33 (1928): 20-24.

Describes Scott's expedition.

754 Kearny, Thomas. GENERAL PHILIP KEARNEY: BATTLE SOLDIER OF FIVE WARS. New York: Putnam, 1937. 406 p.

Biography of Scott's personal bodyguard who was wounded at Churubusco.

755 Kendall, George W. THE WAR BETWEEN THE UNITED STATES AND MEXICO. New York: Appleton, 1851. 520 p.

Account of the war by a newspaper reporter who witnessed most of the battles.

756 Lavender, David S. CLIMAX AT BUENA VISTA: THE AMERICAN CAMPAIGNS IN NORTHEASTERN MEXICO, 1846-1847. Philadelphia: Lippincott, 1966. 252 p.

Story of the decisive battle of the Mexican War. Also deals with the preceeding battles of Palo Alto, Resaca de la Palma, and Monterrey.

757 Lewis, Lloyd. CAPTAIN SAM GRANT. Boston: Little, Brown, 1950. 512 p.

Focuses on Grant's participation in the Mexican War, a story told through Grant's eyes. Reveals Grant as a quiet, unassuming courageous officer. Highly laudable biography of Grant's early years.

758   Livingston–Little, D.E., ed. THE MEXICAN WAR DIARY OF THOMAS D. TENNERY. Norman: University of Oklahoma Press, 1970. 117 p.

Diary of a soldier of a regiment assigned to Scott's command. Emphasizes everyday life of the common soldier.

759   Lofgren, Charles A. "Force and Diplomacy, 1846–1848: The View From Washington." MILITARY AFFAIRS 31 (1967): 57–64.

Discusses how the Polk administration wisely used military force to support political policy.

760   McCornack, Richard B. "The San Patricio Deserters in the Mexican War." AMERICAS 8 (1951): 131–42.

An account of deserters from the American Army who fought with Santa Anna's Army.

761   McSherry, Richard. EL PUNCHERO; OR A MIXED DISH, EMBRACING GENERAL SCOTT'S CAMPAIGN. Philadelphia: Lippincott, 1850. 247 p.

Useful description of Mexican and army life during Scott's campaign by a physician who served under Scott's command.

762   McWhiney, Grady, and McWhiney, Sue, eds. TO MEXICO WITH TAYLOR AND SCOTT, 1845–1847. Waltham, Mass.: Blaisdell, 1969. 214 p.

Collection of excerpts from contemporary accounts.

763   Maguire, T. Miller. "The United States Versus Mexico." ROYAL UNITED SERVICE INSTITUTE JOURNAL 58 (1914): 605–10, 764–70.

American military operations from the British point of view.

764   Mansfield, Edward D. THE MEXICAN WAR: A HISTORY OF ITS ORIGINS. Cincinnati: Derby, Bradley, 1848. 365 p.

Contemporary but nevertheless accurate description of campaigns.

765   Meade, George G. THE LIFE AND LETTERS OF GEORGE MEADE. 2 vols. New York: Scribner, 1913.

Includes material dealing with Meade's service under Taylor and Scott.

766   Meyers, William S.L., ed. MEXICAN WAR DAIRY OF GEORGE B. McCLELLAN. Princeton, N.J.: Princeton University Press, 1917. 333 p.

Covers period from McClellan's departure from West Point in 1846 to the Battle of Cerro Gordo in 1847.

767   Nevins, Allan. FREMONT: PATHMAKER OF THE WEST. New York: Appleton-Century, 1939. 649 p.

Focuses on Fremont as a frontiersman and explorer. Well-researched, well-written, with both a sympathetic and objective point of view.

768   Nichols, Edward J. ZACH TAYLOR'S LITTLE ARMY. Garden City, N.Y.: Doubleday, 1963. 280 p.

Undocumented, but well-written narrative of the army's experiences in the Mexican War under Gen. Taylor.

769   Oswandel, J. Jacob. NOTES ON THE MEXICAN WAR. Philadelphia, 1885. 642 p.

Recollections of a soldier in the Pennsylvania Volunteers.

770   Pohl, James W. "The Influence of Antoine Henri de Jomini on Winfield Scott's Campaign in the Mexican War." SOUTHWEST HISTORICAL QUARTERLY 77 (1973): 85-110.

Argues that Jomini was held in high regard by pre-Civil War American officers because Jomini's theories and principles were put to test and not found wanting by Scott in the Mexican War.

771   Quaife, Milo M. THE DIARY OF JAMES K. POLK. 4 vols. Chicago: McClurg, 1910.

Basic source for the politics of the Mexican War.

772   Ripley, Roswell S. WAR WITH MEXICO. 2 vols. New York: Harper, 1849.

One of the earliest major accounts of the war. Presents the story in surprising detail and balance for its time.

773   Rives, George L. THE UNITED STATES AND MEXICO. 2 vols. New York: Scribner, 1913.

First volume deals with diplomacy, but second covers war with acceptable clarity and correctness.

774   Schroeder, John. MR. POLK'S WAR: AMERICAN OPPOSITION AND DISSENT, 1846-1848. Madison: University of Wisconsin Press, 1973. 184 p.

Discusses how the unpopularity of the war generated widespread opposition, but it never coalesced. Supplements works
by Justin Smith (see entries 782-84) and Otis Singletary (see
entry 778).

775   Scott, Winfield. MEMOIRS OF LIEUTENANT GENERAL SCOTT. 2
       vols. New York: Sheldon, 1864.

       A kind of apologia, but useful for presenting Scott's views.

776   Scribner, Benjamin F. CAMP LIFE OF A VOLUNTEER: A CAMPAIGN
       IN MEXICO. Philadelphia: Grigg-Elliot, 1847. 75 p.

       Scirbner was a private attached to Taylor's army who was dis-
       charged after the Battle of Buena Vista.

777   Sedgwick, John. CORRESPONDENCE OF JOHN SEDGWICK. 2
       vols. New York: Buttel, 1903.

       Officer who served with both Taylor and Scott in every major
       battle. Considered an excellent collection of descriptive let-
       ters.

778   Singletary, Otis A. THE MEXICAN WAR. Chicago: University of
       Chicago Press, 1960. 181 p.

       Treats political, economic, military, and diplomatic aspects
       of the war. Focuses on the ways in which they reflected
       manifest destiny.

779   Smith, Arthur D. Howden. OLD FUSS AND FEATHERS: THE LIFE
       AND EXPLOITS OF LT. GENERAL WINFIELD SCOTT. New York:
       Greystone, 1937. 386 p.

       Popular biography of "The only American Commander never to
       lose a battle," focusing on the Mexican War.

780   Smith, George, and Judah, Charles, eds. CHRONICLES OF THE
       GRINGOS: THE U.S. ARMY IN THE MEXICAN WAR, 1846-1848.
       Albuquerque: University of New Mexico Press, 1968. 523 p.

       Ties together exerpts from eyewitness accounts of the war in
       a chronological story.

781   Smith, Harry A. "Four Interventions in Mexico: A Study in Military
       Government." INFANTRY JOURNAL 18 (1920): 125-31.

782   Smith, Justin. "Our Preparations for the War of 1846-1848." MILI-
       TARY HISTORY AND ECONOMY 2 (1917): 27-42.

This and the following article are taken from chapters in Smith's larger study of the Mexican War.

783 _____. "Sources for a History of the Mexican War." MILITARY HISTORY AND ECONOMY 1 (1916): 18-32.

784 _____. THE WAR WITH MEXICO. 2 vols. New York: Macmillan, 1919.

Well-researched and still considered by many to be the best study of the war. Particularly strong on Mexican sources. Tone is pro-American. Won the Pulitzer prize in 1920.

785 Snoke, Elizabeth. THE MEXICAN WAR: A BIBLIOGRAPHY OF MHRC HOLDINGS, 1835-1850. Carlisle Barracks, Pa.: U.S. Army Military History Research Collections, 1974. 107 p.

A list of holdings at the Military History Research Collections, Carlisle Barracks.

786 Spell, Lota M. "The Anglo-Saxon Press in Mexico." AMERICAN HISTORICAL REVIEW 38 (1932): 20-31.

Discusses how English-language newspapers along the Mexican-American border covered the Mexican War.

787 Stephenson, Nathaniel W. TEXAS AND THE MEXICAN WAR: A CHRONICLE OF WINNING OF THE SOUTHWEST. Yale Chronicle of America Series. New Haven, Conn.: Yale University Press, 1919. 273 p.

Views annexation of Texas as the cause of the war and war with Mexico as imperialistic.

788 Stevens, Isaac I. CAMPAIGNS OF THE RIO GRANDE AND OF MEXICO, WITH NOTICES OF THE RECENT WORK OF MAJOR RIPLEY. New York: Appleton, 1851. 108 p.

789 Tanner, Rhoda, ed. JOURNALS OF MAJOR PHILIP N. BARBOUR. New York: Putnam, 1936. 187 p.

Covers Barbour's service with Taylor, March-September 1846. Barbour was killed at Monterrey.

790 Thorpe, Thomas B. OUR ARMY ON THE RIO GRANDE. Philadelphia: Carey and Hart, 1846. 296 p.

Description of Taylor's army by a probable observer.

791 Vandiver, Frank E. "The Mexican Experiences of Josiah Gorgas." JOURNAL OF SOUTHERN HISTORY 13 (1947): 373-84.

Using Gorgas as an example, author discusses how quartermasters, commissaries, and ordinance officers as well as line officers learned many lessons from the Mexican War that would prove helpful in the Civil War.

792 Wallace, Edward S. "The Battalion of St. Patrick in the Mexican War." MILITARY AFFAIRS 14 (1950): 84-91.

An account of American deserters who fought with Santa Anna.

793 _____. "Deserters on the Mexican War." HISPANIC AMERICAN HISTORICAL REVIEW 15 (1935): 374-83.

A general account of deserters, including the Saint Patrick deserters.

794 _____. "The United States Army in Mexico City." MILITARY AFFAIRS 13 (1949): 158-66.

Discusses the army's experiences during the occupation of Mexico City.

795 Weems, John E. TO CONQUER A PEACE: THE WAR BETWEEN THE UNITED STATES AND MEXICO. Garden City, N.Y.: Doubleday, 1974. 500 p.

Popular narrative based upon observations of key participants, covers the whole of American life during the war.

796 Whiteside, Henry O. "Winfield Scott and the Mexican Occupation." MID-AMERICA 52 (1970): 102-18.

Discusses Scott's occupation policy, arguing that with no precedence, he and his officers evolved and executed a remarkably successful occupation policy.

797 Wilcox, Cadmus M. HISTORY OF THE MEXICAN WAR. Washington, D.C.: Church News, 1892. 711 p.

Though polemical, much material on military campaigns by a participant under Scott's command.

798 Williams, T. Harry. WITH BEAUREGARD IN MEXICO: THE MEXICAN WAR REMINISCENSES OF P.G.T. BEAUREGARD. Baton Rouge: Louisiana State University Press, 1956. 345 p.

Recollections of Beauregard based on diary he kept during the war.

C. THE CIVIL WAR

799 Adams, George W. DOCTORS IN BLUE: THE MEDICAL HISTORY OF THE UNION ARMY IN THE CIVIL WAR. New York: Schuman, 1952. 253 p.

Nontechnical account on the heroic work of doctors during the Civil War, focusing on reforms and the beginnings of an ambulance service.

800 Amann, William F., ed. PERSONNEL OF THE CIVIL WAR. 2 vols. New York: Yoseloff, 1961.

Reprints of rare works including Wright's "Local Designation of Confederate Organizations." Generals are listed alphabetically with an outline of their commands. First volume covers the Confederacy, the second the Union Army.

801 Ambrose, Stephen E. HALLECK: LINCOLN'S CHIEF OF STAFF. Baton Rouge: Louisiana State University Press, 1962. 226 p.

Argues that Halleck served as an essential liaison between Lincoln and Grant and was responsible for professionalizing the Union Army during the war. In addition, believes Halleck may have served as a buffer between his commanders absorbing blame for bad decisions.

802 _____. "Henry Halleck and the Second Bull Run Campaign." CIVIL WAR HISTORY 6 (1960): 238-49.

Story of how Halleck as Chief of Staff tried to manipulate the Union Army in the battle of Second Bull Run. It was his first battle in the east where he tried to apply Jomini's principles to combat. It failed.

803 _____. "The Union Command System and the Donelson Campaign." MILITARY AFFAIRS 24 (1960): 78-86.

Argues that Halleck's motives for attacking the fort were military, not personal, and that its momentous outcome even surprised him.

804 Ballard, Colin R. THE MILITARY GENIUS OF ABRAHAM LINCOLN. London: Oxford University Press, 1926. Reprint. Cleveland: World, 1952. 246 p.

Study by an Englishman who was one of the first to argue that Lincoln's handling of his military commanders was brilliant and correct.

805   Barrett, John G. SHERMAN'S MARCH THROUGH THE CAROLINAS. Chapel Hill: University of North Carolina Press, 1956. 325 p.

Describes how Sherman laid waste to the Carolinas in much the same way as he did in Georgia.

806   Berry, Mary F. MILITARY NECESSITY AND CIVIL RIGHTS POLICY: BLACK CITIZENSHIP AND THE CONSTITUTION, 1861-1868. Port Washington, N.Y.: Kennikat Press, 1977. 132 p.

Argues that the service of black troops in the Civil War was instrumental in bringing about the abolition of slavery and played a large role in securing the civil rights legislation after the war.

807   Bigelow, John. THE CAMPAIGN OF CHANCELLORSVILLE: A STRATEGIC AND TACTICAL STUDY. New Haven, Conn.: Yale University Press, 1910. 528 p.

Massive study of a short campaign ending in a single battle.

808   Bridges, Leonard H. LEE'S MAVERICK GENERAL, DANIEL HARVEY HILL. New York: McGraw-Hill, 1961. 323 p.

Well-researched, scholarly written account of one of Lee's most trusted commanders who played a large role in the first days of Gettysburg.

809   Brownlee, Richard S. GRAY GHOSTS OF THE CONFEDERACY: GUERRILLA WARFARE IN THE WEST, 1861-1865. Baton Rouge: Louisiana State University Press, 1958. 274 p.

An account of the psychological and physical havoc created by obscure Confederate cavalry men.

810   Bruce, Robert V. LINCOLN AND THE TOOLS OF WAR. Indianapolis: Bobbs-Merrill, 1956. 368 p.

Based on solid, detailed research, a study of Lincoln's search for new and improved weapons with which to fight successfully the Civil War. Discusses Lincoln's role in the administration of military procurement.

811   Buel, Clarence C., and Johnson, Robert U. BATTLES AND LEADERS OF THE CIVIL WAR. 1884. Reprint. 4 vols. New York: Yoseloff, 1956.

Significant first-hand accounts, but must be used with care.

812   Burne, Alfred H. LEE, GRANT AND SHERMAN: A STUDY IN LEADERSHIP IN THE 1864-5 CAMPAIGN. New York: Scribner, 1939. 216 p.

A military critique by a British officer who discusses four
campaigns in the war's last years in order to show their unity.

813   Cannon, M. Hamlin. "The United States Christian Commission."
MISSISSIPPI VALLEY HISTORICAL REVIEW 38 (1951): 61-80.

Commission served as an early United Services Organization.
Its aim was to bring religion to Union soldiers, but it also
dispensed much comfort aid. Faced apathy and some antag-
onism from army commanders.

814   Carpenter, John A. SWORD AND OLIVE BRANCH: OLIVER OTIS
HOWARD. Pittsburgh: University of Pittsburgh Press, 1965. 379 p.

Focuses on Howard's work as commissioner of the Freedman's
Bureau and his concern for the education of the freedmen during Reconstruction.

815   Carter, Samuel. THE SEIGE OF ATLANTA 1864. New York: St.
Martin's, 1973. 425 p.

A story of the ordeal in Atlanta during 1864, from the point
of view of both sides.

816   Castel, Albert E. GENERAL STERLING PRICE AND THE CIVIL WAR
IN THE WEST. Baton Rouge: Louisiana State University Press, 1968.
300 p.

Account of the events that took place in the trans-Mississippi
theatre of operations. Price was influential in shaping these
events.

817   Catton, Bruce. "Billy Yank and the Army of the Potomac." MILI-
TARY AFFAIRS 18 (1954): 169-75.

Discusses the life of the enlisted men in the Army of the
Potomac, 1861-64.

818   _____. THE CENTENNIAL HISTORY OF THE CIVIL WAR. 3 vols.
Garden City, N.Y.: Doubleday, 1961-65.

As in other works, skillfully weaves a story of the motives,
the muddling and confusion of Civil War battles.

819   _____. GLORY ROAD. Garden City, N.Y.: Doubleday, 1952.
416 p.

Second volume of the trilogy that deals with the commands
of Burnside, Hooker, and Meade.

820 _____. MR. LINCOLN'S ARMY. Garden City, N.Y.: Doubleday, 1951. 372 p.

First volume of a trilogy on the army of the Potomac, deals with McClellan's command.

821 _____. A STILLNESS AT APPOMATOC. Garden City, N.Y.: Doubleday, 1954. 438 p.

Third volume of the trilogy. An account of Grant's command.

822 _____. THIS HALLOWED GROUND: THE STORY OF THE UNION SIDE OF THE CIVIL WAR. Garden City, N.Y.: Doubleday, 1956. 437 p.

Covers much of the same ground as the trilogy but painted in broader strokes and colored with intimate sketches and new anecdotes.

823 Chambers, Lenoir. STONEWALL JACKSON. 2 vols. New York: Morrow, 1959.

Focuses on Jackson as a military commander. Fullest though not necessarily the most useful biography of Jackson.

824 Chesnut, Mary B. A DIARY FROM DIXIE. New York: Appleton, 1905. Reprint. New York: Peter Smith, 1929. Reprint. Boston: Houghton-Mifflin, 1961. 424 p.

One of the Civil War's most popular diaries. Recounts life in the south during the Civil War by the wife of important southern politician.

825 Cleaves, Freeman. ROCK OF CHICKAMAUGA: THE LIFE OF GENERAL GEORGE H. THOMAS. Norman: University of Oklahoma Press, 1948. 328 p.

Account of a Union officer who, though born a southerner, earned a well-deserved reputation of a competent Union commander.

826 Coddington, Edwin B. THE GETTYSBURG CAMPAIGN: A STUDY IN COMMAND. New York: Scribner, 1968. 866 p.

Based on unfamiliar evidence and sources and contains important insights. Concludes Meade displayed fine generalship in this campaign.

827 Commager, Henry Steele, ed. THE BLUE AND THE GRAY: THE

STORY OF THE CIVIL WAR AS TOLD BY PARTICIPANTS. 2 vols. Indianapolis: Bobbs-Merrill, 1950.

A history of the Civil War in the words of participants. Gives an authentic image of the war.

828   Connelly, Thomas L. ARMY OF THE HEARTLAND: THE ARMY OF TENNESSEE, 1861-1862. Baton Rouge: Louisiana State University Press, 1967. 305 p.

Emphasizes the impact of personalities and politics on the formulation of military policy.

829   _____. AUTUMN OF GLORY: THE ARMY OF TENNESSEE, 1862-1865. Baton Rouge: Louisiana State University Press, 1971. 588 p.

Discusses the decline of the army caused by faulty command structures, squabbling generals and battlefield mistakes.

830   Connelly, Thomas L., and Jones, Archer. THE POLITICS OF COMMAND: FACTIONS AND IDEAS IN CONFEDERATE STRATEGY. Baton Rouge: Louisiana State University Press, 1973. 235 p.

Develops new hypothesis about Confederate strategy: Lee's attachment to Virginia led to a much too provincial southern approach to the war.

831   Cooling, B. Franklin. "Civil War Deterrent: Defenses of Washington." MILITARY AFFAIRS 29 (1965): 164-78.

Describes the work of constructing the intricate earthen fortifications around the capital after the Battle of Bull Run. Concludes they were an effective deterent to Confederate attacks.

832   _____. THE ERA OF THE CIVIL WAR. U.S. Army Military History Research Collection Special Bibliographic Series. Carlisle Barracks, Pa.: U.S. Army Military History Research Collection, 1974. 596 p.

Over five hundred pages of secondary and primary sources held at the U.S. Army Military History Research Collection at Carlisle Barracks.

833   _____. SYMBOL, SWORD, AND SHIELD: DEFENDING WASHINGTON DURING THE CIVIL WAR. Hamden, Conn.: Archon, 1975. 300 p.

Emphasizes military defense processes, focusing on civil relations with garrison soldiers.

834   Cook, Adrian. THE ARMIES OF THE STREET: THE NEW YORK CITY
       DRAFT RIOTS OF 1863. Lexington: University Press of Kentucky,
       1974. 323 p.

       Scholarly analysis of the three-day holocaust that engulfed
       New York City in 1863. Emphasis on mob psychology.

835   Corgdon, Don, ed. COMBAT: THE CIVIL WAR. New York: Dela-
       corte, 1967. 564 p.

       A "complete but compact" story of the sights and sounds of
       Civil War battles.

836   Cornish, Dudley T. THE SABLE ARM: NEGRO TROOPS IN THE
       UNION ARMY, 1861-1865. New York: Longmans, Green, 1956.
       337 p.

       Well-documented account of how, after limitless debate,
       Negro troops were accepted into the Union Army and served
       well.

837   Cotton, Ray C. THE CIVIL WAR IN THE WESTERN TERRITORIES:
       ARIZONA, COLORADO, NEW MEXICO, AND UTAH. Norman:
       University of Oklahoma Press, 1959. 230 p.

       A useful, though undistinguished, treatment of the trans-Mis-
       sissippi theatre of war.

838   Cunnigham, Horace H. DOCTORS IN GRAY: THE CONFEDERATE
       MEDICAL SERVICE. Baton Rouge: Louisiana State University Press,
       1958. 338 p.

       Story of mostly Confederate but some Union medical practices
       during the war.

839   Current, Richard, ed. ADVANCE AND RETREAT: PERSONAL EXPER-
       IENCES IN THE UNITED STATES AND CONFEDERATE STATES ARMIES.
       1880. Reprint. Bloomington: Indiana University Press, 1959. 358 p.

       Memoirs of John B. Hood's personal experiences and thus an
       excellent primary source.

840   Davis, Burke. TO APPOMATTOX: NINE DAYS, 1865. New York:
       Rinehart, 1959. 433 p.

       Day-by-day account, in quotations and paraphrases of partic-
       ipants, of the nine days in April 1865 when Lee's army began
       to disintegrate.

841   _____. JEB STUART: THE LAST CAVALIER. New York: Rinehart,
       1957. 462 p.

Focuses on cavalry tactics and the role of cavalry in Confederate strategy, but also captures the thrill of Stuart's raids.

842   Davis, Carl L. ARMING THE UNION: SMALL ARMS IN THE CIVIL WAR. Port Washington, N.Y.: Kennikat, 1973. 207 p.

Account of arms procurement process during the Civil War. Assesses the impact of weapons technology on the outcome of the war.

843   Davis, Ronald. "The U.S. Army and the Origins of Sharecropping in the Natchez District--A Case Study." JOURNAL OF NEGRO HISTORY 42 (1977): 60-80.

Concludes that the army played a significant role in creating the sharecropping system.

844   Davis, William C. BATTLE AT BULL RUN: A HISTORY OF THE FIRST MAJOR CAMPAIGN OF THE CIVIL WAR. Garden City, N.Y.: Doubleday, 1977. 298 p.

Full scale, scholarly account of the battle at Manassas. Armies portrayed as more capable and generals far abler than most accounts.

845   Donald, David H. "Refighting the Civil War." In LINCOLN RECONSIDERED, edited by David Donald, pp. 82-102. New York: Knopf, 1956.

Discusses the military education of the Union and Confederate commanders in the process of fighting the Civil War.

846   _____. DIVIDED WE FOUGHT: A PICTORIAL HISTORY OF THE WAR 1861-1865. New York: Macmillan, 1952. 452 p.

A selection of over five hundred photographs, some new to publication, along with a lively text by the editor.

847   _____. GONE FOR A SOLDIER: CIVIL WAR MEMOIRS OF PRIVATE ALFRED BELLARD. Boston: Little, Brown, 1975. 298 p.

Personal account focuses on the cruel, brutalizing effect of the Civil War on the common soldier.

848   Donnelly, Ralph D. "Local Defense in the Confederate Munitions Area." MILITARY AFFAIRS 18 (1954): 118-30.

Munitions area includes ore deposits in Tennessee, Alabama, Arkansas, and Missouri. Discusses the problem of defending those areas against anti-Confederate sentiment and Union Army raids, 1861-65.

849   Dowdey, Clifford. LEE'S LAST CAMPAIGN: THE STORY OF LEE
       AND HIS MEN AGAINST GRANT, 1864. Boston: Little, Brown,
       1960. 415 p.

       Argues that Lee's 1864 campaign was by far his most brilliant.
       He did more with less than in any other time during the Civil
       War.

850   _____. THE SEVEN DAYS: THE EMERGENCE OF LEE. Boston:
       Little, Brown, 1964. 380 p.

       Account of the early days of Lee's first command, where he
       displayed the military genius that was to later characterize
       his career.

851   Dowdey, Clifford, and Mananin, Louis H., eds. THE WARTIME PA-
       PERS OF R.E. LEE. Boston: Little, Brown, 1961. 994 p.

       Valuable primary source on Lee's experiences as commander
       of the Confederate forces.

852   Downey, Fairfax D. THE GUNS OF GETTYSBURG. New York:
       McKay, 1958. 290 p.

       Battle from the point of view of the artillery corps.

853   Dufour, Charles L. THE NIGHT THE WAR WAS LOST. Garden City,
       N.Y.: Doubleday, 1960. 427 p.

       The war was the Civil War; the night was April 24, 1862,
       when Farragut captured New Orleans.

854   Dyer, Brainerd. "The Treatment of Colored Union Troops by the Con-
       federates, 1861-1865." JOURNAL OF NEGRO HISTORY 20 (1935):
       273-86.

       Traces the attitude toward black soldiers in the Union Army.
       Confederate government pursued its antebellum views while
       northern government demanded that they be treated as normal
       prisoners of war when captured.

855   Dyer, Frederick H., ed. A COMPENDIUM OF THE WAR OF THE
       REBELLION. 3 vols. Des Moines, Iowa: Dyer Publishers, 1908.
       Reprint. New York: Yoseloff, 1959.

       Gives organization of Union Armies, record of campaigns and
       regimental histories. Compiled from official sources.

856   Dyer, John P. THE GALLANT HOOD. Indianapolis: Bobbs-Merrill,
       1950. 383 p.

Account of Hood's career, focusing on his life at West Point and his military command during the Civil War. Useful for explaining Hood's ultimate failure as a military commander.

857 Eisenschiml, Otto, and Newman, Ralph G., eds. THE AMERICAN ILIAD: THE EPIC STORY OF THE CIVIL WAR AS NARRATED BY EYE-WITNESSES AND CONTEMPORARIES. Indianapolis: Bobbs-Merrill, 1947. 720 p.

Arrangement of selected documents to form a narrative of the Civil War.

858 Esposito, Vincent J., ed. THE WEST POINT ATLAS OF THE CIVIL WAR. New York: Praeger, 1962. 158 p.

Useful collection of multicolored maps with a clear accompanying narrative.

859 Fletcher, Marvin E. "The Negro Volunteer in Reconstruction 1865-1866." MILITARY AFFAIRS 32 (1968): 124-31.

After surveying how historians interpreted the role of the Negro volunteer, concludes that their use was marked by violence and the government withdrew them as quickly as possible.

860 Foote, Shelby. THE CIVIL WAR. 3 vols. New York: Random, 1958-74.

Stresses point of view from both sides, weaving together political, strategic, and personal issues.

861 Freeman, Douglass. LEE'S LIEUTENANTS: A STUDY IN COMMAND. 3 vols. New York: Scribner, 1942-44.

Author's second classic study of the Civil War. An account of Lee's relationship with the commanders who served under him.

862 _____. R.E. LEE: A BIOGRAPHY. 4 vols. New York: Scribner, 1934-37.

The classic biography of Lee.

863 Freidel, Frank. "General Orders 100 and Military Government." MISSISSIPPI VALLEY HISTORICAL REVIEW 32 (1946): 541-56.

Discusses the confusion and uncertainty over civil-military relations that led to G.O. No. 100 which provided instructions for the governing civilians in the field. Remained in effect through the Spanish-American War.

864   Fuller, John F.C. THE GENERALSHIP OF ULYSSES S. GRANT.
New York: Dodd, Mead, 1929. 452 p.

Detailed study of Grant's campaigns with a tendency to apol-
ogize and to defend the Union commander.

865   _____. GRANT AND LEE: A STUDY IN PERSONALITY AND GEN-
ERALSHIP. London: Eyre and Spottiswoods, 1933. 323 p.

Account by a British general which focuses on a detailed
comparison of the personalities of the two leading Civil War
generals. Argues Lee's reputation has been exaggerated while
Grant's has been under-estimated.

866   Futch, Ovid L. HISTORY OF ANDERSONVILLE. Gainesville: University of Florida Press, 1968. 146 p.

Author assesses the matter of responsibility for high mortality
rates at this Confederate prison camp.

867   Goff, Richard D. CONFEDERATE SUPPLY. Durham, N.C.: Duke
University Press, 1969. 275 p.

Account of Confederate logistics covering the activities of
the quartermaster and the subsistence departments as well as
the ordnance bureau.

868   Govan, Gilbert E., and Livingood, James W. A DIFFERENT VALOR:
THE STORY OF GENERAL JOSEPH E. JOHNSTON, C.S.A. Indianapolis: Bobbs-Merrill, 1956. 470 p.

Study of a controversial Confederate general that fails to
fully analyze Johnston's character.

869   Gow, June I. "Military Administration in the Confederate Army of
Tennessee." JOURNAL OF SOUTHERN HISTORY 40 (1970): 183-
98.

Argues that the army of Tennessee experimented with three
administrative heads: the chief of staff, inspector general,
and the adjutant general. It settled upon the latter, which
the author discusses.

870   _____. "Theory and Practice of Confederate Military Administration."
MILITARY AFFAIRS 39 (1975): 119-23.

Argues that Confederates were no more capable of constructing
an effective military staff system than the North and for the
same reasons.

871   Grant, Ulysses S. PERSONAL MEMOIRS OF U.S. GRANT. 2 vols.
New York: Webster, 1885. Reprint. Cleveland: World, 1952.
Interesting and useful autobiography by the Union's most suc-
cessful general.

872   Grant, Ulysses III. "Military Strategy of the Civil War." MILITARY
AFFAIRS 22 (1958): 13-25.
Traces the influence of Jomini on American Civil War strat-
egy.

873   Hagerman, Edward. "The Professionalization of George B. McClellan
and Early Civil War Field Command: An Institutional Perspective."
CIVIL WAR HISTORY 21 (1975): 113-35.
Argues that a military officer subculture developed alongside
other professional groups and drew upon similar ideas and
practices. Uses McClellan as a case study.

874   Hamlin, Percy G. "OLD BALD HEAD": THE PORTRAIT OF A SOL-
DIER. Strasburg, Va.: Shenandoah, 1940. 216 p.
Biography of Gen. R.S. Ewell, commander of one of Lee's
army corps.

875   Harrington, Fred H. FIGHTING POLITICIAN: MAJOR GENERAL
N.P. BANKS. Philadelphia: University of Pennsylvania Press, 1948.
301 p.
Scholarly account of a rather colorful, though less well-known
Union general.

876   Hartje, Robert G. VAN DORN: THE LIFE AND TIMES OF A CON-
FEDERATE GENERAL. Nashville: Vanderbilt University Press, 1962.
359 p.
Not a profound biography, but useful on Van Dorn's generalship.

877   Hassler, Warren W., Jr. COMMANDERS OF THE ARMY OF THE
POTOMAC. Baton Rouge: Louisiana State University Press, 1962.
281 p.
Account of the several commanders that Lincoln pitted against
Lee from 1861 to 1865.

878   _____. CRISIS AT CROSSROADS: THE FIRST DAY AT GETTYSBURG.
Tuscaloosa: University of Alabama Press, 1970. 213 p.
In opposition to most accounts, cites first day as critical in the
three-day conflict. Argues battle was decided on the first day.

879 ____. GENERAL GEORGE B. McCLELLAN: SHIELD OF THE
UNION. Baton Rouge: Louisiana State University Press, 1957.
350 p.

Scholarly account of the career of one of America's most
controversial generals.

880 ____. A.P. HILL: LEE'S FORGOTTEN GENERAL. Richmond,
Va.: Garrett and Massie, 1957. 249 p.

Covers Hill's early life in Virginia, his studies at West Point,
and his commands in the United States and Confederate armies. Focuses on his service under Gen. Robert E. Lee,
particularly on Hill's role in the battle of Gettysburg.

881 Hay, Thomas R. "The South and the Arming of the Slaves." MISSIS-
SIPPI VALLEY HISTORICAL REVIEW 6 (1919): 34-73.

Discusses the temptations in the last of the war for the south-
erners to arm their slaves and send them into battle against
the Union Army. Fear prevented its execution.

882 Henderson, George F. STONEWALL JACKSON AND THE AMERICAN
CIVIL WAR. 1898. Reprint in 1 vol. London: Longmans, Green,
1936. 737 p.

Standard biography of Lee's right-hand man until Jackson's
untimely death.

883 Henry, Robert S. "FIRST WITH THE MOST": FORREST. Indianapolis:
Bobbs-Merrill, 1944. 558 p.

Scholarly and interesting biography of Civil War general who
became a legend in his own time.

884 Hesseltine, William B. CIVIL WAR PRISONS: A STUDY IN WAR
PSYCHOLOGY. Columbus: Ohio State University Press, 1930.
290 p.

The first systematic treatment of the subject. Argues against
wanton cruelty, but does cite lack of foresight and shows inefficiency in management.

885 Higginson, Thomas W. ARMY LIFE IN A BLACK REGIMENT. Boston:
Houghton-Mifflin, 1900. 119 p.

Covers the period 1862-64. Autobiography of a white commander of a black regiment in the Union Army. Focuses on
how he attempted to restore pride to former slaves.

886   Horan, James D. CONFEDERATE AGENT: A DISCOVERY IN HIS-
       TORY. New York: Crown, 1954. 326 p.

       Story of Thomas H. Hines who spied for the Confederacy and
       was involved in the "Northeast Conspiracy" aimed at inciting
       revolution against the United States.

887   Horowitz, Murray M. "Ethnicity and Command: The Civil War Ex-
       perience." MILITARY AFFAIRS 42 (1978): 182-89.

       Argues that ethnic considerations played a large role in the
       appointment of Germans and Irish to positions of military
       leadership. Germans and Irish were singled out because of
       their political strength.

888   Hubbell, John T., ed. BATTLES LOST AND WON: ESSAYS FROM
       CIVIL WAR HISTORY. Westport, Conn.: Greenwood, 1975. 289 p.

       An overview touching upon virtually every military aspect of
       the war from impact of West Point to recruitment of Negro
       soldiers.

889   Hyman, Harold M. "Johnson, Stanton and Grant: A Reconsideration
       of the Army's Role in the Events Leading to Impeachment." AMERI-
       CAN HISTORICAL REVIEW 66 (1959): 85-100.

       Argues that in the political struggle between the President
       and Congress, the military was forced to decide political al-
       legiances and that most officers chose allegiance to the Re-
       publicans in Congress.

890   Jahns, Patricia. MATTHEW FONTAINE MURRAY AND JOSEPH HEN-
       RY: SCIENTISTS OF THE CIVIL WAR. New York: Hastings House,
       1961. 308 p.

       Dual biography of two leading pre-Civil War scientists and
       their contributions to the opposing forces of the Civil War.

891   Jones, Archer. CONFEDERATE STRATEGY FROM SHILOH TO VICKS-
       BURG. Baton Rouge: Louisiana State University Press, 1961. 258 p.

       Describes overall plans of both Confederate and Union Armies
       in the Western Department.

892   Kerby, Robert L. KIRBY SMITH'S CONFEDERACY: THE TRANS-MIS-
       SISSIPPI SOUTH, 1863-1865. New York: Columbia University Press,
       1972. 529 p.

       Traces trans-Mississippi history and offers reasons for its de-
       cline in strength during the Civil War.

893   Key, William. THE BATTLE OF ATLANTA AND THE GEORGIA
       CAMPAIGN. New York: Twayne, 1958. 92 p.

       Popular narrative of Union and Confederate military opera-
       tions in Georgia, focusing on the battle of Atlanta.

894   Kimmons, Neil C. "Federal Draft Exemptions, 1863–1865." MILI-
       TARY AFFAIRS 15 (1951): 25–33.

       Discusses the numerous revisions of the law designed to pre-
       vent exemptions.

895   Lamers, William M. THE EDGE OF GLORY: A BIOGRAPHY OF
       GENERAL WILLIAM S. ROSECRANS, U.S.A. New York: Harcourt,
       Brace, 1961. 499 p.

       Well documented, vigorously written account of brilliant Civil
       War general, focusing on Rosecrans's war service.

896   Lewis, Lloyd. SHERMAN: FIGHTING PROPHET. New York: Har-
       court, Brace, 1932. 614 p.

       Focuses on the views and conduct of Sherman and his rela-
       tions with the men he commanded.

897   Liddell Hart, Basil H. SHERMAN: SOLDIER, REALIST, AMERICAN.
       New York: Dodd, Mead, 1929. 456 p.

       Well-researched, scholarly work that treats Sherman as a sin-
       gularly brilliant genius in the Civil War.

898   Lonn, Ella. DESERTION DURING THE CIVIL WAR. New York:
       Century, 1928. 251 p.

       Deals with causes of desertion, means of escape, and capture
       and punishment.

899   Luvaas, Jay. THE MILITARY LEGACY OF THE CIVIL WAR: THE
       EUROPEAN INHERITANCE. Chicago: University of Chicago Press,
       1959. 252 p.

       Discusses why European officers have studied and written about
       America's Civil War.

900   McCague, James. THE SECOND REBELLION: THE STORY OF THE
       NEW YORK CITY DRAFT RIOTS OF 1863. New York: Dial Press,
       1968. 210 p.

       Descriptive and interpretative account of the anticonscription
       disturbances in New York that became race and class riots.

901   McDonough, James L. SCHOFIELD: UNION GENERAL IN THE
CIVIL WAR AND RECONSTRUCTION. Tallahassee: Florida State
University Press, 1972. 208 p.

Some useful chapters on the war in Missouri and Arkansas.

902   _____. SHILOH: IN HELL BEFORE NIGHT. Knoxville: University
of Tennessee Press, 1977. 260 p.

Balanced narrative, with clear account of the battle. Discounts possibility of southern success. Depicts the battle as
a turning point for Grant's and Beauregard's careers.

903   McFeely, William S. YANKEE STEPFATHER: O.O. HOWARD AND
THE FREEDMEN. New Haven, Conn.: Yale University Press, 1968.
351 p.

Study of the Freedmen's Bureau and its director. Thesis is
that Howard failed to make the bureau an effective agency
because he bowed too much to President Johnson's desires.

904   McKinney, Francis F. EDUCATION IN VIOLENCE: THE LIFE OF
GEORGE H. THOMAS AND THE HISTORY OF THE ARMY OF THE
CUMBERLAND. Detroit: Wayne State University Press, 1961. 530 p.

Depicts Thomas, a Virginian, as a cautious, yet imaginative
commander in the Union Army.

905   McMurray, Richard M. "The Atlanta Campaign: A New Look."
CIVIL WAR HISTORY 22 (1976): 5-15.

Argues for a new framework within which to interpret the
battle, focusing particularly on the need to use more contemporary sources.

906   McMurray, Richard M., and Robertson, James I., Jr., eds. RANK
AND FILE: CIVIL WAR ESSAYS IN HONOR OF BELL IRVIN WILEY.
San Rafael, Calif.: Presidio, 1976. 164 p.

Essays by nine former students of Professor Bell Wiley, prominent Civil War historian, most reflecting Wiley's interest in
the social history of the war and the men who fought it.

907   McWhiney, Grady. BRAXTON BRAGG AND CONFEDERATE DEFEAT:
FIELD COMMAND. 2 vols. New York: Columbia University Press,
1969.

Traces Bragg's career, 1817-63, focusing on his role in con-
tributing to Confederate defeat. Amplifies on the view that
Bragg was an unpopular and ineffective commander.

908   . "Jefferson Davis and the Art of War." CIVIL WAR HISTORY
21 (1975): 101-12.

Traces the historical literature on Davis as commander-in-
chief and goes on to discuss Davis's concept of war and how
it should be fought. Concludes that Davis substituted mere
will to win for systematic planning.

909   , ed. GRANT, LEE, LINCOLN AND THE RADICALS: ESSAYS
ON CIVIL WAR LEADERSHIP. Evanston, Ill.: Northwestern University Press, 1964. 117 p.

Essays by prominent Civil War historians on Lee, Grant, Lincoln, and the Radical Republicans.

910   Maslowski, Pete. "A Study of Morale in Civil War Soldiers." MIL-
ITARY AFFAIRS 34 (1976): 122-26.

Applies Samuel Stouffer's psychological theories (see entry
1405) to morale problems in the Civil War.

911   McNeely, Alexander H. THE WAR DEPARTMENT, 1861: A STUDY
IN MOBILIZATION AND ADMINISTRATION. New York: Columbia
University Press, 1928. 400 p.

Argues that inadequacy of American military organization in
1861 was the product of antimilitaristic tradition, not the
weakness of President Buchanan.

912   Merrill, James M. WILLIAM TECUMSEH SHERMAN. Chicago: Rand
McNally, 1971. 445 p.

Most recent biography of Sherman based on letters never before used by historians.

913   Meyers, Robert M., ed. THE CHILDREN OF PRIDE: A TRUE STORY
OF GEORGIA AND THE CIVIL WAR. New Haven, Conn.: Yale
University Press, 1972. 1,845 p.

Monumental book of letters concerning the life of a prominent
Georgia family. Stands alongside Chesnut's diary (see entry
824) as a primary source.

914   Miers, Earl S. THE WEB OF VICTORY: GRANT AT VICKSBURG.
New York: Knopf, 1955. 320 p.

A detailed account of the campaign that led to the fall of
Vicksburg.

915   , ed. A REBEL WAR CLERK'S DIARY. New York: Oxford,
1957. 545 p.

Diary of a Confederate war office clerk who kept a voluminous account of day-to-day events in Richmond, including some contemporary thinking about military leaders. Useful picture of Richmond life during the war.

916   Milligan, John D. GUNBOATS DOWN THE MISSISSIPPI. Annapolis, Md.: U.S. Naval Institute, 1965. 217 p.

Account of the northern fresh water navy, focusing on the Mississippi. Supports view that Vicksburg, not Gettysburg, was key to northern victory.

917   Monaghan, James. CIVIL WAR ON THE WESTERN BORDER, 1854-1865. Boston: Little, Brown, 1955. 454 p.

Argues that war west of the Mississippi was cruel and useless. It could have been avoided by wiser leadership in Washington.

918   Moore, Albert B. CONSCRIPTION AND CONFLICT IN THE CONFEDERACY. New York: Macmillan, 1924. 367 p.

Account of the conflict, problems, and ultimate failure of conscription in the Confederacy because it was "contrary to the spirit of the people."

919   Murdock, Eugene. ONE MILLION MEN: THE CIVIL WAR DRAFT IN THE NORTH. Madison: State Historical Society of Wisconsin, 1971. 366 p.

A comprehensive study of recruiting and compulsory enlistment efforts of the Union government during the Civil War.

920   _____. PATRIOTISM LIMITED, 1862-1865: THE CIVIL WAR AND THE BOUNTY SYSTEM. Kent, Ohio: Kent State University Press, 1967. 270 p.

A study of Union recruiting efforts focusing on the bounty system in New York state.

921   Murfin, James V. THE GLEAM OF BAYONETS: THE BATTLE OF ANTIETAM AND THE MARYLAND CAMPAIGN OF 1862. New York: Yoseloff, 1965. 451 p.

Useful book (with helpful maps) which argues that Antietam was the high tide of the Confederacy.

922   Nevins, Allan. THE WAR FOR UNION. 4 vols. New York: Scribner, 1959-71.

Rapidly becoming the classic standard general account of the
Civil War. Full of genius and insights.

923 _____, et al., eds. CIVIL WAR BOOKS: A CRITICAL BIBLIOG-
RAPHY. 2 vols. Baton Rouge: Louisiana State University Press,
1970.

Annotated bibliography, covers such topics as government and
politics, economics and social studies, and state and local
politics.

924 Niven, John. GIDEON WELLES: LINCOLN'S SECRETARY OF NAVY.
New York: Oxford University Press, 1973. 676 p.

Provides glimpses into Lincoln's wartime administration, its
jealousies, its infighting, and its problems.

925 Nye, Wilbur S. HERE COMES THE REBELS! Baton Rouge: Louisiana
State University Press, 1965. 412 p.

Story of Lee's invasion of the North to the Battle of Gettysburg.

926 O'Connor, Richard. SHERIDAN: THE INEVITABLE. Indianapolis:
Bobbs-Merrill, 1953. 400 p.

Argues that of all the great Union commanders, Sheridan was
"the youngest, the most aggressive, the most versatile, and
the most uniformly successful." Covers all of Sheridan's life,
but concentrates on his Civil War service.

927 O'Flaherty, Daniel C., Jr. GENERAL JO SHELBY: UNDEFEATED
REBEL. Chapel Hill: University of North Carolina Press, 1954.
437 p.

Concentrates on Shelby's command of Confederate cavalry in
the Trans-Mississippi department and his bizarre effort to lead
disaffected Confederate soldiers in support of Maxmillian of
Mexico after the Civil War.

928 Parish, Peter J. THE AMERICAN CIVIL WAR. London: Holmes and
Meier, 1975. 750 p.

Devotes more to military affairs than Randall's (see entry 934)
standard account. Synthesizes recent findings and interpretations.

929 Parks, Joseph H. GENERAL EDMUND KIRBY SMITH, C.S.A. Baton
Rouge: Louisiana State University Press, 1954. 537 p.

Account of the commander of the Trans-Mississippi West who had the thankless task of organizing a leftover army. Focuses on his Civil War experience but covers early and later life.

930 _____. GENERAL LEONIDAS POLK, C.S.A.: THE FIGHTING BISHOP. Baton Rouge: Louisiana State University Press, 1963. 408 p.

Focuses on Polk's command of a corps in Johnston's army of Tennessee until he was killed in the Battle of Atlanta.

931 Pullen, John J. THE TWENTIETH MAINE: A VOLUNTEER REGIMENT IN THE CIVIL WAR. Philadelphia: Lippincott, 1957. 338 p.

An account of the Maine Volunteers from the battles of Antietam to Appomattox. Based on memoirs, diaries, and letters of participants. A microcosm of the soldier's life in the Civil War.

932 Quarles, Benjamin. THE NEGRO IN THE CIVIL WAR. Boston: Little, Brown, 1953. 379 p.

Argues that Negroes were not merely passive observers but, on their own efforts, were a large factor in establishing their own freedom.

933 Ramsdell, Charles W. BEHIND THE LINES IN THE SOUTHERN CONFEDERACY. Baton Rouge: Louisiana State University Press, 1944. 136 p.

Description of the general economic and social conditions in the South during the Civil War.

934 Randall, James G. LINCOLN THE PRESIDENT. 4 vols. New York: Dodd, Mead, 1945-55.

Standard account (virtually a classic), dealing with Lincoln as a war president.

935 Randall, James G., and Donald, David H. THE CIVIL WAR AND RECONSTRUCTION. 2d ed. Lexington, Mass.: Heath, 1969. 866 p.

Classic and standard history of the Civil War and Reconstruction.

936 Rawley, James A. TURNING POINTS OF THE CIVIL WAR. Lincoln: University of Nebraska Press, 1966. 230 p.

Discusses seven turning points including Battles of Bull Run, Vicksburg, and Gettysburg.

937 Richter, William. "'We Must Rub Out and Begin Over': The Army and the Republican Party in Texas Reconstruction." CIVIL WAR HISTORY 19 (1973): 334–52.

938 Robertson, James I. THE STONEWALL BRIGADE. Baton Rouge: Louisiana State University Press, 1964. 304 p.

Exciting story of the legendary brigade as seen through camp life and personal experiences.

939 _____, ed. FROM MANASSAS TO APPOMATTOX: MEMOIRS OF CIVIL WAR IN AMERICA. Bloomington: Indiana University Press, 1960. 692 p.

Recollections of Gen. James Longstreet, one of Lee's most important and controversial commanders. Provides useful introduction and text notes.

940 Roland, Charles P. ALBERT SIDNEY JOHNSTON: SOLDIER OF THREE REPUBLICS. Austin: University of Texas Press, 1964. 384 p.

Useful biography of one of the Confederate's most competent generals, killed early in the war at Shiloh.

941 Sanger, Donald B., and Hay, Thomas R. JAMES LONGSTREET: SOLDIER, POLITICIAN, OFFICEHOLDER, AND WRITER. Baton Rouge: Louisiana State University Press, 1960. 402 p.

Account of Lee's First Corps commander. Argue that Longstreet was a capable commander who matured in battle and possessed dogged good sense.

942 Sefton, James E. "Gettysburg: An Exercise in the Evaluation of Historical Evidence." MILITARY AFFAIRS 28 (1964): 64–72.

Illustrates some of the problems of evaluating the mass of literature concerning four controversies that resulted from the Battle of Gettysburg.

943 _____. THE UNITED STATES ARMY AND RECONSTRUCTION. Baton Rouge: Louisiana State University Press, 1967. 284 p.

Describes the role of the army as an occupation force, its problems and successes. Gives the army an important role in reconstruction.

944 Shannon, Fred A. "The Federal Government and the Negro Soldier, 1861–1865." JOURNAL OF NEGRO HISTORY 11 (1926): 563–83.

Discusses how the Union government only very reluctantly

accepted blacks in the army and even then discriminated against them.

945   . "The Life of the Common Soldier in the Union Army, 1861-1865." MISSISSIPPI VALLEY HISTORICAL REVIEW 13 (1926): 465-82.

Describes all aspects of the common soldier's life in the Union Army including daily routine of camp life. Concludes there was much suffering.

946   . "The Mercenary Factor in the Creation of the Union Army." MISSISSIPPI VALLEY HISTORICAL REVIEW 12 (1925): 523-49.

Argues that many of those who entered the Union Army did so from the motive of receiving pecuniary reward and this caused a mercenary problem in the army.

947   . THE ORGANIZATION AND ADMINISTRATION OF THE UNION ARMY, 1861-1865. 2 vols. Cleveland: Clark, 1928.

Behind the lines racial history of the military part of the war.

948   . "States Rights and the Union Army." MISSISSIPPI VALLEY HISTORICAL REVIEW 12 (1925): 51-71.

Argues that the states' rights principle was strong in the North and interferred with recruiting, arming, and equipping the Union Army and thereby prolonged the conflict.

949 Sherman, William T. MEMOIRS. 2 vols. New York: Appleton, 1875.

A classic primary source on the Civil War.

950 Simon, John Y., ed. THE PAPERS OF ULYSSES S. GRANT. 4 vols. Carbondale: Southern Illinois University Press, 1967-74.

A collection of widely scattered documents edited with scholarly notes.

951 Singletary, Otis. NEGRO MILITIA AND RECONSTRUCTION. Austin: University of Texas Press, 1957. 181 p.

Discusses how these troops were organized, armed, and trained and their major experiences.

952   . "The Negro Militia During Radical Reconstruction." MILITARY AFFAIRS 19 (1955): 177-86.

Discusses use of black militas by radicals during Reconstruction and how the effort failed.

953   Sparks, David. "General Patrick's Progress: Intelligence and Security in the Army of the Potomac." CIVIL WAR HISTORY 10 (1964): 371-83.

Story of Patrick's experience in providing intelligence and security to McClellan's army on the peninsula. Judges Patrick as quite successful.

954   _____. INSIDE LINCOLN'S ARMY: THE DIARY OF MARSENA R. PATRICK. New York: Yoseloff, 1964. 536 p.

A diary by Lincoln's provost marshall general which throws light on the day-to-day operations of the Union Army.

955   Steer, Edward. THE WILDERNESS CAMPAIGN. Harrisburg, Pa.: Stackpole, 1960. 522 p.

Detailed account of the Battle of the Wilderness, May 5-7, 1864, the first of many inconclusive meetings between Lee and Grant.

956   Stewart, George Ripley. PICKETT'S CHARGE: A MICROHISTORY OF THE FINAL ATTACK AT GETTYSBURG, JULY 3, 1863. Boston: Houghton-Mifflin, 1959. 354 p.

Narrative of the "you-are-there" school, takes the reader through the drama of the climax of the Battle of Gettysburg.

957   Sword, Wiley. SHILOH: BLOODY APRIL. New York: Morrow, 1974. 517 p.

Massive account of an early Civil War battle. Critical of Grant and optimistic about chances for a southern victory.

958   Tanner, Robert G. STONEWALL IN THE VALLEY: THOMAS J. "STONEWALL" JACKSON'S SHENANDOAH VALLEY CAMPAIGN, SPRING, 1862. Garden City, N.Y.: Doubleday, 1976. 436 p.

Account by an amateur historian who depicts Jackson's campaign in the Shenandoah Valley as less a preconceived grand plan than an improvised response to events and conditions.

959   Tate, Allen. STONEWALL JACKSON, THE GOOD SOLDIER. Ann Arbor: University of Michigan Press, 1957. 322 p.

Popular biography of General Jackson.

960   Thomas, Benjamin, and Hyman, Harold. STANTON: THE LIFE AND
       TIMES OF LINCOLN'S SECRETARY OF WAR. New York: Knopf,
       1962. 643 p.

       In-depth study of Stanton. Concludes that he was a good,
       perhaps great, administrator, but he did not dominate Lincoln.

961   Thomas, Wilbur D. GENERAL GEORGE H. THOMAS: THE INDOMI-
       TABLE WARRIOR. New York: Exposition Press, 1963. 649 p.

       Account of a Virginia officer who remained in the Union and
       commanded under Jackson. Laudatory biography.

962   Trefousse, Hans L. "The Joint Committee on the Conduct of the War:
       A Reassessment." CIVIL WAR HISTORY 10 (1965): 5-19.

       Argues that, despite its errors, the committee performed the
       significant service of providing persuasive propaganda.

963   Tucker, Glenn. CHICKAMAUGA: BLOODY BATTLE IN THE WEST.
       Indianapolis: Bobbs-Merrill, 1961. 448 p.

       Step-by-step analysis of the two-day battle with many human
       interest stories. Critical of both Union and Confederate lead-
       ership.

964   _____. HIGH TIDE AT GETTYSBURG: THE CAMPAIGN IN PENN-
       SYLVANIA. Indianapolis: Bobbs-Merrill, 1958. 462 p.

       Account of the strategies, course, and significance of the
       battle. Much detail on military units and life histories of
       the principal participants.

965   _____. LEE AND LONGSTREET AT GETTYSBURG. Indianapolis:
       Bobbs-Merrill, 1968. 301 p.

       A supplement to the author's HIGH TIDE AT GETTYSBURG.
       Dismisses the charges that Longstreet was responsible for the
       failure to attack on July 2.

966   Vandiver, Frank E. JUBAL'S RAID: GENERAL EARLY'S FAMOUS
       ATTACK ON WASHINGTON IN 1864. New York: McGraw-Hill,
       1960. 198 p.

       Accurate, concise account of Early's approach to the Capitol.

967   _____. MIGHTY STONEWALL. New York: McGraw-Hill, 1957.
       Reprint. Westport, Conn.: Greenwood, 1974. 547 p.

       A standard study of Jackson's strategy and tactics.

968 _____. PLOUGHSHARES INTO SWORDS: JOSIAH GORGAS AND
CONFEDERATE ORDNANCE. Austin: University of Texas Press, 1952.
349 p.

Based on public and private papers of Gorgas's, focuses on
the Confederate Ordnance Department and Gorgas's role in it.

969 _____. REBEL BRASS: THE CONFEDERATE COMMAND SYSTEM.
Baton Rouge: Louisiana State University Press, 1956. 142 p.

Discusses the direction of the southern war effort from the
point of view of the Confederate high command, both civilian and military.

970 _____. THEIR TATTERED FLAGS: THE EPIC OF THE CONFEDERACY.
New York: Harper, 1970. 362 p.

Account of the South's daily life--its politics, professions,
literature, social groups, and its military--during the Confederacy. Useful introduction to Confederate history.

971 _____, ed. WAR MEMOIRS: AUTOBIOGRAPHICAL AND NARRA-
TIVE SKETCH OF THE WAR BETWEEN THE STATES. Bloomington:
Indiana University Press, 1960. 496 p.

Recollections of Jubal Early covering his experiences in the
Civil War.

972 Wagandt, Charles L. "The Army Versus Maryland Slavery, 1862-
1864." CIVIL WAR HISTORY 10 (1964): 141-48.

Discusses how even though the government promised not to
interfere with slavery in Maryland, army officers paid no attention to that promise and proceeded to undermine the institution.

973 Walters, John B. MERCHANT OF TERROR: GENERAL SHERMAN
AND TOTAL WAR. Indianapolis: Bobbs-Merrill, 1973. 267 p.

Castigates Sherman's total war strategy as unnecessary brutali-
zation of a defenseless people.

974 Warner, Ezra J. GENERALS IN BLUE; THE LIVES OF THE UNION
COMMANDERS. Baton Rouge: Louisiana State University Press, 1964.
679 p.

Short biographical sketches of all major Union commanders.

975 _____. GENERALS IN GRAY: LIVES OF CONFEDERATE COM-
MANDERS. Baton Rouge: Louisiana State University Press, 1959.
420 p.

Biographical sketches of all Confederate commanders in the first four grades.

976　Weigley, Russell F. "Military Strategy and Civilian Leadership." In HISTORICAL DIMENSIONS OF NATIONAL SECURITY PROBLEMS, edited by Klaus Knorr, pp. 38–77. Lawrence: University Press of Kansas, 1976.

General discussion of civilian leadership's influence on military strategy but uses President Lincoln's experience during the Civil War as a case study.

977　_____. QUARTERMASTER GENERAL OF THE UNION ARMY: A BIOGRAPHY OF M.C. MEIGS. New York: Columbia University Press, 1959. 396 p.

Useful biography of the officer responsible for feeding and transporting the Union Army.

978　Wesley, Charles H. "The Employment of Negroes as Soldiers in the Confederate Army." JOURNAL OF NEGRO HISTORY 4 (1919): 239-53.

Discusses the use of slaves by the Confederate Army despite fears of insurrection.

979　Wiley, Bell I. THE LIFE OF BILLY YANK. Indianapolis: Bobbs-Merrill, 1952. 454 p.

The definitive study of the common soldier in the Union Army during the Civil War. As in THE LIFE OF JOHNNY REB, covers all aspects of soldiering.

980　_____. THE LIFE OF JOHNNY REB. Indianapolis: Bobbs-Merrill, 1943. 444 p.

Definitive study of the common soldier in the Confederate Army. Covers all aspects of soldiering--recruiting, training, health conditions, deeds, and misdeeds.

981　Williams, George W. A HISTORY OF THE NEGRO TROOPS IN THE WAR OF THE REBELLION, 1861-1865. 1888. Reprint. Westport, Conn.: Greenwood, 1977. 353 p.

An early attempt to depict the role of the blacks in the Civil War.

982　Williams, Kenneth. LINCOLN FINDS A GENERAL: A MILITARY STUDY OF THE CIVIL WAR. 4 vols. New York: Macmillan, 1956.

Comprehensive study of the inadequacies of eight Union generals and Lincoln's search for a commanding general of the Union Army. Emphasis on command problems.

983   Williams, T. Harry. "The Attack Upon West Point During the Civil War." MISSISSIPPI VALLEY HISTORICAL REVIEW 25 (1939): 491-504.

Discusses the criticism of West Point during the Civil War as an elitist institution. Radical Republicans especially feared its graduates would stage a military coup d' etat.

984   _____. LINCOLN AND HIS GENERALS. New York: Knopf, 1952. 380 p.

Discusses Lincoln as director of the war and his role in high-command decisions.

985   _____. McCLELLAN, SHERMAN, AND GRANT. New Brunswick, N.J.: Rutgers University Press, 1962. 113 p.

Three character studies that also include much discussion of American military thought.

986   _____. P.G.T. BEAUREGARD: NAPOLEON IN GRAY. Baton Rouge: Louisiana State University Press, 1955. 345 p.

Scholarly, interestingly written, perhaps the definitive biography of the Confederate's first military leader. Concludes Beauregard was a good but not great general.

987   _____. "Voters in Blue, The Citizen Soldiers of the Civil War." MISSISSIPPI VALLEY HISTORICAL REVIEW 31 (1944): 187-204.

Argues that the common Union soldier, when he was not fighting, was criticizing the conduct of his general or engaging in the popular American pastime of political debate.

988   Wood, W.B., and Edmonds, J.E. MILITARY HISTORY OF THE CIVIL WAR. New York: Putnam, 1937. 327 p.

A kind of minor classic in its own field with particular focus on the struggle between the armies commanded by Lee and Grant.

989   Wyeth, John Allan. THAT DEVIL FORREST: LIFE OF GENERAL NATHAN BEDFORD FORREST. 1899. Reprint. New York: Harper, 1959. 614 p.

A detailed, dated but still useful, biography of Forrest.

Chapter 5

THE MILITARY AND AMERICA'S RISE TO WORLD POWER

A. THE MILITARY AND THE CLOSING OF THE FRONTIER

990   Andrist, Ralph K. THE LONG DEATH: THE LAST DAYS OF THE
PLAINS INDIANS. New York: Macmillan, 1964. 371 p.

Broad but thin coverage of the military conquest of the Plains
Indians from the rebellion of the Sioux in 1862 to the white
settlement of Oklahoma.

991   Athearn, Robert G. FORTS OF THE UPPER MISSOURI. Englewood
Cliffs, N.J.: Prentice-Hall, 1967. 339 p.

Focuses on encounters between the cavalry stationed in the
"picket lines of civilization" and the Missouri River Valley
Indians.

992   _____. WILLIAM TECUMSEH SHERMAN AND THE SETTLEMENT OF
THE WEST. Norman: University of Oklahoma Press, 1956. 371 p.

Argues that Sherman's attitude toward the Indians was moder-
ate and that he saw his principal function as using the army
to protect the building of railroads.

993   Bigelow, John, Jr. ON THE BLOODY TRAIL OF GERONIMO.
1890. Reprint. Los Angeles: Westernlore, 1955. 237 p.

Story of Gen. Crook's campaign against the Apaches, as told
by a participant.

994   Bourke, John G. ON THE BORDER WITH CROOK. 1891. Reprint.
Westport, Conn.: Greenwood, 1977. 491 p.

A valuable firsthand account of army life in the Southwest
and of Indian campaigns against the Apaches.

995   Brimlow, George F. CAVALRYMAN OUT OF THE WEST: LIFE OF
       GENERAL WILLIAM CAREY BROWN. Caldwell, Ind.: Caxton, 1944.
       442 p.

       Somewhat pedestrian account of a minor figure.

996   Brown, Dee. BURY MY HEART AT WOUNDED KNEE: AN INDIAN
       HISTORY OF THE AMERICAN WEST. New York: Holt, 1971.
       487 p.

       Indian perspective of the military conquest of the West. Re-
       lies heavily on the words of Indian participants.

997   _____. FORT PHIL KEARNEY: AN AMERICAN SAGA. New York:
       Putnam, 1962. 251 p.

       Account of the Fetterman Massacre when eighty U.S. soldiers
       were wiped out by Indians at Fort Kearney in 1866. Focuses
       on two dissimilar officers, Carrington and Fetterman, with
       common missions.

998   Carriker, Robert C. FORT SUPPLY, INDIAN TERRITORY: FRONTIER
       OUTPOST ON THE PLAINS. Norman: University of Oklahoma Press,
       1970. 241 p.

       Biography of a fort in western Oklahoma, focusing on the
       military efforts to pacify the Indians.

999   Carroll, John M., comp. GENERAL CUSTER AND THE BATTLE OF
       LITTLE BIG HORN: THE FEDERAL VIEW. New Brunswick, N.J.:
       Gary Owen, 1976. 177 p.

       Collection of official reports written by army officers and
       government officials.

1000   _____, ed. THE BLACK MILITARY EXPERIENCE IN THE WEST.
       New York: Liveright, 1971. 591 p.

       Selected essays on outstanding accomplishments of black mil-
       itary unit experiences.

1001   Carroll, John M., and Frost, Lawrence, eds. PRIVATE THEODORE
       EWERT'S DIARY OF THE BLACK HILLS EXPEDITION OF 1874. Pis-
       cataway, N.J.: CRI Books, 1976. 131 p.

       One of few enlisted men's accounts of Indian fighting, viv-
       idly describes army life on the post-Civil War frontier.

1002   Clendenen, Clarence C. BLOOD ON THE BORDER: THE UNITED
       STATES ARMY AND THE MEXICAN IRREGULARS. New York: Mac-
       millan, 1969. 390 p.

Account of the sporadic border hostilities (1848–1919) between Mexico and United States, includes Pershing's expedition against Pancho Villa.

1003   Coffman, Edward M.   "Army Life on the Frontier, 1865–1868."   MILITARY AFFAIRS   20 (1956):   193–201.

Brief account of the garrison life in frontier posts, and its hardships, its monotony, and its few amusements.

1004   D'Elia, Donald J.   "The Argument Over Civilian or Military Indian Control, 1865–1880."   HISTORIAN   24 (1962):   207–25.

Discusses the debate over whether the military who subdued the Indians ought also to have administered them.

1005   Dillon, Richard.   BURNT-OUT FIRES: CALIFORNIA'S MODOC INDIAN WAR.   Englewood Cliffs, N.J.:   Prentice-Hall, 1973.   371 p.

Discusses the military and governmental destruction of the Modoc Indian civilization.

1006   Downey, Fairfax.   THE INDIAN FIGHTING ARMY.   New York: Scribner, 1941.   329 p.

History of Indian Wars, 1865–1915, focusing on the role of officers and enlisted men in pacifying the Plains Indians. Though sympathetic to the Indians, presents the army's view.

1007   Downey, Fairfax, and Jacobsen, Jacques N.   THE RED/BLUECOATS: THE INDIAN SCOUTS, U.S. ARMY.   Fort Collins, Colo.:   Old Army Press, 1973.   204 p.

Covers military campaigns in the West, discussing the role of native scouts in the Indian-fighting army.

1008   Ellis, Richard N.   GENERAL POPE AND U.S. INDIAN POLICY. Albuquerque: University of New Mexico Press, 1970.   287 p.

Discusses Indian wars from the point of view of army headquarters.

1009   _____.   "The Humanitarian Generals."   WESTERN HISTORICAL QUARTERLY   3 (1972):   169–78.

Argues that most of the generals who fought the Indians were personally concerned with the welfare of the Indian.   They were "sincere and benevolent men performing a difficult job."

1010   _____.   "Volunteer Soldiers in the West, 1865."   MILITARY AFFAIRS

34 (1971): 53-56.

Argues that early failures in wars against the Indians after the Civil War came because volunteers were mutinous, ineffective and wanted to go home.

1011   Emmett, Chris. FORT UNION AND THE WINNING OF THE SOUTH-WEST. Norman: University of Oklahoma Press, 1965. 436 p.

A biography of a fort, focusing on the army and its efforts to pacify the Indians of the Southwest.

1012   Faulk, Odie B. THE GERONIMO CAMPAIGN. New York: Oxford University Press, 1969. 245 p.

Account of the last Apache campaign showing that both the army and the Indians lost--the winners being rapacious Americans, the "Tucson Ring."

1013   Finerty, John F. WAR-PATH AND BIVOUAC: THE BIG HORN AND YELLOWSTONE EXPEDITION. Edited by Milo Quaife. Chicago: Donnelley, 1955. 379 p.

Recollections of a reporter's experiences with Gen. George Crook and Gen. George Custer in campaigns against the Sioux in 1876.

1014   Fite, Gilbert C. "The United States Army and Relief to Pioneer Settlers, 1874-1875." JOURNAL OF THE WEST 6 (1961): 99-107.

1015   Forsyth, George A. THE STORY OF THE SOLDIER. New York: Appleton, 1900. 389 p.

Useful autobiography of the author's Indian fighting experience.

1016   Fowler, Arlen F. THE BLACK INFANTRY IN THE WEST, 1869-1891. Westport, Conn.: Greenwood, 1971. 167 p.

Tells the story of the 24th and 25th Colored Infantry Regiments which manned forts throughout the West. Useful chapter on the black soldier and army education.

1017   Frazer, Robert W. FORTS OF THE WEST. Norman: University of Oklahoma Press, 1963. 246 p.

An alphabetical list of forts in twenty-two western states. Sketches each subject, giving reasons for establishment, its important officers, and events in the fort's history.

1018   Graham, W.A. THE STORY OF LITTLE BIG HORN. Harrisburg, Pa.:

Military Service, 1941. 174 p.

Dated but still useful account of the battle by a former judge advocate of the U.S. Army.

1019   Gray, John S. CENTENNIAL CAMPAIGN: THE SIOUX WAR OF 1876. Fort Collins, Colo.: Old Army Press, 1977. 392 p.

Places Battle of Little Big Horn in the broader perspective of the 1876 campaign against the Sioux. Focuses on detail of the military campaign.

1020   Haley, James L. THE BUFFALO WAR: THE HISTORY OF THE RED RIVER INDIAN UPRISING OF 1874. Garden City, N.Y.: Doubleday, 1976. 290 p.

Deals with the last of the wars with southern Plains Indians.

1021   Hoig, Stan. THE BATTLE OF WASHITA: THE SHERIDAN-CUSTER INDIAN CAMPAIGN OF 1867-69. Garden City, N.Y.: Doubleday, 1976. 268 p.

Detailed account of events preceding and following an important event in the southern Plains Wars.

1022   Horn, Tom. LIFE OF TOM HORN, GOVERNMENT SCOUT AND INTERPRETER. Denver: Louthan, 1904. Reprint. Norman: University of Oklahoma Press, 1964. 277 p.

Reissue of an autobiography of one of the Southwest's most colorful characters. Captures the atmosphere of Indian fighting in the Southwest.

1023   Howard, Oliver O. MY LIFE AND EXPERIENCES AMONG OUR HOSTILE INDIANS. New York: DaCapo, 1972. 570 p.

Valuable primary source of government policy by a sympathetic, though ethnocentric general.

1024   Johnson, Virginia W. UNREGIMENTED GENERAL: A BIOGRAPHY OF NELSON A. MILES. Boston: Houghton-Mifflin, 1961. 401 p.

Covers Miles's career, focusing on his role in western campaigns against the Indians. Overly sympathetic, ignoring Miles's flaws.

1025   Josephy, Alvin M. "The Last Stand of Chief Joseph." AMERICAN HERITAGE 9 (1958): 36-43.

Narrative of the 1,300 mile bitter chase that Nez Perces led the army in 1877.

141

1026 King, Charles. CAMPAIGNING WITH CROOK. 1880. Reprint.
Norman: University of Oklahoma Press, 1964. 166 p.

A first-hand account by Crook's regimental adjutant.

1027 King, James T. WAR EAGLE: A LIFE OF GENERAL EUGENE A.
CARR. Lincoln: University of Nebraska Press, 1963. 323 p.

Account of an officer who spent four decades fighting the
Plains Indians, and Apaches of the Southwest. Carr participated in the Wounded Knee incident.

1028 Knight, Oliver. FOLLOWING THE INDIAN WARS: THE STORY OF
THE NEWSPAPER CORRESPONDENTS AMONG THE INDIAN CAM-
PAIGNERS. Norman: University of Oklahoma Press, 1960. 348 p.

Account with emphasis on the history journalism, considerable
material included on the Indian war the journalists covered.

1029 _____. LIFE AND MANNERS IN THE FRONTIER ARMY. Norman:
University of Oklahoma Press, 1978. 280 p.

A social history of the U.S. Army on the western frontier,
1866-90, based on the novels of Charles King, thus forced
to present King's view of the army.

1030 Lane, Jack C., ed. CHASING GERONIMO: THE JOURNAL OF
LEONARD WOOD, MAY-SEPTEMBER, 1886. Albuquerque: University of New Mexico Press, 1970. 152 p.

Journal of an officer who played a prominent role in the
final capture of Geronimo and his band. Includes introduction, epilogue, and ample notes.

1031 Leckie, William H. THE BUFFALO SOLDIERS: A NARRATIVE OF
THE NEGRO CAVALRY IN THE WEST. Norman: University of Oklahoma Press, 1967. 290 p.

Very useful account of the 9th and 10th Cavalry Regiments,
drawing upon post returns and military reports. Argues that
operating under great disadvantages, the units developed into
effective regiments.

1032 Leonard, Thomas C. "Red, White and Army Blue: Empathy and Anger
in the American West." AMERICAN QUARTERLY 26 (1974): 176-90.

Argues that, although they have been treated badly by most
authors, army officers were sympathetic with and even em-
pathetic to Indian problems and conditions.

1033   McNitt, Frank. NAVAJO WARS: MILITARY CAMPAIGNS, SLAVE
RAIDS AND REPRISALS. Albuquerque: University of New Mexico
Press, 1972. 477 p.

Bulk of book deals with Navaho military engagements with
the American Army. Mostly a narrative of military and strategic maneuvers against the Navahos.

1034   Marquis, Thomas B. KEEP THE LAST BULLET FOR YOURSELF: THE
TRUE STORY OF CUSTER'S LAST STAND. New York: Reference,
1976. 203 p.

Blames Custer for the defeat, but introduces other factors such
as low army morale and misinformation. Concludes troopers
panicked.

1035   Marshall, S.L.A. CRIMSONED PRAIRIE: 'THE WARS BETWEEN THE
UNITED STATES AND THE PLAINS INDIANS DURING THE WINNING
OF THE WEST. New York: Scribner, 1972. 256 p.

Focuses on how Army and Indian leaders made command and
tactical decisions and how these two affected the outcome of
battles.

1036   Miles, Nelson A. SERVING THE REPUBLIC: MEMOIRS OF THE
CIVIL AND MILITARY LIFE OF NELSON A. MILES. New York:
Scribner, 1889. 339 p.

Useful primary source, though somewhat self-serving.

1037   Ogle, Ralph H. FEDERAL CONTROL OF THE WESTERN APACHES,
1848-1886. Albuquerque: University of New Mexico Press, 1970.
259 p.

Scholarly, well-researched study of American Indian policy
in the Southwest.

1038   Parker, James. THE OLD ARMY: MEMORIES, 1872-1918. Philadelphia: Dorrance, 1929. 454 p.

Interesting and useful autobiography by an officer whose military experience extended from Southwest Indian fighting to
World War I.

1039   Pratt, Richard H. BATTLEFIELD & CLASSROOM: FOUR DECADES
WITH THE AMERICAN INDIAN, 1867-1904. New Haven, Conn.:
Yale University Press, 1964. 358 p.

Memoirs of Gen. Richard Pratt who first fought the Indians
and then founded the Carlisle Indian School.

1040   Rickey, Don, Jr. "The Enlisted Men of the Indian Wars." MILITARY AFFAIRS 23 (1959): 91-96.

Discusses how individual Americans as soldiers reacted to and lived on the frontier.

1041   _____. FORTY MILES A DAY ON BEANS AND HAY: THE EN-LISTED SOLDIER FIGHTING THE INDIAN WARS. Norman: University of Oklahoma Press, 1963. 353 p.

Well researched, scholarly account of army life in the Indian-fighting army after the Civil War.

1042   Rister, Carl C. BORDER COMMAND: GENERAL PHIL SHERIDAN IN THE WEST. Norman: University of Oklahoma Press, 1944. Reprint. Westport, Conn.: Greenwood, 1974. 244 p.

Scholarly account of Sheridan's attempt to advance the settlement of the west after the Civil War.

1043   Schmitt, Martin F., ed. GENERAL GEORGE CROOK: HIS AUTO-BIOGRAPHY. Norman: University of Oklahoma Press, 1946. 326 p.

Rudely written but extremely useful source on Indian fighting in the West and Southwest by a leading participant.

1044   Schneider, George A. THE FREEMAN JOURNAL: THE INFANTRY IN THE SIOUX CAMPAIGN OF 1876. San Rafael, Calif.: Presidio Press, 1978. 104 p.

Account of a captain who arrived at the Little Big Horn battlefield shortly after Custer's defeat. Substantiates the claim that the dead soldiers' bodies had been mutilated.

1045   Summerhayes, Martha. VANISHED ARIZONA: RECOLLECTIONS OF ARMY LIFE OF A NEW ENGLAND WOMAN. Philadelphia: Lippincott, 1908. Reprint. Tucson: Arizona Silhouetts, 1960. 269 p.

Vivid descriptions of frontier army life by the wife of an army officer.

1046   Thrapp, Dan L. AL SIEBER: CHIEF OF SCOUTS. Norman: University of Oklahoma Press, 1964. 342 p.

Important study of one of the Southwest's most famous and colorful Indian scouts.

1047   _____. THE CONQUEST OF APACHERIA. Norman: University of Oklahoma Press, 1967. 405 p.

Story of how at one time one fourth of the American Army

was involved in chasing down a few hundred Apache warriors.

1048 _____. GENERAL CROOK AND THE SIERRE MADRE ADVENTURE. Norman: University of Oklahoma Press, 1972. 196 p.

Account of the problems facing the army in attempts to follow the Apache Indians into the Sierre Madre mountains.

1049 Utley, Robert M. CUSTER AND THE GREAT CONTROVERSY: THE ORIGIN AND DEVELOPMENT OF A LEGEND. Los Angeles: Westernlore, 1962. 184 p.

1050 _____. FRONTIER REGULARS: THE UNITED STATES ARMY AND THE INDIAN, 1886-1891. New York: Macmillan, 1974. 462 p.

Earlier chapters discuss military organization, doctrine, and frontier conditions; last part focuses on Indian campaigns.

1051 _____. THE LAST DAYS OF THE SIOUX NATION. New Haven, Conn.: Yale University Press, 1963. 314 p.

Account of the Sioux, leading to the Battle of Wounded Knee.

1052 _____, ed. LIFE IN CUSTER'S CAVALRY: DIARIES AND LETTERS OF ALBERT AND JENNIE BARNITZ, 1867-1868. New Haven, Conn.: Yale University Press, 1977. 302 p.

Presents vivid picture of the daily life in the old frontier army as it patrolled the plains. Considerable material on the army family and much information on the life of a woman on the military frontier.

1053 Vogel, Virgil T. THIS COUNTRY WAS OURS: A DOCUMENTARY HISTORY OF THE AMERICAN INDIAN. New York: Harper, 1972. 473 p.

Contains many documents on conflict between Indians and American military.

1054 Wade, Arthur P. "The Military Command Structure: The Great Plains, 1853-1891." JOURNAL OF THE WEST 25 (1976): 5-22.

1055 White, Lonnie, et al. HOSTILES AND HORSE SOLDIERS: INDIAN BATTLES AND CAMPAIGNS IN THE WEST. Boulder, Colo.: Pruett, 1972. 231 p.

Accounts of battles in the plains wars by several competent scholars.

B. THE MILITARY AND OVERSEAS EMPIRE

1056   Alger, Russell A. "The Food of the Army During the Spanish War."
NORTH AMERICAN REVIEW 172 (1901): 39-58.

Secretary of war's apologia against the criticism that he mis-
managed the war.

1057   _____. THE SPANISH-AMERICAN WAR. New York: Harper, 1901.
465 p.

Book length apologia of a secretary of war who was charged
with ineptness in managing the Spanish-American War.

1058   Bacon, Robert, and Scott, James B., eds. THE MILITARY AND CO-
LONIAL POLICY OF THE UNITED STATES: ADDRESSES AND RE-
PORTS BY ELIHU ROOT. Cambridge, Mass.: Harvard University
Press, 1924. 511 p.

Useful primary source on a formative period of American military history.

1059   Berthoff, Rowland T. "Taft and MacArthur, 1900-1901: A Study in
Civil-Military Relations." WORLD POLITICS 5 (1953): 196-213.

Discusses the conflict between Gen. Arthur MacArthur, commander of the Army in the Philippines, and William Howard
Taft, Philippine Commissioner, over the task of ruling an imperial colony. Argues that the colonial governmental structure was as much at fault as the two personalities.

1060   Bigelow, John. REMINISCENCES OF THE SANTIAGO CAMPAIGN.
New York: Harper, 1898. 187 p.

Useful memoir by one of the participants in the Spanish-American
War.

1061   Blount, James H. THE AMERICAN OCCUPATION OF THE PHILIP-
PINES, 1898-1912. New York: Putnam, 1912. 644 p.

Account of an officer and a judge who spent six years in the
Islands. Argues for Filipino self-government, and opposed
American imperialism in Asia.

1062   Bolton, Grania. "Military Diplomacy and National Liberation: Insur-
gent-American Relations After the Fall of Manila." MILITARY AF-
FAIRS 36 (1972): 99-104.

Traces the deterioration of relations between Aguinaldo and
his forces and the American military, 1898-99. Argues that

American military commander took too narrow of a military view of diplomacy.

1063   Chadwick, French E. THE RELATIONS OF THE UNITED STATES TO SPAIN: THE SPANISH-AMERICAN WAR. 2 vols. New York: Scribner, 1911.

Still a useful, detached account of American relations with Spain, focusing on the clash in 1898.

1064   Clendenen, Clarence C. THE UNITED STATES AND PANCHO VILLA: A STUDY IN UNCONVENTIONAL DIPLOMACY. Ithaca, N.Y.: Cornell University Press, 1961. 352 p.

Deals mostly with diplomatic relations with Pancho Villa but contains a good discussion on frontier troubles in 1910.

1065   Cooper, Jerry. "National Guard Reform, the Army, and the Spanish-American War: The View From Wisconsin." MILITARY AFFAIRS 42 (1978): 20-23.

Using Wisconsin as a case study, author argues that National Guardsmen opposed the Hull bill of 1898 and tried to use the Spanish-American War to further the militia citizen-soldier tradition.

1066   Cosmas, Graham A. AN ARMY FOR EMPIRE: THE UNITED STATES ARMY IN THE SPANISH-AMERICAN WAR. Columbia: University of Missouri Press, 1971. 334 p.

Comprehensive account of the structure and composition of the U.S. Army prior to and during the war, focusing on military policy and the men who made it.

1067   _____. "From Order to Chaos: The War Department, The National Guard and Military Policy, 1898." MILITARY AFFAIRS 29 (1965): 105-21.

Argues that rather than incompetency, a "complex chain of events," hindered the War Department's preparation for war with Spain and they disrupted what preparations it had made.

1068   _____. "Military Reform After the Spanish-American War: The Army Reorganization Fight of 1898-1899." MILITARY AFFAIRS 35 (1972): 12-18.

Discusses how debate over the Army Reorganization Bill of 1898 became entangled with other issues as the annexation of the Philippines.

1069 _____. "Securing the Fruits of Victory: The U.S. Army Occupies Cuba, 1898-1899." MILITARY AFFAIRS 38 (1974): 85-91.

Discusses how the war department managed the organization of the Army of Occupation after the Spanish-American War with a minimum of confusion.

1070 Daggett, Aaron S. AMERICA IN THE CHINA RELIEF EXPEDITION. Kansas City, Kans.: Hudson-Kimberly, 1903. 267 p.

Early account of America's participation in the successful effort to relieve the beseiged foreign legation in Peking in 1900.

1071 Davis, Richard H. THE CUBAN AND PUERTO RICAN CAMPAIGNS. New York: Scribner, 1898. Reprint. New York: Arno, 1979. 360 p.

Valuable, sometimes irreverent, account of the American experience in the Cuban and Puerto Rican expeditions.

1072 Dierks, Jack C. A LEAP TO ARMS: THE CUBAN CAMPAIGN OF 1898. Philadelphia: Lippincott, 1970. 240 p.

Brief introductory account with much detail on the naval battle of Santiago Bay.

1073 Fletcher, Marvin. "The Black Volunteers in the Spanish-American War." MILITARY AFFAIRS 38 (1974): 48-53.

Discusses how blacks saw the war as an opportunity but were discriminated against in recruitment. Those who were accepted for service, faced similar fates.

1074 Foner, Philip S. THE SPANISH-CUBAN-AMERICAN WAR AND THE BIRTH OF AMERICAN IMPERIALISM, 1895-1902. 2 vols. New York: Monthly Review, 1972.

Revisionist treatment of the war from a Cuban point of view. Emphasizes economic causation and imperialistic consequences.

1075 Freidel, Frank B. THE SPLENDID LITTLE WAR. Boston: Little, Brown, 1958. 314 p.

A useful pictorial history of the Spanish-American War which attempts to capture the realism and seriousness of the war rather than its more ludicrous aspects.

1076 Funston, Frederick. MEMORIES OF TWO WARS: CUBAN AND PHILIPPINE EXPERIENCES. New York: Scribner, 1911. 451 p.

An informative, at times racy, account of Funston's experiences in the Spanish-American War both in Cuba and in the
Philippines.

1077   Gates, John M. SCHOOLBOOKS AND KRAGGS: THE UNITED
STATES ARMY IN THE PHILIPPINES, 1898-1902. Westport, Conn.:
Greenwood, 1973. 315 p.

Account of the army's dual role in the Philippine occupation:
military pacification and the building of benevolent, humanitarian programs.

1078   Gatewood, Willard B., comp. SMOKED YANKEES AND THE STRUG-
GLE FOR EMPIRE: LETTERS FROM NEGRO SOLDIERS, 1898-1902.
Urbana: University of Illinois Press, 1971. 328 p.

Comprehensive collection of letters from black soldiers in the
Spanish-American War and Philippine Insurrection.

1079   Gillett, Howard, Jr. "Military Occupation of Cuba, 1899-1902:
Workshop for Progressivism." AMERICAN QUARTERLY 25 (1973):
410-25.

Argues military government in Cuba instituted progressive-like
reforms and served as a model for American Progressivism.

1080   Hagedorn, Hermann. LEONARD WOOD: A BIOGRAPHY. Vol. I.
New York: Harper, 1931. 436 p.

Focuses on Wood's role in the capture of Geronimo and particularly his work as a leading pro-consul of America's new
empire.

1081   Healy, David F. THE UNITED STATES IN CUBA, 1898-1902: GEN-
ERALS, POLITICIANS AND THE SEARCH FOR A POLICY. Madison:
University of Wisconsin Press, 1963. 260 p.

Focuses on the politics of military administration of Cuba.
Argues policy developed out of circumstances.

1082   Jessup, Philip C. ELIHU ROOT. Vol. I. New York: Dodd-Mead,
1938. 450 p.

Several chapters deal with Root as secretary of war immediately after the Spanish-American War.

1083   Jones, Virgil C. ROOSEVELT'S ROUGH RIDERS. Garden City, N.Y.:
Doubleday, 1971. 345 p.

Story of men from all walks of life thrown together in a

unique regiment. Avoids ridicule of prior works on Spanish-American War.

1084 Kenchel, Edward F. "Chemicals and Meat: The Embalmed Beef Scandal of the Spanish-American War." BULLETIN OF THE HISTORY OF MEDICINE 48 (1974): 249-64.

1085 Kennan, George. CAMPAIGNING IN CUBA. New York: Century, 1899. 229 p.

One of the best of many reportorial works by war correspondents.

1086 Lane, Jack C. ARMED PROGRESSIVE: GENERAL LEONARD WOOD. San Rafael, Calif.: Presidio, 1978. 329 p.

A study of the military and public career of one of America's most controversial generals. Focusing on Wood's experience as a colonial pro consul and his role as a preparedness advocate.

1087 _____. "Instrument for Empire: The American Military Government in Cuba, 1899-1902." SCIENCE AND SOCIETY 36 (1972): 314-30.

Argues that the main concern of Leonard Wood's military government was to place Cuba securely in America's new empire.

1088 Leech, Margaret. IN THE DAYS OF McKINLEY. New York: Harper, 1959. 686 p.

Describes administration of Spanish-American War. Focuses on McKinley, who emerges as a limited but nevertheless honest, principled, effective leader.

1089 Lindeman, Gerald F. THE MIRROR OF WAR: AMERICAN SOCIETY AND THE SPANISH-AMERICAN WAR. Ann Arbor: University of Michigan Press, 1974. 227 p.

Argues Spanish-American War was the dividing line between nineteenth century localism and twentieth century nationalism.

1090 Longacre, Edward G. FROM UNION STARS TO TOP HAT: A BIOGRAPHY OF THE EXTRAORDINARY GENERAL JAMES HARRISON WILSON. Harrisburg, Pa.: Stackpole, 1972. 320 p.

Biography of a Civil War "boy" general, successful businessman, officer in the Spanish-American War, and imperialist.

1091   Miley, John D. IN CUBA WITH SHAFTER. New York: Scribner, 1899. 228 p.

Significant narrative memoir by a participant on Shafter's staff.

1092   Millett, Allan. "'Cleansing the Augean Stables': The American Armed Forces in the Caribbean, 1898-1934." ESSAYS ON NEW DIMENSIONS IN MILITARY HISTORY 4 (1976): 123-41.

1093   _____. "The General Staff and the Cuban Intervention of 1906." MILITARY AFFAIRS 39 (1967): 113-19.

Discusses how in the case of the Cuban intervention of 1906, the general staff performed its proper function by drafting and carrying out contingency plans.

1094   _____. THE POLITICS OF INTERVENTION: THE MILITARY OCCUPATION OF CUBA, 1906-1909. Columbus: Ohio State University Press, 1968. 306 p.

Argues Roosevelt was less than enthusiastic about intervention and that Cuban factions had their own reasons for desiring intervention.

1095   Millis, Walter. THE MARTIAL SPIRIT: A STUDY OF OUR WAR WITH SPAIN. Boston: Houghton-Mifflin, 1931. Reprint. New York: Arno, 1979. 427 p.

Classic study of the origins, conduct, and outcome of the Spanish-American War. Author's criticism is softened by his capable style.

1096   Post, Charles J. THE LITTLE WAR OF PRIVATE POST. Boston: Little, Brown, 1960. 340 p.

Almost a classic now. Depicts his experiences in the Spanish-American War with color, vividness, and a sense of humor amid scenes of death and dying.

1097   Ranson, Edward. "The Investigation of the War Department, 1898-1899." HISTORIAN 34 (1971): 78-99.

Discusses the origins and work of the famous Dodge commission, arguing that the commission's report, though replete with political overtones, was substantial enough to influence army reform in 1899.

1098   _____. "Nelson A. Miles as Commanding General." MILITARY AFFAIRS 29 (1965): 179-200.

Trials and tribulations of Gen. Miles as commanding general prior to and during the Spanish-American War.

1099 Roosevelt, Theodore. THE ROUGH RIDERS. New York: Scribner, 1899. 214 p.

Colorful personal account of Roosevelt's role in Spanish-American War. Particularly biased, but still useful as a first-hand account if used with caution.

1100 Sarqent, Herbert H. THE CAMPAIGN OF SANTIAGO DE CUBA. 3 vols. Chicago: McClurg, 1914.

Detailed and useful account by a first-hand observer, with some research in published documents. Highly critical of American war effort.

1101 Sexton, William T. SOLDIERS IN THE SUN: AN ADVENTURE IN IMPERIALISM. Harrisburg, Pa.: Military Service, 1939. 297 p.

Comprehensive account covering the entire period of military occupation, May 1898–June 1901, in the Philippines.

1102 Smythe, Donald. GUERILLA WARRIOR: THE EARLY LIFE OF JOHN J. PERSHING. New York: Scribner, 1973. 370 p.

Discusses Pershing's career when he was involved with unconventional enemies: American Indians, Filipinos, and Mexican revolutionaries.

1103 U.S. Department of War. CORRESPONDENCE RELATING TO THE WAR WITH SPAIN. 2 vols. Washington, D.C.: Government Printing Office, 1902.

Basic and indispensible collection of official government correspondence relating to the American war effort in 1898.

1104 U.S. Senate. "Report of the Commission Appointed by the President to Investigate the Conduct of the War Department in the War With Spain." 8 vols. Senate Document no. 221. 56th Cong., 1st Sess. Washington, D.C.: Government Printing Office, 1902.

Basic document for researching the war and the controversies of administration.

1105 Vandiver, Frank E. BLACK JACK: THE LIFE AND TIMES OF JOHN J. PERSHING. Vol. I. College Station: Texas A & M University Press, 1977. 594 p.

Describes Pershing's career as commander in the Spanish-American War, in the Punitive Expedition, and as a colonial administrator.

1106   Welch, Richard E., Jr. "American Atrocities in the Philippines: The Indictment and the Response." PACIFIC HISTORICAL REVIEW 43 (1974): 233-53.

Discusses several verifiable American atrocities and the public's lack of concern. Argues racism the cause.

1107   Wheeler, Joseph. THE SANTIAGO CAMPAIGN. Boston: Lamson, Wolffe, 1898. 369 p.

Moderately useful memoir of the Cuban Campaign by one of the leading generals, but limited by Wheeler's brief participation.

1108   White, John R. BULLETS AND BOLOS: FIFTEEN YEARS IN THE PHILIPPINE ISLANDS. New York: Century, 1928. 348 p.

An exceptional personal narrative of the author's experiences with the Philippine Constabulary. Contains a particularly good description of the Battle of Mount Dajo.

1109   Wilson, James H. UNDER THE OLD FLAG: RECOLLECTIONS OF MILITARY OPERATIONS IN THE WAR FOR UNION, THE SPANISH-AMERICAN WAR AND THE BOXER REBELLION. 2 vols. New York: Appleton, 1912. Reprint. Westport, Conn.: Greenwood, 1971.

Memoirs of a controversial general officer who served prominently in three wars. Most useful on the Spanish American War and the Boxer Rebellion where Wilson established himself as an outspoken expansionist.

Chapter 6

THE MILITARY IN THE AGE OF TOTAL WAR (1914-45)

A. WORLD WAR I

1110   Alexander, Robert. MEMORIES OF THE WORLD WAR, 1917-1918.
New York: Macmillan, 1931. 309 p.

Recollections by one of Pershing's division commanders.

1111   American Battle Monuments Commission. AMERICAN ARMIES AND
BATTLEFIELDS IN EUROPE: A HISTORY, GUIDE, AND REFERENCE
BOOK. Washington, D.C.: Government Printing Office, 1938.

Indispensible for locating units on the World War I battlefields.

1112   Asprey, Robert. AT BELLEAU WOODS. New York: Putnam, 1965.
375 p.

An important study of the battle involving the American Second Division. Well documented from interviews and primary
sources.

1113   Beardsley, Edward H. "Allied Against Sin: American and British Responses to Venereal Disease in World War I." MEDICAL HISTORY
20 (1976): 189-202.

Composes British and American responses to the problem of
venereal disease among the troops and concludes that Americans were more successful because they treated it as a medical not a moral problem.

1114   Barbeau, Arthur E., and Henri, Florette. THE UNKNOWN SOLDIERS:
BLACK AMERICAN TROOPS IN WORLD WAR I. Philadelphia: Tem-
ple University Press, 1974. 279 p.

Dispels the myth that blacks acted cowardly in World War I.
Provides evidence of widespread discrimination and abuse

against black troops during the war.

1115   Baruch, Bernard M. AMERICAN INDUSTRY IN THE WAR. New
        York: Prentice Hall, 1961. 498 p.

        Includes Baruch's official report on the activity of the War
        Industries Board (Baruch was the director). A significant pri-
        mary source on the economics of World War I.

1116   _____. BARUCH: MY OWN STORY. New York: Holt, 1957.
        337 p.

        Portions concerned with Baruch's experiences as director of
        the War Industries Board.

1117   Beaver, Daniel R. NEWTON D. BAKER AND THE AMERICAN WAR
        EFFORT 1917-1919. Lincoln: University of Nebraska Press, 1966.
        273 p.

        Study of Baker as Secretary of War. Assigns Baker a large
        role in the war effort.

1118   _____. "Newton D. Baker and the Genesis of the War Industries
        Board." JOURNAL OF AMERICAN HISTORY 52 (1965): 43-58.

        Account of how "personal beliefs, institutional loyalties and
        party politics" interacted to shape the American war effort
        during World War I.

1119   Blumenson, Martin, ed. THE PATTON PAPERS: 1885-1940. Vol. I.
        Houghton-Mifflin, 1972. 966 p.

        Covers Patton's career before World War II, with a focus on
        Patton's experience with World War I armored warfare.

1120   Broun, Heywood. A.E.F.: WITH GENERAL PERSHING AND THE
        AMERICAN FORCES. New York: Appleton, 1918. 297 p.

        Description by one of the few correspondents Pershing allowed
        in the trenches of the day-to-day life of the American sol-
        dier on the front during World War II.

1121   Bullard, Robert L. AMERICAN SOLDIERS ALSO FOUGHT. New
        York: Longmans, Green, 1936. 118 p.

        A brief narrative of the war by the Second Army (American
        Expeditonary Forces) commander. He attempts to disprove
        the theory that Americans played a small role in final out-
        come of the First World War.

1122 _____. PERSONALITIES AND REMINISCENCES OF THE WAR. Garden City, N.Y.: Doubleday, 1925. 347 p.

Memoirs of the commander of Pershing's Second Army commander.

1123 Camfield, Thomas M. "'Will to Win'--The U.S. Army Troop Morale Program of World War I." MILITARY AFFAIRS 41 (1977): 125-28.

Account of the efforts to establish a systematic program for influencing the minds of World War I soldiers. Concludes the program had little effect but idea survived for use in World War II.

1124 Clarkson, Grosvenor B. INDUSTRIAL AMERICA IN THE WORLD WAR: THE STRATEGY BEHIND THE LINE, 1917-1918. Boston: Houghton-Mifflin, 1923. 573 p.

Still the standard account of industrial mobilization by the former director of the Council of National Defense. Based on War Industries Board records and interviews. Useful not for its historical analysis, but as a major source for historians of American participation in the war.

1125 Clifford, John G. THE CITIZEN SOLDIERS: THE PLATTSBURG TRAINING CAMP MOVEMENT, 1913-1920. Lexington: University of Kentucky Press, 1972. 326 p.

Scholarly work presents a favorable view of the movement. Denies Plattsburgers were militarists and undemocratic, and argues they demonstrated the effectiveness of universal training.

1126 Coffman, Edward M. "The Battle Against Red Tape: Business Methods of the War Department General Staff, 1917-1918." MILITARY AFFAIRS 26 (1962): 1-10.

Discusses how under the leadership of Peyton March the general staff was efficiently organized and successfully met its first wartime test.

1127 _____. HILT OF THE SWORD: THE CAREER OF PEYTON C. MARCH. Madison: University of Wisconsin Press, 1966. 346 p.

Biography of the chief of staff during World War I. Also focuses on the modernization of the army after the Spanish-American War.

1128 _____. THE WAR TO END ALL WARS: THE AMERICAN MILITARY EXPERIENCE IN WORLD WAR I. New York: Oxford University Press, 1968. 396 p.

Narrative of American military participation. Focuses on the planning, organization, and fighting of the American Expeditionary Forces.

1129 Coit, Margaret. MR. BARUCH. Boston: Houghton-Mifflin, 1957. 784 p.

Covers well Baruch's work as War Industries Board director during World War I. Well written but not interpreted with scholarly precision.

1130 Cooperman, Stanley. WORLD WAR I AND THE AMERICAN NOVEL. Baltimore: Johns Hopkins University Press, 1967. 273 p.

Using literature and conventional historical sources, author attempts to reconstruct the World War I experience. Organization topical rather than chronological, focusing on fictional literature.

1131 Crowder, Enoch. THE SPIRIT OF SELECTIVE SERVICE. New York: Century, 1920. 353 p.

Account by the provost marshall who headed the Selective Service during World War I. Concludes Selective Service successful because American citizens were involved in the system.

1132 Crowell, Benedict, and Wilson, Robert. THE ROAD TO FRANCE. 2 vols. New Haven, Conn.: Yale University Press, 1921.

Useful for human interest stories and information on troop movements.

1133 Crozier, William. ORDNANCE IN THE WORLD WAR: A CONTRIBUTION TO AMERICAN PREPAREDNESS. New York: Scribner, 1920. 292 p.

Former member of the War Department discusses the processes of arming the American Expeditionary Forces. Mostly an apology for the department and the author.

1134 Cuff, Robert S. "Business, the State, and World War I: The American Experience." In WAR AND SOCIETY IN NORTH AMERICA, edited by J.S. Granatstein and R.S. Cuff. Nelson, 1971. 199 p.

Discusses America's first total war experience and the need for business-military cooperation.

1135 _____. "'A Dollar-A-Year Man' in Government: George N. Peek and the War Industries Board." BUSINESS HISTORY REVIEW 41 (1967): 404-20.

Discusses the role that business executives played in economic
mobilization during World War I, using Peek as a case study.

1136 _____. "Newton D. Baker, Frank Scott and THE AMERICAN REIN-
FORCEMENT IN THE WORLD WAR." MILITARY AFFAIRS 34 (1970):
11-13.

Argues that the book, THE AMERICAN REINFORCEMENT IN
THE WORLD WAR (see entry 1151) was written at the sugges-
tion of Baker and Scott who wanted the public to know their
role in industrial mobilization.

1137 _____. WAR INDUSTRIES BOARD: BUSINESS-GOVERNMENT RE-
LATIONS DURING WORLD WAR I. Baltimore: Johns Hopkins University Press, 1973. 304 p.

Account of the War Industries Board from the point of view
of organizational theory.

1138 Davis, Allan. "Welfare, Reform, and World War I." AMERICAN
QUARTERLY 19 (1967): 516-33.

Discusses how reformers used the crusading spirit of the war to
push for more progressive reforms, arguing that in a sense the
war made reform possible.

1139 Dawes, Charles G. A JOURNAL OF THE GREAT WAR. 2 vols.
Boston: Houghton-Mifflin, 1921.

Account by the purchasing agent for the American Expeditionary Forces. Covers the day-by-day operations of an army
in combat. Particularly sympathetic to Pershing.

1140 Deutrich, Mabel E. STRUGGLE FOR SUPREMACY: THE CAREER OF
FRED C. AINSWORTH. Washington, D.C.: Public Affairs Press,
1962. 170 p.

A sympathetic account of a bureaucratic adjutant general who
fought and lost the struggle to prevent the growth of the
army's general staff system.

1141 Deweerd, Harvey. "The American Adoption of French Artillery, 1917-
1918." JOURNAL OF AMERICAN MILITARY INSTITUTE 3 (1939):
104-16.

Discusses how United States, famed for its technological developments, nevertheless accepted artillery advances of another nation during World War I.

1142 _____. PRESIDENT WILSON FIGHTS HIS WAR: WORLD WAR I

AND THE AMERICAN INTERVENTION. New York: Macmillan, 1968. 457 p.

Conventional narrative of America's war effort, with considerable space given to the operation of European Armies.

1143   Dickinson, John M. BUILDING OF AN ARMY: A DETAILED ACCOUNT OF LEGISLATION, ADMINISTRATION AND OPINION IN THE UNITED STATES, 1915-1920. New York: Century, 1922. 398 p.

Deals extensively with the manner in which the United States placed over three million men under arms by 1918.

1144   Dos Passos, John. MR. WILSON'S WAR. Garden City, N.Y.: Doubleday, 1962. 517 p.

Account by the famous novelist written in a light, almost whimsical style. Useful, vividly written accounts of battles, but work not well researched.

1145   Dubay, Robert. "Opposition to Selective Service, 1916-1918." SOUTHERN QUARTERLY 7 (1969): 301-22.

Discusses the opposition to conscription, but fails to show that it was widespread.

1146   Dupuy, R. Ernest. FIVE DAYS TO WAR. Harrisburg, Pa.: Stackpole, 1967. 224 p.

Pictorially (photos, cartoons, news reports) describes major events immediately prior to American intervention in April 1917.

1147   Durham, Weldon B. "'Big Brother' and the 'Seven Sisters': Camp Life Reforms in World War I." MILITARY AFFAIRS 42 (1978): 57-60.

Describes the work of the Commission on Training Camp Activities created by Secretary of War Newton Baker in order to reduce the evil effects of drunkenness, disease, and boredom in World War I army camps.

1148   Finnegan, John P. AGAINST THE SPECTER OF A DRAGON: THE CAMPAIGN FOR AMERICAN MILITARY PREPAREDNESS, 1914-1917. Westport, Conn.: Greenwood, 1974. 253 p.

Account of the plans, actors and motives in the movement to strengthen American military power just prior to intervention in 1917.

1149 Fredericks, Pierce G. THE GREAT ADVENTURE: AMERICA IN THE
FIRST WORLD WAR. New York: Dutton, 1960. 253 p.

A light, popular, brief account of a very complex topic
written in a narrative, unanalytical style.

1150 Freidel, Frank B. OVER THERE: THE STORY OF AMERICA'S FIRST
GREAT OVERSEAS CRUSADE. Boston: Little, Brown, 1964. 385 p.

Popular, pictorial account with quotations from diaries and
letters.

1151 Frothingham, Thomas G. THE AMERICAN REINFORCEMENT IN THE
WORLD WAR. Introduction by Newton D. Baker. New York: Doran,
1928. 388 p.

Supplements Clarkson's work (see entry 1124) on military and
industrial organization.

1152 Gibbons, Floyd. AND THEY THOUGHT WE WOULDN'T FIGHT.
New York: Doran, 1918. 410 p.

Account by a correspondent who was at the front for quite
awhile and was wounded.

1153 Gilbert, Charles. AMERICAN FINANCING OF WORLD WAR I.
Westport, Conn.: Greenwood, 1970. 259 p.

Account on how the U.S. government raised money to fi-
nance World War I. Useful as a first work on the topic but
based on printed material.

1154 Goldhurst, Richard. THE MIDNIGHT WAR: THE AMERICAN INTER-
VENTION IN RUSSIA, 1918-1920. New York: McGraw-Hill, 1978.
288 p.

A popular, yet vivid story of the futile effort of President
Wilson to influence the course of the Bolshevik Revolution
through force.

1155 Gorrell, Edgar S. THE MEASURE OF AMERICA'S WORLD WAR AER-
ONAUTICAL EFFORT. Northfield, Vt.: Norwich University Press,
1940. 78 p.

Much useful information by a former chief of staff of the
American Expeditionary Forces Air Service.

1156 Gow, Kenneth. LETTERS OF A SOLDIER. New York: Covert, 1920.
457 p.

Provides useful description of author's experiences.

1157   Graves, William S. AMERICA'S SIBERIAN ADVENTURE, 1918-1920.
        New York: Cape, Smith, 1931. 363 p.

        A personal account by the commanding general of the Siberian
        adventure attempting to justify the decision to send American
        troops.

1158   Gruber, Carol S. MARS AND MINERVA: WORLD WAR I AND THE
        USES OF HIGHER LEARNING IN AMERICA. Baton Rouge: Louisiana
        State University Press, 1975. 293 p.

        An account of how academic institutions willingly joined the
        war propaganda effort and how academicians became the serv-
        ants of government power.

1159   Hagedorn, Hermann. LEONARD WOOD: A BIOGRAPHY. Vol. II.
        New York: Harper, 1931. 524 p.

        Focuses on Wood's role in preparedness and his inactive role
        in World War I. Sympathetic with Wood in his struggle with
        the Wilson administration.

1160   Hagood, Johnson. THE SERVICES OF SUPPLY: A MEMOIR OF THE
        GREAT WAR. Boston: Houghton, 1927. 408 p.

        Account by the chief of staff of the Services of Supply de-
        scribing the organization and administration of the service.
        Many documents included.

1161   Harbord, James G. THE AMERICAN ARMY IN FRANCE, 1917-1919.
        Boston: Little, Brown, 1936. 632 p.

        Both a memoir and a narrative account. Critical of the War
        Department in the Pershing-March controversy. Weak as his-
        tory, but useful as a first-hand account.

1162   _____. LEAVES FROM A WAR DIARY. New York: Dodd, Mead,
        1925. 407 p.

        Memories of an officer on Pershing's staff. More than a mil-
        itary record, it tells a full story of the men and women of
        the American Expeditionary Forces.

1163   Henri, Florette, and Stillman, Richard. BITTER VICTORY: A HIS-
        TORY OF BLACK SOLDIERS IN WORLD WAR I. Garden City, N.Y.:
        Doubleday, 1970. 120 p.

        Argue that even though black soldiers were subjected to wide-
        spread practices of discrimination, most performed with bravery
        and efficiency.

1164   Herring, George C.   "James Hay and the Preparedness Controversy,
        1915-1916." JOURNAL OF SOUTHERN HISTORY 30 (1964): 383-
        404.

        Discusses Representative Hay's successful opposition to the
        Wilson administration's national defense policy.

1165   Hirschfield, Charles.   "The Transformation of American Life."   In
        WORLD WAR I: A TURNING POINT IN MODERN HISTORY, edited
        by Jack Roth. New York: Knopf, 1967. 136 p.

        Useful introduction to the meaning of World War I to Ameri-
        can society.

1166   Holley, Irving B.   IDEAS AND WEAPONS: EXPLORATION OF THE
        AERIAL WEAPON BY THE UNITED STATES DURING WORLD WAR I.
        New Haven, Conn.: Yale University Press, 1971. 222 p.

        An account of America's aviation production during World
        War I and the problems facing military leaders of turning
        ideas into weapons.

1167   Hudson, James J.   HOSTILE SKIES: A COMBAT HISTORY OF THE
        AMERICAN AIR SERVICE IN WORLD WAR I. Syracuse, N.Y.: Syra-
        cuse University Press, 1968. 338 p.

        Both an operational history of the Air Service and an account
        of individuals assigned to units.

1168   Hurley, Alfred F.   BILLY MITCHELL: CRUSADER FOR AIR POWER.
        New York: Watts, 1964. 180 p.

        Sympathetic account of the first crusader for an Army Air
        Force.

1169   James, D. Clayton.   THE YEARS OF MacARTHUR. Vol. I. 1880-
        1941. Boston: Houghton-Mifflin, 1970. 740 p.

        Thoroughly researched with balanced, unprejudiced judgments.
        Covers early life and West Point years, but focuses on World
        War I and chief of staff experiences.

1170   Johnson, Donald O.   THE CHALLENGE TO AMERICAN FREEDOMS:
        WORLD WAR I AND THE RISE OF THE AMERICAN CIVIL LIBERTIES
        UNION. Lexington: University of Kentucky Press, 1963. 243 p.

        Account of how a group of liberals upheld civil liberties in
        the face of war hysteria.

1171   Johnson, Thomas.   WITHOUT CENSOR. Indianapolis: Bobbs-Merrill,
        1928. 411 p.

By an American correspondent covering the St. Mihiel–Meuse–Argonne battles, based on observation and interviews.

1172   Johnson, Thomas, and Pratt, Fletcher. THE LOST BATTALION. Indianapolis: Bobbs-Merrill, 1938. 338 p.

Story of the battalion cut off from its parent organization in October 1918.

1173   Josephson, Harold. "History for Victory: The National Board for Historical Service." MID-AMERICA 52 (1970): 205–14.

Discusses the historical scholar's dilemma during World War I. Argues that historians tended to prostitute their scholarship, to trade historical accuracy for persuasion.

1174   Kennett, Lee. "The A.E.F. Through French Eyes." MILITARY REVIEW 52 (1972): 3–11.

Discusses the French image of the American Expeditionary Force as humorous, critical, but in the end, fundamentally laudatory.

1175   Kevles, Daniel J. "Testing the Army's Intelligence: Psychologists and the Military in World War I." JOURNAL OF AMERICAN HISTORY 55 (1968): 565–82.

Recounts the work of Robert Yerkes in establishing intelligence testing and the difficulties he had in getting the military to accept it.

1176   Koistenen, Paul A.C. "The Industrial Military Complex in Historical Perspective: World War I." BUSINESS HISTORY REVIEW 41 (1967): 378–403.

Argues that the War Department was not prepared to run the war and thus turned over economic mobilization to business-men.

1177   Langer, William. GAS AND FLAME IN WORLD WAR I. Brooklyn: Holton, 1919. Reprint. New York: Knopf, 1965. 120 p.

Originally entitled WITH "E" OF THE FIRST GAS. Provides useful description of author's experiences with a gas company during World War I. Useful field history.

1178   Liggett, Hunter. COMMANDING AN AMERICAN ARMY. Boston: Houghton-Mifflin, 1925. 257 p.

Commander of the First Army Corps who trained them and

then took them into battle on the western front. Somewhat detached with few personal stories.

1179 Lockmiller, David A. ENOCH H. CROWDER: SOLDIER, LAWYER AND STATESMAN. Columbia: University of Missouri Press, 1955. 286 p.

Study of a leading judge advocate general who directed America's first Selective Service System, 1917-18.

1180 Lowry, Bullit. "Pershing and the Armistice." JOURNAL OF AMERICAN HISTORY 55 (1968): 281-91.

Discusses how Pershing first supported the Armistice and then changed his mind because he believed Wilson's terms would sacrifice allied victory.

1181 Malan, Nancy E. "How 'Ya Gonna Keep Them Down?': Women and World War I." PROLOGUE 5 (1973): 208-39.

A collection of interesting and informative photographs documenting the role of women in World War I.

1182 McCarthy, Joe. "The Lost Battalion." AMERICAN HERITAGE 28 (1977): 88-93.

Determines that the force was neither a battalion nor was it lost. A group of 550 men were cut off from their regiment during five days of fighting in the Argonne Forest.

1183 McLean, Ross H. "Troop Movements on the American Railroads During the Great War." AMERICAN HISTORICAL REVIEW 26 (1921): 464-88.

Account of the experience of the Railroad War Board during World War I. Favorably assesses the work of the board.

1184 March, Peyton C. THE NATION AT WAR. Garden City, N.Y.: Doubleday, Doran, 1932. 407 p.

Recollections of the army's chief of staff during World War I. With devasting bluntness, describes the incredible problems associated with training, equipping, and transporting the American Expeditionary Forces to France.

1185 Marshall, George C. MEMOIRS OF MY SERVICES IN THE WORLD WAR, 1917-1918. Boston: Houghton-Mifflin, 1976. 268 p.

Memoirs by the now famous general, focuses on the strengths and weaknesses of the army and the men who fought the war.

1186 Marshall, S.L.A. THE AMERICAN HERITAGE HISTORY OF WORLD
WAR I. New York: American Heritage, 1964. 384 p.

Popular history by a leading military historian.

1187 Matloff, Maurice. "The American Approach to War, 1919-1945." In
THE THEORY AND PRACTICE OF WAR: ESSAYS PRESENTED TO
CAPT. SIR BASIL LIDDELL HART, edited by Michael Howard. London:
Cassell, 1965.

1188 Millett, Allan R. THE GENERAL: ROBERT L. BULLARD AND OF-
FICERSHIP IN THE UNITED STATES ARMY, 1881-1925. Westport,
Conn.: Greenwood, 1975. 499 p.

Study of a World War I commander as a typical pre-World
War I officer. Focuses on broader aspects of military professionalism.

1189 Millis, Walter. ROAD TO WAR: AMERICA, 1914-1917. Boston:
Houghton-Mifflin, 1935. 466 p.

Critical, somewhat irreverant, account of America's intervention in World War I, focusing on public opinion and propaganda. Traces of pacifism evident.

1190 Mitchell, William. MEMOIRS OF WORLD WAR I. New York: Random House, 1960. Reprint. Westport, Conn.: Greenwood, 1976.
312 p.

Account by a veteran correspondent who understood military
strategy and tactics.

1191 Mock, James R., and Larsen, Cedric. WORDS THAT WON THE WAR:
THE STORY OF THE COMMITTEE ON PUBLIC INFORMATION, 1917-
1919. Princeton, N.J.: Princeton University Press, 1939. 372 p.

Useful for its information but very uncritical of George Creel
and the Committee on Public Information.

1192 Mooney, Chase C., and Layman, Martha. "Some Phases of Compulsory Military Training Movement, 1914-1920." MISSISSIPPI VALLEY
HISTORICAL REVIEW 38 (1952): 633-56.

Traces the progress of the first compulsory training movement,
focusing on prevailing public opinion of universal military
training.

1193 Nash, Gerald D. "Experiments in Industrial Mobilization: WIB and
NRA." MID-AMERICA 45 (July, 1963): 157-74.

Argues that the war experience with the War Industries Board greatly influenced Roosevelt's major New Deal policies, particularly the National Recovery Administration.

1194 O'Connor, Richard. BLACK JACK PERSHING. Garden City, N.Y.: Doubleday, 1961. 431 p.

Narrative account of Pershing's life, focusing on Pershing's American Expeditionary Forces experience. Weak on research and documentation.

1195 Ohl, John K. "Hugh Johnson and the Draft, 1917-1918." PROLOGUE 8 (1976): 85-96.

Discusses Johnson's experience as a kind of handy man who planned and organized the draft during World War I.

1196 Palmer, Frederick. BLISS, PEACEMAKER: THE LIFE AND LETTERS OF GENERAL TASKER BLISS. New York: Dodd, Mead, 1934. 477 p.

Based on Bliss papers and interviews. A sympathetic, somewhat uncritical, account.

1197 _____. JOHN J. PERSHING, GENERAL OF THE ARMIES: A BIOGRAPHY. Harrisburg, Pa.: Military Service, 1948. 380 p.

Not close to Pershing, therefore based mostly on observations.

1198 _____. NEWTON D. BAKER: AMERICA AT WAR. 2 vols. New York: Dodd, Mead, 1931.

An early biography of Baker but more history of the War Department than biography of its secretary. Sympathetic to Baker.

1199 _____. OUR GREATEST BATTLE. New York: Dodd, Mead, 1919. 629 p.

A journalist's view of the war, based on some records.

1200 _____. WITH MY OWN EYES: A PERSONAL STORY OF BATTLE YEARS. Indianapolis: Bobbs-Merrill, 1933. 396 p.

Experienced reporter, acquainted with many military men, makes important observations on World War I. Drawn from first-hand knowledge.

1201 Paxson, Frederic L. AMERICAN DEMOCRACY AND THE WORLD. 3 vols. Boston: Houghton-Mifflin, 1936.

Standard account of the war with material on military, political, and economic aspects of the war.

1202 _____. "The American War Government, 1917-1918." AMERICAN HISTORICAL REVIEW 26 (1920): 54-76.

Surveys the transformation to a war government after April 1917, which the author states was accomplished by September 1918.

1203 _____. "The Great Demobilization." AMERICAN HISTORICAL RE-VIEW 44 (1939): 237-51.

Surveys the effort of the Americans to raze the jerry-built structures of war, generally without much planning or foresight.

1204 Perry, Ralph B. THE PLATTSBURG MOVEMENT: A CHAPTER IN AMERICA'S PARTICIPATION IN WORLD WAR I. New York: Dutton, 1921. 275 p.

A sympathetic account of the movement by a participant. Clifford's recent work (see entry 1125) is more scholarly.

1205 Pershing, John J. MY EXPERIENCES IN THE WORLD WAR. 2 vols. New York: Stokes, 1931.

Indispensible, detailed source on the American Expeditionary Forces. Refights the battle to maintain a unified American force, but neglects problems with his own subordinates.

1206 Peterson, H.C. PROPAGANDA FOR WAR. Norman: University of Oklahoma Press, 1939. 357 p.

Discusses the British campaign against American neutrality.

1207 Pogue, Forrest. GEORGE C. MARSHALL: EDUCATION OF A GEN-ERAL, 1880-1939. New York: Viking, 1963. 370 p.

Covers larger period but significant account of Marshall's participation in World War I. Definitive study of a three-volume project.

1208 Schlesinger, Arthur M. "The Khaki Journalist, 1917-1919." MISSIS-SIPPI VALLEY HISTORICAL REVIEW 6 (1920): 350-59.

Discusses the activities and effort of the "soldier press" in creating a sense of obedience and esprit de corps among the disparate citizen army conscriptees during World War II.

1209   Seldes, George.   IRON, BLOOD AND PROFITS.   New York: Harper,
       1934.   397 p.

       A muckraking account of the munitions industry, useful as
       evidence of post-World War I American attitudes toward the
       war.

1210   Skeykill, Tom, ed.   SERGEANT YORK: HIS OWN LIFE STUDY AND
       WAR DIARY.   Garden City, N.Y.:   Houghton-Mifflin, 1928.   490 p.

       Describes life in the World War I army with mountain humor,
       focusing on York's amazing feat in the Argonne Forest on
       October 8, 1918.

1211   Smythe, Donald.   "Battle of the Books: Pershing Versus March."
       ARMY   22 (1972):   30-33.

       Argues that controversy between three officers--Pershing,
       March, and Harbord--produced three books of high quality.

1212   _____.   "Venereal Disease: The A.E.F.'s Experience."   PROLOGUE
       9 (1977):   65-74.

       Discusses how Pershing, although he hoped for sexual contin-
       ence from the American soldier, finally acquiesced to con-
       trolling its social consequences.

1213   Snell, John L.   "Wilsonian Rhetoric Goes to War."   HISTORIAN   14
       (1952):   191-208.

       Argues that Woodrow Wilson created and organized the "first
       top-level ideological campaign of the twentieth century."
       Sees it as a World War I version of "organized psychological
       warfare."

1214   Soule, George.   "The Brain of the Army."   NEW REPUBLIC   13 (22
       December 1917):   203-5.

       Critical examination of the lack of coordination between the
       general staff and the American Expeditionary Forces.

1215   Spector, Ronald.   "You're Not Going to Send Soldiers Over There
       Are You?:   The American Search for an Alternate to the Western
       Front, 1916-1917."   MILITARY AFFAIRS 36 (1972):   1-4.

       Traces the reluctance of American leaders to accept the idea
       of fighting battles in France.

1216   Stallings, Laurence.   THE DOUGHBOYS: THE STORY OF THE AEF,
       1917-1918.   New York: Harper, 1963.   404 p.

Recent account of personal recollections by a participant.

1217 _____. THE FIRST WORLD WAR: A PHOTOGRAPHIC HISTORY. New York: Simon and Schuster, 1933. 298 p.

A collection of over five hundred photographs arranged chronologically.

1218 Swisher, C.B. "Control of the War Preparations." AMERICAN POLITICAL SCIENCE REVIEW 34 (1940): 1085-1103.

Analyzes the war preparations of the Wilson administration, arguing that the initial phase was characterized by fumbling and ineffeciency.

1219 Taft, William H., ed. SERVICE WITH FIGHTING MEN. 2 vols. New York: Association Press, 1922.

Account of the work of the YMCA during World War I.

1220 Tate, Michael L. "Pershing's Punitive Expedition: Pursuer of Bandits or Presidential Panacea?" AMERICAS 32 (1975): 46-71.

Argues that Wilson manipulated the expedition for the purpose of protecting vested interests in Mexico for moral reasons.

1221 Thomason, John W. FIX BAYONETS! New York: Blue Ribbon, 1926. 245 p.

Partially fictional, but good descriptions of battles, including Belleau Woods and Soissons, by a participant.

1222 Toulmin, H.A. AIR SERVICE: AMERICAN EXPEDITIONARY FORCES, 1918. New York: Van Nostrand, 1921. 388 p.

Useful on the administrative problems of the American Expeditionary Forces Air Service.

1223 Trask, David F. THE UNITED STATES IN THE SUPREME WAR COUNCIL: AMERICAN WAR AIMS AND INTERALLIED STRATEGY, 1917-1918. Middletown, Conn.: Wesleyan University Press, 1961. 244 p.

Focuses on difficulties of military decisions in coalition warfare.

1224 _____, ed. WORLD WAR I AT HOME: READINGS ON AMERICAN LIFE, 1914-1920. New York: Wiley, 1970. 212 p.

Collection of forty-four documents indicating American responses to the nation's experiences in the First World War.

A kind of impressionistic picture of America at war.

1225 Twichell, Heath, Jr. ALLEN: A BIOGRAPHY OF AN ARMY OF-
FICER. New Brunswick, N.J.: Rutgers University Press, 1974.
358 p.

Account of a second echelon military figure, but deals with
the many dimensions of military professionalism.

1226 U.S. Department of the Army. THE UNITED STATES IN THE WORLD
WAR. 17 vols. Washington, D.C.: Government Printing Office,
1948.

A collection of primary documents on the war.

1227 Unterberger, Betty M. "President Wilson and the Decision to Send
American Troops to Siberia." PACIFIC HISTORICAL REVIEW 24
(1955): 63-74.

Argues that the primary motive for intervention was to assure
American control over the affair in the hopes of maintaining
the open door policy.

1228 Vandiver, Frank E. BLACK JACK: THE LIFE AND TIMES OF JOHN
J. PERSHING. Vol. II. College Station: Texas A & M University
Press, 1977. 590 p.

Discusses Pershing's experience as the American Expeditionary
Force commander, focusing on organizational problems and
the effort of Pershing to maintain a separate command.

1229 Van Every, Dale. THE A.E.F. IN BATTLE. New York: Appleton-
Century-Crofts, 1928. 385 p.

Dated but still useful for details of battles of the American
Expeditionary Forces.

1230 Ward, Robert D. "Against the Tide: The Preparedness Movement,
1923-1924." MILITARY AFFAIRS 38 (1974): 59-61.

Discusses how old preparedness organizations as the American
Security League and the National Security Council marshalled
their forces for one last preparedness effort in the early 1920s.

1231 Wecter, Dixon. WHEN JOHNNY COMES MARCHING HOME. Cambridge, Mass.: Harvard University Press, 1944. 588 p.

Study of the return of Americans from three wars: American
Revolution, Civil War, and World War I, with emphasis on
the latter. A useful historical survey.

1232   Wilgus, W.J. TRANSPORTING THE A.E.F. TO EUROPE, 1917-1918.
New York: Columbia University Press, 1931. 612 p.

Detailed account by the director of military railways during
World War I.

1233   Wiltz, John E. IN SEARCH OF PEACE: THE SENATE MUNITIONS
INQUIRY, 1934-36. Baton Rouge: Louisiana State University Press,
1963. 277 p.

Claims Nye Committee was not hostile to business, nor did
it pursue predetermined theories.

1234   Wise, Jennings C. THE TURN OF THE TIDE. New York: Holt,
1920. 255 p.

First-hand recollections by a staff officer at Pershing's headquarters.

1235   Yoshpe, Henry B. "Bernard Baruch: Civilian Godfather of the Military M Day Plan." MILITARY AFFAIRS 29 (1965): 1-15.

Story of how Baruch worked after World War I to establish a
war mobilization plan. He was only partially successful.

1236   Young, Hugh. A SURGEON'S AUTOBIOGRAPHY. New York: Harcourt, Brace, 1940. 554 p.

Describes the venereal disease problem in the American Expeditionary Forces.

B. WORLD WAR II

1237   Adams, Henry H. A NARRATIVE HISTORY OF WORLD WAR II. 4
vols. New York: McKay, 1970-73.

A comprehensive historical narrative with emphasis on American participation. Strongest on the Pacific campaigns.

1238   Ambrose, Stephen. EISENHOWER AND BERLIN, 1945: THE DECI-
SION TO HALT AT THE ELBE. New York: Norton, 1967. 119 p.

Examines the complex issues and defends Eisenhower's decision.

1239   _____. THE SUPREME COMMANDER: THE WAR YEARS OF GEN-
ERAL DWIGHT D. EISENHOWER. Garden City, N.Y.: Doubleday,
1970. 732 p.

A major study of the allied commander. Sometimes overly
sympathetic, but not uncritical.

1240 Amrine, Michael. THE GREAT DECISION: THE SECRET HISTORY OF THE ATOMIC BOMB. New York: Putnam, 1959. 251 p.

Account of the complex events that led to the dropping of the bombs on Hiroshima and Nagasaki.

1241 Armstrong, Anne. UNCONDITIONAL SURRENDER. New Brunswick, N.J.: Rutgers University Press, 1961. 304 p.

Argues that policy too narrow in the range of possibilities and it did have an impact of Germany's surrender decision.

1242 Arnold, Henry H. GLOBAL MISSION. New York: Harper, 1949. Reprint. New York: Arno, 1979. 626 p.

Account by former head of the Air Force, which combines autobiography with historical narrative in describing the role he and the Air Force played in World War II. Many anecdotes, impressions, and personal views.

1243 Ayer, Fred. BEFORE THE COLORS FADE: PORTRAIT OF A SOLDIER, GEORGE S. PATTON. Boston: Houghton-Mifflin, 1964. 266 p.

A friendly, affectionate portrait, focusing on Patton's military career in World War II.

1244 Baldwin, Hanson. BATTLES LOST AND WON: GREAT CAMPAIGNS OF WORLD WAR II. New York: Harper, 1966. 532 p.

Prominent military reporter and analyst discusses seven major battles.

1245 _____. GREAT MISTAKES OF THE WAR. New York: Harper, 1950. 114 p.

An essentially personal statement of the author's views concerning "mistakes" (mostly political) made during World War II that led to the cold war.

1246 _____. "The New American Army." FOREIGN AFFAIRS 19 (1940): 34-54.

The "new" army was the one being organized after the passage of the Selective Service Act in May 1940.

1247 Bateson, Charles. THE WAR WITH JAPAN: A CONCISE HISTORY. Ann Arbor: University of Michigan Press, 1968. 417 p.

The Pacific war from the point of view of a New Zealander.

1248   Beck, John. MacARTHUR AND WAINWRIGHT: SURRENDER OF THE
       PHILIPPINES. Albuquerque: University of New Mexico Press, 1974.
       302 p.

       Narrative of relations between Philippine high command and
       authorities in Washington, December 1941-May 1942.

1249   Belote, James H., and Belote, William H. CORREGIDOR: THE
       SAGA OF A FORTRESS. New York: Harper, 1967. 273 p.

       Analysis of why and how the rock in Manila harbor was de-
       fended.

1250   _____. TYPHOON OF STEEL: THE BATTLE FOR OKINAWA. New
       York: Harper, 1970. 368 p.

       Account of the last military campaign in the Pacific war from
       the point of view of both Japanese and Americans. A useful
       battle and campaign history written in exciting narrative.

1251   Bernstein, Barton J. "Roosevelt, Truman and the Atomic Bomb, 1941-
       1945: A Reinterpretation." POLITICAL SCIENCE QUARTERLY 90
       (1975): 23-69.

       Argues that FDR always saw the bomb as a legitimate weapon
       and understood it could serve as a bargaining lever.

1252   Blum, Albert A. "Roosevelt, the M-Day Plans and the Military Indus-
       trial Complex." MILITARY AFFAIRS 36 (1972): 44-46.

       Discusses the cooperation between the military and industry in
       an attempt to push through a mobilization plan prior to World
       War II.

1253   Blum, John M. V WAS FOR VICTORY: POLITICS AND AMERICAN
       CULTURE DURING WORLD WAR II. New York: Harcourt, Brace,
       1976. 372 p.

       An account of the home front from a liberal perspective. Fo-
       cuses on struggle between free competition and a managed
       economy.

1254   Blumenson, Martin. ANZIO: THE GAMBLE THAT FAILED. Philadel-
       phia: Lippincott, 1963. 212 p.

       Study of the effort to break the impasse in the Italian Cam-
       paign by an amphibious landing. Discusses the controversy
       surrounding the effort, concluding that it failed in its objec-
       tives.

1255 _____. BLOODY RIVER: THE REAL TRAGEDY OF THE RAPIDO. Boston: Houghton-Mifflin, 1970. 150 p.

Account of a controversial episode in the Italian campaign with focus on the interplay of individual personalities as affecting the outcome of the battle.

1256 _____. THE DUEL FOR FRANCE, 1944. Boston: Houghton-Mifflin, 1963. 432 p.

Covers the Normandy campaign and the liberation of France. Discusses strategic maneuvers from both sides, giving full treatment to German counter moves.

1257 _____. KASSERINE PASS. Boston: Houghton-Mifflin, 1967. 341 p.

Recounts battle in North African campaign. Concludes that battle was lost because of American inexperience. Focuses on commanders under battle stress.

1258 _____. THE PATTON PAPERS. Vol. II. Boston: Houghton-Mifflin, 1972-74. 889 p.

Presents important insights into Patton's personality and character, concluding that the general was "complex, paradoxical and many faceted."

1259 Bradley, Omar N. A SOLDIER'S STORY. New York: Holt, 1951. Reprint. Westport, Conn.: Greenwood, 1977. 618 p.

Tells of Bradley's extensive role in the European war from Tunisia to Berlin. Frank, frequently blunt, but not malicious.

1260 Bray, Charles W. PSYCHOLOGY AND MILITARY PROFICIENCY: A HISTORY OF THE APPLIED PSYCHOLOGY PANEL OF THE NATIONAL DEFENSE RESEARCH COMMITTEE. Princeton, N.J.: Princeton University Press, 1968. 242 p.

Account of how psychologists served America's armed forces during World War II.

1261 Brereton, Lewis H. THE BRERETON DIARIES. New York: Morrow, 1946. 450 p.

The personal account of a prominent American general who served in every major theater of war from the Pacific to the Middle East to Europe. Heavily burdened with technical and military data, and thus useful for campaign histories.

1262 Brines, Russell. MacARTHUR'S JAPAN. Philadelphia: Lippincott, 1948. 315 p.

Account of the American occupation of Japan after World War II which focuses on MacArthur as the moving spirit.

1263   Buchanan, A. Russell. THE UNITED STATES AND WORLD WAR II. 2 vols. New York: Harper, 1963.

Important and useful narrative which covers military, political, and economic phases of the war.

1264   _____, ed. and comp. THE UNITED STATES AND WORLD WAR II: MILITARY AND DIPLOMATIC DOCUMENTS. Columbia: University of South Carolina Press, 1972. 303 p.

Useful collection of documents, intelligently selected.

1265   Burns, James M. ROOSEVELT: THE SOLDIER OF FREEDOM. New York: Harcourt Brace Jovanovich, 1970. 722 p.

Recognizes FDR's qualities of war leadership but critical of his administrative shortcomings. Successfully combines domestic politics and war strategy.

1266   Burtness, Paul S., and Ober, Warren. "Research Methodology Problems of Pearl Harbor Intelligence Reports." MILITARY AFFAIRS 25 (1961): 132-46.

Discusses poor interpretation of intelligence reports by officials.

1267   Butcher, Harry C. MY THREE YEARS WITH EISENHOWER. New York: Simon and Schuster, 1946. 911 p.

A personal diary of the naval aide to Eisenhower, 1942-45. If carefully used, helpful as a primary source on Eisenhower's experiences.

1268   Chandler, Alfred, and Ambrose, Stephen, ed. THE PAPERS OF DWIGHT D. EISENHOWER: THE WAR YEARS. 5 vols. Baltimore: Johns Hopkins University Press, 1967.

Important source material on the planning and conduct of World War II.

1269   Chandler, Harriette L. "Another View of Operation Crossword: A Revision of Kolko." MILITARY AFFAIRS 42 (1978): 68-73.

Effort to refute revisionist assertions that the Soviet Union was excluded from the Italian surrender negotiations was politically motivated. Argues the Allied objectives were purely military.

1270 Chennault, Claire L. WAY OF A FIGHTER: THE MEMOIRS OF CLAIRE CHENNAULT. New York: Putnam, 1949. 375 p.

Highly critical of Roosevelt, Churchill, and Marshall for having thrown away chances for winning the struggle for the Far East.

1271 Christman, Calvin L. "Donald Nelson and the Army: Personality as a Factor in Civil-Military Relations During World War II." MILITARY AFFAIRS 37 (1973): 81-83.

Argues personality factors made civil-military relations more complex than simple civilian military struggle for power. War Production Board Director Nelson used as a case study.

1272 Clark, Mark W. CALCULATED RISK. New York: Harper, 1950. 500 p.

Personal account of author's experiences as a commander in the North African and Italian Campaigns. Particularly useful for the long and bitter struggle in Italy.

1273 Clay, Lucius D. DECISION IN GERMANY. Garden City, N.Y.: Doubleday, 1950. 522 p.

Account of Clay's experiences as post-war military governor of Berlin and Germany. Measured and restrained in telling of the struggles with Russia over Berlin.

1274 Clifford, John G. "Grenville Clark and the Origins of Selective Service." REVIEW OF POLITICS 35 (1973): 17-40.

Discusses the four-month campaign by former "Plattsburgers," led by Clark, which culminated in the passage of the Selective Service Act of 1940.

1275 Cole, Wayne. CHARLES LINDBERG AND THE BATTLE AGAINST AMERICAN INTERVENTION IN WORLD WAR II. New York: Harcourt Brace Jovanovich, 1974. 298 p.

Monograph based on exhaustive use of sources including Lindberg papers and many interviews.

1276 Collier, Basil. THE SECOND WORLD WAR, A MILITARY HISTORY: FROM MUNICH TO HIROSHIMA. New York: Morrow, 1967. 640 p.

Account by an Englishman. A well-written, competently researched study of World War II. Greatly critical of American strategy and operations.

1277 ____. THE WAR IN THE FAR EAST, 1941-1945: A MILITARY HIS-
TORY. New York: Morrow, 1969. 530 p.

Sound history, yet limited only to Anglo-American involvement in the Far-Eastern War.

1278 Collins, John M. "Depression Army." ARMY 22 (1972): 8-14.

Good, useful description of the "Old Army" as it struggled
through the Depression.

1279 Conn, Stetson. "Changing Concepts of National Defense in the United
States, 1937-1947." MILITARY AFFAIRS 28 (1964): 1-7.

Changed from one based on defense of U.S. territory in 1937
to one of entangling alliances and active opposition to Communist aggression.

1280 Craven, Wesley Frank, and Cate, James L. THE ARMY AIR FORCES
IN WORLD WAR II. 7 vols. Chicago: University of Chicago Press,
1948-58.

Official history but written by historians commissioned to write
critically of the Air Forces' role in World War II.

1281 Cousins, Norman. "Douglas MacArthur." SATURDAY REVIEW, May
2, 1964, pp. 18-19.

A pacifist's sympathetic view of MacArthur.

1282 Dalfiume, Richard. DESEGREGATION OF THE U.S. ARMY FORCES:
FIGHTING ON TWO FRONTS, 1939-1953. Columbia: University of
Missouri Press, 1969. 252 p.

Well-researched, well-documented account of the battle to
desegregate the armed forces. Argues military problem with
segregation comprised the seedbed for the black revolt in the
1960s. Argues also that resistance came from civilians not
the military.

1283 Daniels, Roger. THE BONUS MARCH: AN EPISODE OF THE GREAT
DEPRESSION. Westport, Conn.: Greenwood, 1971. 289 p.

Sympathetic with army's role in the bonus affairs but critical
of President Hoover and General MacArthur. Believes Mac-
Arthur exceeded his authority.

1284 Davis, Burke. THE BILLY MITCHELL AFFAIR. New York: Random,
1967. 373 p.

Well researched, interestingly written, but mostly narrative, and short on analysis and evaluation.

1285   Davis, Franklin M. COME AS A CONQUEROR: THE UNITED STATES
ARMY'S OCCUPATION OF GERMANY 1945-1949. New York: Macmillan, 1967. 288 p.

A popular, somewhat discursive account of the U.S. occupation of Germany. Sees the occupation as an overall success.

1286   Dobran, Edward. P.O.W.: THE STORY OF AMERICAN PRISONERS
OF WAR DURING WORLD WAR II. New York: Exposition, 1953.
123 p.

A former prisoner held by the Germans, graphically tells of
life in a POW camp during World War II.

1287   Dulles, Allen. THE SECRET SURRENDER. New York: Harper, 1966.
268 p.

Account by a leading participant of the secret negotiations
by the Office of Strategic Services for the surrender of German forces in Italy.

1288   Edmonds, Walter D. THEY FOUGHT WITH WHAT THEY HAD: THE
STORY OF THE ARMY AIR FORCES IN THE SOUTHWEST PACIFIC,
1941-1942. Boston: Little, Brown, 1951. 532 p.

Semiofficial narrative of the Army Air Force in the Philippines and the Pacific, 1941-42. Based on interviews, written
statements, and squadron diaries.

1289   Eichelberger, Robert L. OUR JUNGLE ROAD TO TOKYO. New
York: Viking Press, 1950. 306 p.

Personal account by the commander of the Pacific Theater
from the early days to the fall of the Philippines. Particularly useful on the dark, early days of the war.

1290   Eisenhower, Dwight D. CRUSADE IN EUROPE. Garden City, N.Y.:
Doubleday, 1948. 559 p.

Focuses on high strategy and the organization for victory in
Europe, but contains information on political decisions during
the war.

1291   Eisenhower, John. THE BITTER WOODS. New York: Putnam, 1969.
506 p.

Account of the Battle of the Bulge by the general's son.
Useful particularly on high strategy and coalition warfare.

Not surprisingly supports his father in controversial matters.

1292   Eisenhower Foundation. D-DAY: THE NORMANDY INVASION IN
        RETROSPECT. Lawrence: University Press of Kansas, 1971. 354 p.

        Essays by military historians analyzing and evaluating D-Day
        landing twenty-five years later.

1293   Emerson, William M. "Franklin Roosevelt as Commander in Chief in
        World War II." MILITARY AFFAIRS 22 (1958): 181-207.

        Discusses how FDR more than any president before, broadly
        construed his constitutional powers of commander-in-chief
        and wielded them so vigorously.

1294   Essame, Herbert. PATTON: A STUDY IN COMMAND. New York:
        Scribner, 1974. 280 p.

        A work sympathetic to Patton's career. Plays down personal-
        ity flaws. Focuses on Patton as a combat commander.

1295   Esthus, Raymond A. "President Roosevelt's Commitment to Britain to
        Intervene in a Pacific War." MISSISSIPPI VALLEY HISTORICAL RE-
        VIEW 50 (1963): 28-38.

        Concludes Roosevelt did make a firm commitment to British
        for armed support if Japan attacked the British or Dutch East
        Indies.

1296   Fahey, James J. PACIFIC WAR DIARY, 1942-1945. Boston: Hough-
        ton-Mifflin, 1963. Reprint. Westport, Conn.: Greenwood, 1977.
        404 p.

        Diary of Fahey's experiences in the Pacific, with emphasis on
        the human dimension of war.

1297   Falk, Stanley L. BATAAN: THE MARCH OF DEATH. New York:
        Norton, 1962. 256 p.

        Describes the march after the surrender of Bataan from both
        the American and the Japanese viewpoint. Written from per-
        sonal interviews and correspondence with survivors.

1298   Farago, Ladislas. THE BROKEN SEAL: THE STORY OF "ORPERA-
        TION MAGIC" AND THE PEARL HARBOR DISASTER. New York:
        Random, 1967. 439 p.

        History of the Japanese and American code-breaking opera-
        tions, 1921-41. Concludes there was no plot at Pearl Harbor.

1299   ____. PATTON: ORDEAL AND TRIUMPH. New York: Obolen-
sky, 1964. 886 p.

Focuses on the duality of Patton's character: at one time a
flop, a martinet, at another a sensitive human being. Contains a bibliography of Patton's writings.

1300   Freeman, Roger A. THE MIGHTY EIGHTH: UNITS, MEN, AND
MACHINES. Garden City, N.Y.: Doubleday, 1970. 311 p.

History of the Eighth Army Air Force, 1942–45, with emphasis on its operations in World War II.

1301   Funk, Arthur L. "Eisenhower, Giraud and the Command of 'Torch.'"
MILITARY AFFAIRS 3 (1971): 103–8.

Discusses Eisenhower's struggle with the French general, Giraud, over command of the allied forces after they landed in
North Africa.

1302   ____. THE POLITICS OF TORCH: THE ALLIED LANDINGS AND
THE ALGIERS PUTSCH, 1942. Lawrence: University Press of Kansas,
1974. 322 p.

A study of the political maneuverings surrounding the Anglo-
American landings in North Africa.

1303   Gimbel, John. THE AMERICAN OCCUPATION OF GERMANY: POL-
ITICS AND THE MILITARY, 1945–1949. Stanford, Calif.: Stanford
University Press, 1968. 335 p.

Exhaustive survey of the military occupation of Germany after
World War II. Argues officials bowed to the exigencies of
the Cold War.

1304   Giovannitti, Len, and Freed, Fred. THE DECISION TO DROP THE
BOMB. New York: Coward-McCann, 1965. 348 p.

Useful account of the complex issues that led to the decision
to use the atomic bomb against Japan.

1305   Glines, Carroll V. DOOLITTLE'S TOKYO RAIDERS. New York: Van
Nostrand, 1964. 447 p.

A comprehensive narrative of the often told colorful and dar-
ing bomber raid on Tokyo. Includes Japanese response.

1306   Gray, Glenn. THE WARRIORS: REFLECTIONS ON MEN IN BATTLE.
New York: Harcourt, 1959. 242 p.

An account of the author's experiences in World War II from

which he draws reflective and philosphical conclusions. Antiwar in its tone.

1307 Greenfield, Kent R. AMERICAN STRATEGY IN WORLD WAR II: A
RECONSIDERATION. Baltimore: Johns Hopkins Press, 1963. 145 p.

Essays that examine basic strategic decisions and relate them
to military versus political objectives.

1308 _____. "Forging the U.S. Army in World War II into a Combat Arms
Team." MISSISSIPPI VALLEY HISTORICAL REVIEW 34 (1947): 443-
50.

Discusses in brief the kind of army the United States had in
World War II and how it performed its task.

1309 _____, ed. COMMAND DECISIONS. Washington, D.C.: Government Printing Office, 1960. 560 p.

Prominent historians examine twenty major military decisions
made during World War II. Decisions ranged from high strategy to local campaign tactics.

1310 Griffith, Samuel B. THE BATTLE FOR GUADALCANAL. Philadelphia:
Lippincott, 1963. 282 p.

Account of the struggle for a strategic island based on American and Japanese documents. Focuses on the command point
of view.

1311 Groves, Leslie R. NOW IT CAN BE TOLD: THE STORY OF THE
MANHATTAN PROJECT. New York: Harper, 1962. 464 p.

Account by the chief executive of the project. Useful as a
detailed, straightforward record by a participant.

1312 Hackey, Thomas E. "Jim Crow with an Accent: Attitudes of London
Government Officials Toward American Negro Soldiers in England During World War II." JOURNAL OF NEGRO HISTORY 59 (1974):
65-77.

Uses a collection of documents to show that black American
soldiers were subjected to covert condescension and racial
bigotry by the British government while the troops were stationed in England.

1313 Hart, Robert A., ed. MILITARY GOVERNMENT JOURNAL: NOR-
MANDY TO BERLIN. Amherst: University of Massachusetts Press,
1971. 355 p.

Day-by-day account of Gen. John A. Maginnis's experience with military government from the Normandy invasion to the occupation of Berlin.

1314 Hechler, Kenneth W. THE BRIDGE AT REMAGEN. Foreward by S.L.A. Marshall. New York: Ballantine, 1957. 238 p.

Story of the struggle over two key bridges in World War II-- the Ludendorf and the Remagen.

1315 Higgins, Trumbull. SOFT UNDERBELLY: THE ANGLO-AMERICAN CONTROVERSY OVER THE ITALIAN CAMPAIGN. New York: Macmillan, 1968. 275 p.

Account of the allied planning and operations in the eastern Mediterranean, focusing on the controversy over strategy.

1316 Hobbs, Joseph P., ed. DEAR GENERAL: EISENHOWER'S WARTIME LETTERS TO MARSHALL. Baltimore: Johns Hopkins University Press, 1971. 255 p.

Letters show how Marshall guided Eisenhower toward greater growth as a military commander.

1317 Hoehling, A.A. HOME FRONT, U.S.A. New York: Crowell, 1966. 178 p.

Vignettes of American life during World War II. Light popular reading.

1318 Holborn, Hajo. AMERICAN MILITARY GOVERNMENT: ITS ORGANIZATION AND POLICIES. Washington, D.C.: Infantry Journal Press, 1947. 243 p.

Early account of American military government during and after World War II. Contains over one hundred pages of documents which are useful.

1319 Hoopes, Roy, comp. AMERICANS REMEMBER THE HOME FRONT: AN ORAL NARRATIVE. New York: Hawthorn, 1977. 398 p.

Two hundred interviews with a wide variety of people who lived through World War II.

1320 Houston, Donald E. HELL ON WHEELS: THE 2ND ARMORED DIVISION. San Rafael, Calif.: Presidio Press, 1977. 466 p.

Traces the unit from the Sicily landing to its entry into Berlin in 1945. Well researched though sheds little new light on World War II military affairs.

1321   Howe, George, F. THE BATTLE HISTORY OF THE 1ST ARMORED
        DIVISION "OLD IRONSIDES." Washington, D.C.: Combat Forces
        Press, 1954. 417 p.

        Useful divisional history. Particularly helpful on the North
        Africa campaign.

1322   Huie, William B. THE EXECUTION OF PRIVATE SLOVIK. New
        York: Duell, Sloan, and Pearce, 1954. 247 p.

        Story of the life of Edward Slovikowski, his service in the
        109th Infantry, 28th Division in France; and his execution for
        desertion, the first since 1864. Includes documents, letters
        from Slovik, and interviews with officers and the men in the
        firing squad.

1323   Hurley, Alfred F. BILLY MITCHELL: CRUSADER FOR AIR POWER.
        Bloomington: Indiana University Press, 1975. 200 p.

        Full story of Mitchell's life, his ideas on air power, and
        his stubborn effort to create a united air force.

1324   Huston, James A. U.S. AIRBORNE OPERATIONS IN WORLD WAR II.
        Lafayette, Ind.: Purdue University Press, 1975. 327 p.

        Analyzes overall effectiveness of airborne operations in World
        War II. Also examines evolution of airborne doctrine, organ-
        ization, and training.

1325   Irving, David. THE DESTRUCTION OF DRESDEN. New York: Holt,
        Rinehart, Winston, 1964. 208 p.

        A reconstruction of the bombing of Dresden by U.S. and Brit-
        ish bombers, killing over 135,000 people. Does not believe
        the raids were justified.

1326   Isely, Jeter A., and Crowl, Philip A. THE U.S. MARINES AND
        AMPHIBIOUS WAR: ITS THEORIES AND ITS PRACTICE IN THE PA-
        CIFIC. Princeton, N.J.: Princeton University Press, 1951. 636 p.

        Account of the campaigns involving marines during World War
        II. Focuses on the role of the Marine Corps in developing
        amphibious landing doctrine.

1327   Jackson, W.G.F. THE BATTLE FOR ITALY. New York: Harper,
        1967. 372 p.

        Examines both allied and axis strategy and tactics, focusing
        on dissension among allied planners.

1328 _____ . THE BATTLE FOR ROME. London: William Clowes, 1969.
224 p.

Account of the 1944 spring offensive in Italy aimed at divert-
ing Germans from the Normandy invasion. Written by a British participant.

1329 James, D. Clayton. THE YEARS OF MacARTHUR, 1941-45. Vol. 2.
New York: Houghton-Mifflin, 1975.

A life-and-time account. Admires the general but does not
overlook shortcomings. Story to 1945, focusing on the general's World War II experiences.

1330 Janeway, Eliot. STRUGGLE FOR SURVIVAL: A CHRONICLE OF
ECONOMIC MOBILIZATION IN WORLD WAR II. New Haven,
Conn.: Yale University Press, 1951. 382 p.

Discusses the methods of economic mobilization during World
War II, focusing particularly on manpower acquisitions and
traces the development of various mobilization agencies from
1939 through 1945.

1331 Johnson, Charles W. "Army and the Civilian Conservation Corps,
1933-1942." PROLOGUE 4 (1972): 139-52.

Discusses the manner in which the army managed the Civilian
Conservation Corps and concludes that the army refrained from
militarizing the Corps.

1332 Kenney, George C. GENERAL KENNEY REPORTS, A PERSONAL
HISTORY OF THE PACIFIC WAR. New York: Duell, Sloan and
Pierce, 1949. 549 p.

Story of the Fifth Air Force in the Pacific, 1942-45 by the
commander of the unit. Not so much a personal account as
old-fashioned narrative history.

1333 Killibrew, John W. "The Army and the Bonus Incident." MILITARY
AFFAIRS 26 (1962): 59-65.

Describes rout of the Bonus Marchers when MacArthur was
chief of staff. Concludes public opinion unfavorable toward
the army's role although the soldiers did not fire a shot.

1334 Kimmel, Husband E. ADMIRAL KIMMEL'S STORY. Chicago: Regnery, 1955. 206 p.

Former commander of the Pacific fleet tells his side of the
Pearl Harbor debacle. Accepts the conspiracy theory that
the Pacific fleet was placed at Pearl Harbor as a lure for a
Japanese attack.

1335   Koistinen, Paul A.C. "The 'Industrial-Military Complex' in Historical Perspective: The Interwar Years." JOURNAL OF AMERICAN HISTORY 56 (1970): 819-32.

Shows how the War Department, although reluctant to cooperate with business during World War I, afterwards recognized the need for a planned war economy and began working with business in the interwar period, preparing the way for today's military-industrial complex.

1336   _____. "Mobilizing the World War II Economy: Labor and the Industrial Military Alliance." PACIFIC HISTORICAL REVIEW 42 (1973): 443-78.

Argues that military-labor-industrial cooperation reached full flowering during World War II, preparing the way for post-war cooperation.

1337   Krueger, Walter. FROM DOWN UNDER TO NIPPON; THE STORY OF THE SIXTH ARMY IN WORLD WAR II. Washington, D.C.: Combat Forces Press, 1953. 393 p.

Rather than a personal account, a narrative of the experience of the Sixth Army in the Pacific, based upon author's official reports.

1338   Leahy, William D. I WAS THERE. New York: McGraw-Hill, 1950. Reprint. New York: Arno, 1979. 527 p.

A personal account by the chief of staff to Presidents Roosevelt and Truman. Direct, with little effort to hide opinions, but important because Leahy was involved in the major decisions of the war.

1339   Leckie, Robert. CHALLENGE FOR THE PACIFIC: GUADALCANAL, THE TURNING POINT OF THE WAR. Garden City, N.Y.: Doubleday, 1965. 372 p.

Account by a participant based on written sources. Focuses on Battle of Bloody Ridge, with portraits of Puller, Edson, and Foss.

1340   _____. STRONG MEN ARMED: THE UNITES STATES MARINES AGAINST JAPAN. New York: Random, 1963. 563 p.

Military history of the Marines from Guadalcanal to Okinawa. Weak on strategy and political problems but strong on description of the Marine as a fighting man.

1341   Lee, R. Alton. "The Army 'Mutiny of 1946.'" JOURNAL OF AMERICAN HISTORY 53 (1967): 555-71.

Discusses the demobilization riots and demonstrations by American soldiers after World War II in a desperate attempt to
speed up mobilization. Blames the Truman administration for
not developing a coherent demobilization plan.

1342   Leighton, Richard M. "Allied Unity of Command in the Second World
War: A Study in Regional Military Organization." POLITICAL SCI-
ENCE QUARTERLY 67 (1952): 399-425.

Argues that General Eisenhower's SHAPE command after World
War II was the first international peace-keeping constabulary
and required complicated international military cooperation.

1343   _____. "Overlord Revisited: An Interpretation of American Strategy
in the European War, 1942-1944." AMERICAN HISTORICAL REVIEW
68 (1963): 919-37.

Surveys and analyzes American strategy during World War II.
Sees strategy as coming from no single source but a "blend
of competing views."

1344   LeMay, Curtis E., and Kantor, McKinley. MISSION WITH LEMAY:
MY STORY. Garden City, N.Y.: Doubleday, 1965. 581 p.

Autobiography of the former Air Force chief of staff, focusing
on the evolution of the Strategic Air Command. Tends toward polemics when discussing Secretary of War McNamara.

1345   Liang, Chin-Tung. GENERAL STILWELL: THE FULL STORY. Jamai-
ca, N.Y.: St. John's University Press, 321 p.

Account of why Chiang dropped Stilwell. Based on sources
from the Kuomintang archives.

1346   Lingeman, Richard R. "DON'T YOU KNOW A WAR IS ON?" THE
AMERICAN HOME FRONT, 1941-1946. New York: Putnam, 1970.
400 p.

Carefully researched, lively written account of the domestic
scene during World War II.

1347   Lord, Walter. DAY OF INFAMY. New York: Holt, 1957. 243 p.

Account of the events immediately preceding the Japanese
attack on Pearl Harbor on December 7, 1941. Popularly
written, hour-by-hour story.

1348   Lukas, Richard C. "The Big Three and the Warsaw Uprising." MILI-
TARY AFFAIRS 39 (1975): 129-34.

Discusses the impact of the Warsaw uprising on Big Three relations. Argues it may well have been the starting point of
the Cold War.

1349   Luvaas, Jay. DEAR MISS EMS: GENERAL EICHELBERGER'S WAR IN
THE PACIFIC. Westport, Conn.: Greenwood, 1973. 322 p.

Revelation of personal rivalries and jealousies among senior
officers in the Pacific war by one of MacArthur's primary
subordinates.

1350   MacArthur, Douglas. REMINISCENCES. New York: McGraw-Hill,
1964. 438 p.

Autobiography which covers fifty years and eight presidents.
Must be used carefully. Does not tell the whole story and
the book tends to take on the characteristic of an apologia.

1351   _____. A SOLDIER SPEAKS: PUBLIC PAPERS AND SPEECHES OF
GENERAL MacARTHUR. New York: Praeger, 1965. 467 p.

Projects image of MacArthur as a leader and military hero.

1352   MacDonald, Charles B. THE BATTLE OF HUERTGEN FOREST. Philadelphia: Lippincott, 1963. 215 p.

Thoroughly a combat history of a battle fought a few miles
south of the Battle of the Bulge. Thesis that commanders
should have paid closer attention to the dams on the Roer
River.

1353   _____. THE MIGHTY ENDEAVOR: AMERICAN ARMED FORCES IN
THE EUROPEAN THEATER IN WORLD WAR II. New York: Oxford
University Press, 1969. 576 p.

One-volume comprehensive synthesis of the American contribution in World War II. Useful on critical battles, but less
well-informed on strategic decisions.

1354   McFarland, Keith D. "F.D.R. and the Great War Department Feud."
ARMY 26 (1976): 36-42.

Discusses the power struggle between the War Department's
top civilian officials. Argues this was encouraged by President Roosevelt.

1355   McGuire, Philip. "Judge William H. Hastie and Army Recruitment,
1940-1942." MILITARY AFFAIRS 42 (1978): 75-79.

Discusses the effort of Hastie, a black civilian aide to the
Secretary of War, to persuade the War Department to place

more recruitment advertisements in the black press. The Department refused and Hastie resigned in protest, citing racial prejudice.

1356   Manchester, William. AMERICAN CEASAR: DOUGLAS MacARTHUR, 1880-1964. Boston: Little, Brown, 1978. 793 p.

Popular, competently researched, well-written biography of MacArthur by a famous author. Covers longer period than James' work (see entry 1329), but not as scholarly detached.

1357   Margolin, Leo J. PAPER BULLETS: A BRIEF STORY OF PSYCHOLOGICAL WARFARE IN WORLD WAR II. New York: Freben, 1946. 149 p.

Account of both allied and enemy propaganda in the Second World War, written in a journalistic style.

1358   Marshall, S.L.A. BASTOGNE, THE STORY OF THE FIRST EIGHT DAYS IN WHICH THE 101ST AIRBORNE DIVISION WAS CLOSED WITHIN THE RING OF GERMAN FORCE. Washington, D.C.: Infantry Journal Press, 1944. 261 p.

Narrative of the events that led to the battle of Bastogne, where the inexperienced VIII Corps was struck by twenty-five German divisions, and how the order to "hold the line" was carried out.

1359   _____. MEN AGAINST FIRE. Washington, D.C.: Morrow, 1947. 215 p.

A classic series of case studies of junior officers and enlisted men interviewed concerning their attitudes toward combat. Makes the startling discovery that large numbers of men in World War II did not fire their weapons in combat.

1360   _____. NIGHT DROP: THE AMERICAN AIRBORNE INVASION OF NORMANDY. Boston: Little, Brown, 1962. 425 p.

Story of the parachute drop by the 101st and 82nd Airborne behind Utah beach several hours before dawn of June 6, 1944.

1361   Mauldin, William H. UP FRONT. Cleveland and New York: World Press, 1945. 228 p.

Collection of Willie and Joe cartoons along with a narrative by the then 23-year-old cartoonist. With sardonic humor, graphically depicts dirt and terror of the "dog faces'" war.

1362   Mayo, Lida. BLOODY BUNA. Garden City, N.Y.: Doubleday, 1974. 222 p.

Account of the American campaign in New Guinea. Mostly battle history, but does cover the squabble between Australians and Americans over strategy.

1363   Mazuzan, George T. "The National War Service Controversy, 1942-1945." MID-AMERICA 57 (1975): 246-58.

Discusses the effort to establish a compulsory national service law which would draft men into defense-related jobs. Discusses the reasons it failed.

1364   Miller, John R. "The Chaing-Stilwell Conflict, 1942-1944." MILITARY AFFAIRS 43 (1979): 59-62.

Argues that the conflict was more than just a clash of two obstinate personalities; it arose also from differences over strategic policy in China.

1365   Millett, John D. "The War Department in World War II." AMERICAN POLITICAL SCIENCE REVIEW 40 (1946): 863-97.

Early study of the War Department, focusing on its organizational functions during World War II, discussing problems it faced and solutions it found.

1366   Millis, Walter. THIS IS PEARL!: THE UNITED STATES AND JAPAN. New York: Morrow, 1947. 384 p.

Suspenseful story of the events, politics and attitudes leading to the attack on Pearl Harbor in 1941.

1367   Morganstern, George E. PEARL HARBOR: THE STORY OF THE SECRET WAR. New York: Devin-Adair, 1947. 425 p.

A revisionist indictment of the Roosevelt administration's Pacific policy that led to war with Japan.

1368   Morison, Elting E. TURMOIL AND TRADITION: A STUDY OF THE LIFE AND TIMES OF HENRY L. STIMSON. Boston: Houghton-Mifflin, 1960. 686 p.

Account of an important early twentieth century statesman. Significant chapters on Stimson as secretary of war during World War II.

1369   Morison, Samuel E. STRATEGY AND COMPROMISE. Boston: Little, Brown, 1958. 120 p.

Examines and appraises allied strategic decisions during World War II. Describes disputes and compromises between British and American strategists.

1370   Morton, Louis. "Origins of Pacific Strategy." MARINE CORPS GA-
        ZETTE 41 (1957): 36-43.

        Traces development of American strategies in the Far East,
        1900-1907.

1371   _____. "War Plan Orange: Evolution of a Strategy." WORLD
        POLITICS 11 (1959): 22-50.

        Describes the development of American Pacific strategy prior
        to World War II.

1372   Murphy, Audie. TO HELL AND BACK. New York: Holt, 1949.
        274 p.

        Account in diary form of America's most decorated soldier's
        experiences in World War II. Considered one of the best
        enlisted man's personal accounts of World War II combat.

1373   Nelson, Donald M. ARSENAL OF DEMOCRACY: THE STORY OF
        AMERICAN WAR PRODUCTION. New York: Harcourt, Brace, 1946.
        439 p.

        Account by former director of the War Production Board de-
        scribing economic mobilization during World War II. Useful
        in its revelations on American civil-military relations during
        the war.

1374   O'Connor, Raymond C. DIPLOMACY FOR VICTORY: FDR AND
        UNCONDITIONAL SURRENDER. New York: Norton, 1971. 143 p.

        Considers unconditional surrender to have been a sensible pol-
        icy, particularly necessary for coalition warfare.

1375   Ogburn, Charlton, Jr. THE MARAUDERS. New York: Harper, 1956.
        307 p.

        Account of the Merrill Marauders' experiences in Burma in
        1944 by a participant. Details hardships and strains of jungle
        fighting.

1376   Patton, Beatrice A., ed. WAR AS I KNEW IT. Boston: Houghton-
        Mifflin, 1947. 425 p.

        Collection of letters from Gen. George Patton to his wife
        written during the African and Sicilian Campaigns. Blunt,
        candid opinions expressed.

1377   Peers, William. BEHIND THE BURMA ROAD: THE STORY OF AMER-
        ICA'S MOST SUCCESSFUL GUERRILLA FORCE. Boston: Atlantic-Lit-
        tle, 1963. 246 p.

A full account of the 1943-45 guerrilla operations in Burma by an Office of Strategic Services participant.

1378   Polenberg, Richard J. WAR AND SOCIETY: THE UNITED STATES, 1941-1945. Philadelphia: Lippincott, 1972. 297 p.

Argues that in its response to World War II, the nation employed and thus cemented New Deal techniques.

1379   Poque, Forrest C. "George C. Marshall and His Commanders, 1942-1945." ESSAYS ON NEW DIMENSIONS IN MILITARY HISTORY 4 (1976): 80-90.

1380   _____. GEORGE C. MARSHALL: ORDEAL AND HOPE 1939-1942. Vol. II. New York: Viking, 1973. 491 p.

Second of projected four volumes deals with Marshall as chief of staff during World War II. Balances the subject and the war he fought.

1381   _____. GEORGE C. MARSHALL, ORGANIZER OF VICTORY 1943-1945. Vol. III. New York: Viking, 1973. 683 p.

Covers the period 1943-45. Emphasizes manpower problems, interservice rivalry, and relations with Congress. Clear but sympathetic.

1382   Power, Thomas, and Arnhym, Albert. DESIGN FOR SURVIVAL. New York: Coward-McCann, 1965. 225 p.

A polemic by the former commander of the Strategic Air Command warning of the military threat from the Soviet Union. Highly critical of McNamara, book was originally suppressed by the Department of Defense and when published became a cause celebre.

1383   Pyle, Ernest T. BRAVE MEN. New York: Grosset and Dunlap, 1945. Reprint. New York: Arno, 1979. 328 p.

Collection of famous war correspondent's dispatches from Sicily through the liberation of Paris.

1384   _____. HERE IS YOUR WAR. New York: Holt, 1943. 304 p.

Human interest stories of the African Campaign by the famous war correspondent. Depicts the agony of the common soldier.

1385   Ross, Davis R. PREPARING FOR ULYSSES: POLITICS AND VETERANS DURING WORLD WAR II. New York: Columbia University Press, 1969. 315 p.

A useful monograph on America's demobilization policy after World War II, focusing on the reintegration of veterans into American society.

1386　Rundell, Walter. BLACK MARKET MONEY: THE COLLAPSE OF U.S. MILITARY CURRENCY CONTROL IN WORLD WAR II. Baton Rouge: Louisiana State University Press, 1964. 125 p.

Account of how dishonest soldiers made fortunes on the black market because of the breakdown of the U.S. Army's control of currency.

1387　Rupp, Lelia J. MOBILIZING WOMEN FOR WAR: GERMAN AND AMERICAN PROPAGANDA, 1939-1945. Princeton, N.J.: Princeton University Press, 1978. 243 p.

Notes that while the Germans legislated women into civilian jobs, Americans achieved better results through propaganda. Both depicted this as unusual assignments and therefore did not change social ideology.

1388　Rutkowski, Edwin H. THE POLITICS OF MILITARY AVIATION PRO-CUREMENT 1926-1934: A STUDY IN THE POLITICAL ASSERTION OF CONSENSUAL VALUES. Columbus: Ohio State University Press, 1967. 318 p.

Useful as a case study of American civil-military relations, and the complex nature of policy determinants. Much prewar military history here.

1389　Ryan, Cornelius. A BRIDGE TOO FAR. New York: Simon and Schuster, 1974. 670 p.

Popular, colorful account of the battle for Arnhem aimed at seizing five bridges and hopefully ending the war. Focuses on the conflict of personalities.

1390　_____. THE LAST BATTLE. New York: Simon and Schuster, 1966. 571 p.

Absorbing account of the assault on Berlin in 1945, focusing on study of individuals.

1391　_____. THE LONGEST DAY: JUNE 6, 1944. Greenwich, Conn.: Fawcett, 1960. 288 p.

Popular account of the Normandy invasion.

1392　Schoenberger, Walter S. DECISION OF DESTINY. Athens: Ohio University Press, 1969. 319 p.

Discussion of the steps leading to the final decision to drop the atomic bomb.

1393   Scott, Robert L. GOD IS MY CO-PILOT. New York: Scribner, 1943. 277 p.

Popular narrative of an American Army pilot detailing his experience flying in Burma and under Chennault in China. Some views on air tactics and the war in Asia.

1394   Sherry, Michael S. PREPARING FOR THE NEXT WAR: AMERICAN PLANS FOR POSTWAR DEFENSE, 1941-1945. New Haven, Conn.: Yale University Press, 1977. 260 p.

Examines such themes as the campaign for Universal Military Training, the partnership between scientists and soldiers, and between industrialists and soldiers, and the influence of nuclear weapons on strategy. Argues that the war created an ideology of preparedness and thus inaugurated the Cold War even before V-J day.

1395   Sherwin, Martin J. A WORLD DESTROYED: THE ATOMIC BOMB AND THE GRAND ALLIANCE. New York: Knopf, 1975. 315 p.

Concludes that the bomb was dropped more to justify the massive expenditure of public's funds than out of considerations of strategy or diplomacy.

1396   Sherwood, Robert E. ROOSEVELT AND HOPKINS: AN INTIMATE HISTORY. New York: Harper, 1950. 1,002 p.

One of the most useful studies of civilian leadership during World War II.

1397   Smith, Jean E. "Selection of a Proconsul for Germany: The Appointment of Gen. Lucius Clay, 1945." MILITARY AFFAIRS 40 (1976): 123-29.

Argues that Clay, an officer close to New Dealers, was chosen because civilians in the administration wanted him rather than a "military" man.

1398   _____, ed. THE PAPERS OF GENERAL LUCIUS D. CLAY: GERMANY, 1945-1949. 2 vols. Bloomington: Indiana University Press, 1974.

Papers of Clay when he was military governor of Germany after World War II. An important contribution to the primary sources on the Cold War.

1399   Smith, R. Harris. OSS: THE SECRET HISTORY OF AMERICA'S FIRST
        INTELLIGENCE AGENCY. Berkeley and Los Angeles: University of
        California Press, 1972. 450 p.

        Account of the Office of Strategic Services which focuses on
        OSS cooperation with various resistance forces and the con-
        flict of ideological forces within the organization.

1400   Smith, Walter B. EISENHOWER'S SIX GREAT DECISIONS. New
        York: Longmans, Green, 1956. 237 p.

        Eisenhower's chief of staff reviews six critical decisions rang-
        ing from the date of D-Day to the pursuit of German forces
        deep into Germany. A kind of brief, minor commentary,
        yet Smith's relationship with Eisenhower makes it a useful
        source.

1401   Sparrow, John C. HISTORY OF PERSONEL DEMOBILIZATION IN
        THE UNITED STATES ARMY. Department of Army Pamphlet 20-210.
        Washington, D.C.: Department of the Army, 1956. 358 p.

        Covers demobilization during and after the Second World War
        but also includes a historical introduction on demobilization.

1402   Steele, Richard W. THE FIRST OFFENSIVE, 1942: ROOSEVELT,
        MARSHALL AND THE MAKING OF AMERICAN STRATEGY. Bloom-
        ington: Indiana University Press, 1973. 239 p.

        Traces complex forces which led to Torch invasion of North
        Africa. Emphasizes lack of conflict between American and
        British strategists.

1403   _____. "Political Aspects of American Military Planning, 1941-
        1942." MILITARY AFFAIRS 35 (1971): 68-73.

        Discusses conflict between the British and the Americans over
        the goals of World War II strategy.

1404   Stoler, Mark A. THE POLITICS OF THE SECOND FRONT: AMERI-
        CAN MILITARY PLANNING AND DIPLOMACY IN COALITION WAR-
        FARE, 1941-1943. Westport, Conn.: Greenwood, 1977.

        Explores the relationship between politics and military plan-
        ning for the cross-channel invasion. Claims army had ulterior
        motives for developing the second front.

1405   Stouffer, Samuel A., et al. STUDIES IN SOCIAL PSYCHOLOGY IN
        WORLD WAR II. 4 vols. Princeton, N.J.: Princeton University
        Press, 1949.

        A major classic which deals with the behavior of soldiers in

and out of combat during World War II. Covers such topics
as the adjustment to army life; the soldiers' behavior in combat; and experiments in mass communication.

1406   Thomas, Gordon. ENOLA GAY. New York: Stein and Day. 327 p.

Presented from Japanese and American perspective, a detailed
story of dropping the first atomic bomb.

1407   Toland, John. BATTLE: THE STORY OF THE BULGE. New York:
Random, 1959. 400 p.

Based upon newspaper accounts, some official sources and
interviews with hundreds of G.I.'s and Nazi officers. Weakened by a novelistic method which depicts conversation as if
historically occurred.

1408   _____. THE LAST HUNDRED DAYS. New York: Random, 1966.
622 p.

Describes the last three months of World War II, within which
Roosevelt, Hitler, Mussolini, Nazism, and Fascism all died.
Draws heavily on interviews with eyewitnesses.

1409   Tregaskis, Richard W. GUADALCANAL DIARY. New York: Random,
1955. 180 p.

Popular wartime account by an observer.

1410   Truscott, Lucian K. COMMAND MISSIONS: A PERSONAL STORY.
New York: Dutton, 1954. Reprint. New York: Arno, 1979.
570 p.

A military memoir by a general who describes his experiences
in North Africa, Italy, and Germany. Focuses on strategic
and tactical affairs.

1411   Tuchman, Barbara W. STILWELL AND THE AMERICAN EXPERIENCE
IN CHINA. New York: Macmillan, 1971. 621 p.

Well-researched, well-told story of U.S.-China relations
during World War II focusing on the experiences of Joseph
Stilwell. Sees success of Communist forces quite predictable,
perhaps inevitable.

1412   Tute, Warren, et al. D-DAY. New York: Macmillan, 1974.
256 p.

Competent short account of the Normandy landing on June 6,
1944.

1413   U.S. Army Center for Military History. UNITED STATES ARMY IN
        WORLD WAR II. 80 vols. Washington, D.C.: Government Printing
        Office, 1950-75.

        These eighty volumes are the results of a prodigious effort on
        the part of several eminent military historians. Supported by
        the Department of Army, this is the official, but nevertheless
        interpretative, military history, based on solid research in
        the sources. Those interested in the history of World War II
        must begin here.

        Space prevents even a listing of the volumes. All are avail-
        able at Depository Libraries and an annotated list of the works
        is available in a pamphlet entitled "Publications of the Army
        Center of Military History" published by the U.S. Superin-
        tendent of Documents, Government Printing Office, Washing-
        ton, D.C.

1414   U.S. Department of War. PRELUDE TO INVASION: AN ACCOUNT
        BASED UPON OFFICIAL REPORTS BY HENRY L. STIMSON, SECRE-
        TARY OF WAR. Washington: Government Printing Office, 1944.
        322 p.

        Covers period from December 1941 to June 1944, and deals
        with the invasion of Europe.

1415   Villa, Brian L. "The U.S. Army, Unconditional Surrender and the
        Potsdam Proclamation." JOURNAL OF AMERICAN HISTORY 43
        (1976): 66-92.

        Argues that unconditional surrender was a presidential policy
        not supported enthusiastically by the army.

1416   Watson, Mark. "First Vigorous Steps in Rearing, 1938-1939." MILI-
        TARY AFFAIRS 12 (1948): 65-78.

        Discusses the effort on the part of the General Staff to achieve
        a degree of preparedness in the critical period before World
        War II.

1417   Wedemeyer, Albert. WEDEMEYER REPORTS. New York: Holt, 1958.
        497 p.

        Highly critical account of American effort in World War II
        by an officer who served in Washington and the Far East.
        Argues United States waited too long to invade Europe and
        ought not have attempted to reconcile Nationalist and Chi-
        nese communists.

1418   Werstein, Irving. GUADALCANAL. New York: Crowell, 1963.
        186 p.

Discusses the battle from the point of view of both sides, based on personal accounts and letters of participants.

1419 Whitcomb, Edgar D. ESCAPE FROM CORREGIDOR. Chicago: Regnery, 1958. 274 p.

Author tells of experiences as he twice escaped Japanese custody, withstood beatings, and was repatriated.

1420 White, Theodore, ed. THE STILWELL PAPERS. New York: Sloane, 1948. 357 p.

Constructed by White from Joseph Stilwell's notes, journals and letters from the period 1941-44, when he was relieved of command in China. Stilwell has caustic remarks on many people, namely Chiang Kai-Shek.

1421 Whitney, Courtney. MacARTHUR: HIS RENDEZVOUS WITH HISTORY. New York: Knopf, 1956. 547 p.

Biography by MacArthur's aide. Marred by author's overweening sympathy for his subject, but useful as a resource for a critical biography.

1422 Williams, Justin. "Completing Japan's Political Reorientation, 1947-1952: Crucial Phase of the Allied Occupation." AMERICAN HISTORICAL REVIEW 74 (1968): 1454-69.

Account of the military occupation of Japan. Author concludes that American policy was clear and consistent and made by civilians in Washington, not by General MacArthur's command.

1423 Willoughby, Charles A., and Chamberlain, John. MacARTHUR, 1941-1951. New York: McGraw-Hill, 1954. 441 p.

A "headquarters" book on the experiences of Willoughby who served under MacArthur in the Pacific. Presents a "devil theory" when explaining MacArthur's conflicts with civilian leaders and the Joint Chiefs of Staff.

1424 Wilmot, Chester. THE STRUGGLE FOR EUROPE. New York: Harper, 1952. 766 p.

Massive account of first-hand war correspondent experience and credible research. Argues for Montgomery strategy over America and that faulty American strategy allowed for Russian expansion.

1425 Wittner, Lawrence S. "MacArthur and the Missionaries: God and

Man in Occupied Japan." PACIFIC HISTORICAL REVIEW 40 (1971): 77-98.

Discusses how MacArthur attempted but failed to Christianize Japan during American occupation.

1426   Wohlstetter, Roberta. PEARL HARBOR: WARNING AND DECISION. Stanford, Calif.: Stanford University Press, 1962. 426 p.

Study of why the United States was surprised at Pearl Harbor, focusing on the intelligence process. Concludes United States had too much information and too little experience in deciphering.

Chapter 7

THE MILITARY IN THE NUCLEAR AGE (SINCE 1945)

A. CREATION OF THE DEFENSE ESTABLISHMENT

1427   Art, Robert J.   THE TFX DECISION: McNAMARA AND THE MILI-
        TARY.   Boston: Little, Brown, 1968.   202 p.

        A useful case study of civil-military relations in the defense
        department during the McNamara era.

1428   Blum, Albert A.   "Soldier or Worker: A Re-evaluation of the Selec-
        tive Service System."   MID-WEST QUARTERLY 13 (1972):   147-67.

        Discusses the variety of pressures on the Selective Service
        System for manpower needs from the War Department to col-
        leges.

1429   Bogart, Leo, ed.   SOCIAL RESEARCH AND THE DESEGREGATION
        OF THE ARMY.   Chicago: Markham, 1969.   393 p.

        Reports from a research project designed to examine the ef-
        fects of the initial stages of integration in the U.S. Army in
        the early 1950s.

1430   Bolles, Blair.   MILITARY ESTABLISHMENT OF THE UNITED STATES.
        Foreign Policy Reports, vol. 25, no. 9.   New York: Foreign Policy
        Association, 1949.   25 p.

        Discusses growth of Defense Department after World War II.

1431   Borklund, C.W.   THE DEPARTMENT OF DEFENSE.   New York: Prae-
        ger, 1968.   342 p.

        Factual, informed account of twenty years of history of the
        department, which focuses on the McNamara era.

1432   _____.   MEN OF THE PENTAGON: FROM FORRESTAL TO McNA-
        MARA.   New York: Praeger, 1966.   236 p.

A historical survey of the Department of Defense traced
through the profiles of eight men who headed the department
from its formation to 1966.

1433   Burt, Richard, ed. and comp. CONGRESSIONAL HEARINGS ON
AMERICAN DEFENSE POLICY, 1947-1971: AN ANNOTATED BIBLI-
OGRAPHY. Lawrence: University Press of Kansas, 1974. 377 p.

Important reference for the serious scholar of American military policy after World War II. Arranged chronologically,
according to congressional session.

1434   Caraley, Demetrios. THE POLITICS OF MILITARY UNIFICATION: A
STUDY OF CONFLICT AND THE POLICY PROCESS. New York:
Columbia University Press, 1966. 345 p.

Account of the conflict (1943-47) over unification of the
armed forces. Contains much game-theory jargon.

1435   Cline, Ray S., and Matloff, Maurice. "Development of War Department Views on Unification." MILITARY AFFAIRS 13 (1949): 65-74.

Discusses various efforts and proposals to develop institutional
cooperation between the War and Navy Departments prior to
post-World War II unification. Good on historical background
to the creation of the Department of Defense.

1436   Fulbright, J. William. THE PENTAGON PROPAGANDA MACHINE.
New York: Liveright, 1970. 166 p.

Account of how the Defense Department uses its military information budget to propagandize political points of view
rather than perfectly legitimate reasons for dispensing information.

1437   Gerhardt, James M. THE DRAFT AND PUBLIC POLICY: ISSUES IN
MILITARY MANPOWER PROCUREMENT, 1945-1970. Columbus: Ohio
State University Press, 1971. 425 p.

Account of America's struggle with the draft after World War
II. Judges the Selective Service System as inequitable.

1438   Gropman, Alan L. THE AIR FORCE INTEGRATES, 1945-1964. Washington, D.C.: Government Printing Office, 1978. 384 p.

Discusses the forces that led the Air Force to integrate even
before President Truman's famous executive edict ordering integration.

1439   Huntington, Samuel P. "Interservice Competition and the Political

Roles of the Armed Services." AMERICAN POLITICAL SCIENCE RE-
VIEW 55 (1961): 40-52.

Argues that the conventional belief that interservice rivalry
is inefficient and that military action threatens civilian control needs rethinking, which author does.

1440 Kintner, William R. FORGING A NEW SWORD: A STUDY OF THE
DEPARTMENT OF DEFENSE. New York: Harper, 1958. 238 p.

Reviews experience of the department since 1947, and then
suggests areas for improvement.

1441 Korb, Lawrence J. THE JOINT CHIEFS OF STAFF: THE FIRST
TWENTY-FIVE YEARS. Bloomington: University of Indiana Press,
1976. 210 p.

Focuses on the strengths and weaknesses of the Joint Chiefs
of Staff as a bureaucracy and on the men responsible for its
development.

1442 _____. THE PRICE OF PREPAREDNESS: THE FY 1978-1982 DEFENSE
PROGRAM. Washington, D.C.: American Enterprise Institute For
Public Policy, 1977. 43 p.

Study of defense priorities as projected in the defense budget
for fiscal years 1978-82.

1443 McMahon, Chalmers A., and Combs, J.W. "The Age of Military
Leaders and the Expansion of the Armed Forces." SOUTHWESTERN
SOCIAL SCIENCE QUARTERLY 36 (1956): 365-75.

Argues that the period during and immediately after the Second World War could be termed the age of military leaders
because of their high prestige during the war and the expansion of the armed forces afterward made them indispensible.

1444 Mrozek, Donald J. "The Truman Administration and the Enlistment of
the Aviation Industry in Postwar Defense." BUSINESS HISTORY RE-
VIEW 48 (1974): 73-94.

Argues neither military nor the aviation industry, but the
Truman administration played the leading role in integrating
aviation industry into national defense and thus helping create
the military-industrial complex.

1445 Powers, Patrick W. A GUIDE TO NATIONAL DEFENSE: THE OR-
GANIZATION AND OPERATIONS OF THE U.S. MILITARY ESTAB-
LISHMENT. New York: Praeger, 1964. 326 p.

Useful source on plans, policies, and status of America's

military forces after World War II.

1446   Pursell, Carroll W., Jr., ed. THE MILITARY-INDUSTRIAL COMPLEX. New York: Harper, 1972. 341 p.

Collection of superior essays from historical, economic, and sociological perspectives.

1447   Raymond, Jack. POWER AT THE PENTAGON. New York: Harper, 1964. 363 p.

First third of the book surveys World War II build up and the atomic bomb project. Last two-thirds cover the growth of the Pentagon. Reportorial, anecdotal, and critical of McNamara.

1448   Rice, Berkeley. THE C-5A SCANDAL: AN INSIDE STORY OF THE MILITARY-INDUSTRIAL COMPLEX. New York: Macmillan, 1971. 238 p.

Traces the procurement of Department of Defense's most expensive defense systems. Exposes waste and inefficiency.

1449   Ries, John C. THE MANAGEMENT OF DEFENSE: ORGANIZATION AND CONTROL OF THE U.S. ARMED SERVICES. Baltimore: Johns Hopkins University Press, 1964. 228 p.

A narrative of the relationship of management theory to the changes that took place in the War Department after World War II.

1450   Rodberg, Leonard S., and Shearer, Derek, eds. THE PENTAGON WATCHERS: STUDENTS REPORT ON THE NATIONAL SECURITY STATE. Garden City, N.Y.: Doubleday, 1970. 416 p.

Based on research done by a group of students, but not a sign of lesser quality. Thesis is that United States had developed a national security state with an economy that requires preparation for war as its sine qua non.

1451   Rogow, Arnold A. JAMES FORRESTAL: A STUDY OF PERSONALITY, POLITICS AND POLICY. New York: Macmillan, 1963. 397 p.

A sympathetic but not uncritical biography of America's leading cold warrior who served as the first secretary of defense.

1452   Roherty, James M. DECISIONS OF ROBERT S. McNAMARA: A STUDY OF THE ROLE OF THE SECRETARY OF DEFENSE. Coral Gables, Fla.: University of Miami Press, 1970. 223 p.

Discusses McNamara as a unique secretary of defense: a

functionalist who relied on technical and managerial processes
rather than a traditionalist who reached decisions by a political process.

1453   Schiller, Herbert [I.], and Phillips, Joseph [D.]., eds. SUPER STATE
READINGS IN THE MILITARY-INDUSTRIAL COMPLEX. Urbana: University of Illinois Press, 1970. 353 p.

Collection of current essays, addresses, and charts on military
expenditure.

1454   Slater, Jerome, and Nardin, Terry. "The 'Military-Industrial Complex'
Muddle." YALE REVIEW 65 (1975): 1-23.

Argues that Military-Industrial Complex presupposes a theory
of politics that is deficient in analysis and short on substance.

1455   Stillman, Richard J. II. INTEGRATION OF THE NEGRO IN THE
U.S. ARMED FORCES. New York: Praeger, 1968. 167 p.

Thinly researched, cursory review of the effects of military
integration on race relations in the United States.

1456   Swomley, John M., Jr. THE MILITARY ESTABLISHMENT. Boston:
Beacon, 1964. 266 p.

Polemical in tone. Attempts to show the overriding influence
of the military establishment over American society.

1457   Taylor, Maxwell D. RESPONSIBILITY AND RESPONSE. New York:
Harper, 1967. 84 p.

Argued that United States faced with multipolar forces as represented by the war in Vietnam. Argues that all enemies had
to be dealt with individually, not with one policy.

1458   Trager, Frank N. "The National Security Act of 1947: It's Thirtieth
Birthday." AIR UNIVERSITY REVIEW 29 (1977): 2-15.

Evaluates the creation of the Department of Defense which
combined all services into one department in 1947. Believes,
after thirty years, there is room for reform and suggests some.

1459   Trewhitt, Henry L. McNAMARA: HIS ORDEAL IN THE PENTAGON.
New York: Harper, 1971. 307 p.

Objective, yet sympathetic, very human account of the former
secretary of defense, focusing on McNamara's experiences in
the defense department.

1460   U.S. Selective Service System. SPECIAL MONOGRAPHS ON THE
        SELECTED SERVICE SYSTEM OF WORLD WAR II, 1940-1947. 10 vols.
        Washington, D.C.: Government Printing Office, 1948-1950.

        Although self-serving, contains much useful information and
        data. Topics influence classification, conscientious objection,
        quotas, reemployment, and enforcement.

1461   Watson, Mark S. "Two Years of Unification." MILITARY AFFAIRS
        13 (1949): 193-94.

1462   Wolk, Herman. "The Defense Unification Battle, 1947-1950: The Air
        Force." PROLOGUE 7 (1975): 18-31.

        Discusses how the Air Force, believing that they had a dom-
        inant position in the defense structure after World War II,
        pressed for unification of the services.

B. THE COLD WAR AND NUCLEAR STRATEGY

1463   Abel, Elie. THE MISSILE CRISIS. Philadelphia: Lippincott, 1966.
        200 p.

        A journalist's well-written account of the October 1962 Cuban
        Missile Crisis.

1464   Ackley, Charles W. THE MODERN MILITARY IN AMERICAN SOCI-
        ETY: A STUDY IN THE NATURE OF MILITARY POWER. Philadel-
        phia: Westminster, 1972. 400 p.

        A moral and evaluative account with some useful material on
        recent strategic thought among professional officers.

1465   Adams, Benson D. BALLISTIC MISSILE DEFENSE. New York: Amer-
        ican Elsevier, 1971. 274 p.

        A description of American missile defense, focusing on the
        antimissile program.

1466   Armacost, Michael H. THE POLITICS OF WEAPONS INNOVATION:
        THE THOR-JUPITER CONTROVERSY. New York: Columbia University
        Press, 1969. 304 p.

        Study of the Thor-Jupiter project. Focuses on the interrela-
        tionship between politics and weapons policies and more
        broadly between politics and technology.

1467   Baldwin, Hanson. POWER AND POLITICS: THE PRICE OF SECURITY
        IN THE ATOMIC AGE. Claremont, Calif.: Claremont College Press,
        1950. 117 p.

NEW YORK TIMES military writer's account of what he considers the mistakes made in World War II that led to the Cold War.

1468 _____. STRATEGY FOR TOMORROW. New York: Harper, 1970. 377 p.

Account by prominent military writer who maintains that United States should build military strength while it negotiates. Argues for more weapons, more research, more intelligence.

1469 Barnet, Richard J. THE ECONOMY OF DEATH. New York: Atheneum, 1970. 201 p.

Polemical yet powerful indictment of the "military-industrial complex" and the "dangerous irrationality" of American defense policy.

1470 _____. INTERVENTION AND REVOLUTION: AMERICA'S CONFRONTATION WITH INSURGENT MOVEMENTS AROUND THE WORLD. New York: World, 1968. 302 p.

Argues that although the Cold War was begun over the fate of Europe, it has been fought in Asia. Covers interventions in Greece, Lebanon, Dominican Republic, and Vietnam.

1471 _____. ROOTS OF WAR: THE MEN AND INSTITUTIONS BEHIND UNITED STATES FOREIGN POLICY. New York: Atheneum, 1972. 350 p.

Focuses on the composition and attitudes of what the author calls the "national defense establishment."

1472 Berkes, Ross N. "Weapons Development in the United States." CURRENT HISTORY 47 (1964): 71-76.

Briefly discusses the technological development of U.S. weaponry, focusing on the post World War II era.

1473 Betts, Richard K. SOLDIERS, STATESMEN AND COLD WAR CRISIS. Cambridge, Mass.: Harvard University Press, 1977. 215 p.

Analysis of the nature and influence of military advice on American policy decisions made in such crises as the Berlin Blockade, Cuban Missile Crisis, and Vietnam War.

1474 Bottome, Edgar. THE BALANCE OF TERROR: A GUIDE TO THE

ARMS RACE. Boston: Beacon, 1972. 215 p.

An account of the development of the nuclear arms race. Concludes United States has always held a two-one advantage.

1475 Brayton, Abbott A. "American Reserve Policies Since World War II." MILITARY AFFAIRS 36 (1972): 139-44.

Traces development of American reserve policies, concluding that policy arises from compromise between conflicting constituencies.

1476 Brodie, Bernard. ESCALATION AND THE NUCLEAR OPTION. Princeton, N.J.: Princeton University Press, 1966. 151 p.

Presents views on nuclear escalation and argues for the use of "tactical" nuclear weapons as an American option.

1477 _____. "The McNamara Phenomenon." WORLD POLITICS 17 (1965): 672-86.

Critically reviews Kaufman's McNAMARA STRATEGY (see entry 1527) but also provides a penetrating evaluation of that strategy.

1478 _____. "Strategy as a Science." WORLD POLITICS 11 (1959): 467-88.

An early analysis of American nuclear strategic policy.

1479 _____. STRATEGY IN THE MISSILE AGE. Princeton, N.J.: Princeton University Press, 1959. 423 p.

Focuses on deterrence and its bearing on such doctrines as massive retaliation, limited war and defense posture. Critical of prevailing American nuclear strategy.

1480 Brown, Neville. NUCLEAR WAR: THE IMPENDING STRATEGIC DEADLOCK. New York: Praeger, 1965. 238 p.

First part describes various types of nuclear weapons; second part provides a handy reference to military doctrine.

1481 Canan, James W. SUPERWARRIORS: THE FANTASTIC WORLD OF PENTAGON SUPERWEAPONS. New York: Weybright and Talley, 1975. 375 p.

Popular guided tour through the world of U.S. weapons production. Focus is on the Pentagon.

1482 Canby, Steven L. MILITARY MANPOWER PROCUREMENT: A POL-
ICY ANALYSIS. Lexington, Mass.: Lexington Books, 1972. 291 p.

Written from an analytical framework of cost techniques.
Highly specialized.

1483 Chayes, Abram, and Wiesner, Jerome, eds. ABM: AN EVALUATION
OF THE DECISION TO DEPLOY AN ANTIBALLISTIC MISSILE SYS-
TEM. New York: Harper, 1969. 282 p.

A collection of essays by scientists and diplomats assessing
the wisdom of the safeguard system.

1484 Clark, John J. THE NEW ECONOMICS OF NATIONAL DEFENSE.
New York: Random, 1966. 242 p.

Summary of existing literature in 1966 dealing with the ap-
plication of economics to military and defense problems.

1485 Clark, Keith C., and Lagere, Laurence J., eds. THE PRESIDENT
AND THE MANAGEMENT OF NATIONAL SECURITY. New York:
Praeger, 1969. 274 p.

An extended analytical discussion of the problems the president must face in conducting national security.

1486 Coffin, Tristram. THE PASSION OF THE HAWKS: MILITARISM IN
MODERN AMERICA. New York: Macmillan, 1964. 280 p.

Indictment of American "militarism" that is weakened by polemics and a potpourri of questions and anecdotes.

1487 Cook, Fred J. THE WARFARE STATE. New York: Macmillan, 1962.
376 p.

Indictment of American policy makers, military and civilian,
for turning a peace-loving democracy into a war state. Polemical and conspiratorial in tone.

1488 Cooling, Franklin. "Civil Defense and the Army: The Quest For Responsibility." MILITARY AFFAIRS 36 (1972): 11-14.

Discusses how the armed forces avoided responsibility for civil
defense in the immediate prewar years.

1489 _____. "U.S. Army Support of Civil Defense: The Formative Years."
MILITARY AFFAIRS 35 (1971): 7-11.

Discusses how the army assisted the civilian defense program
through advice, planning, training, and equipment, but it
avoided direct responsibility.

1490   Cottrell, Alvin J. "U.S. Military Posture Today." CURRENT HIS-
        TORY 47 (1964): 71–76.

        Believes most significant aspect of recent U.S. military policy
        has been the development of a nuclear strategy based on the
        second–strike concept.

1491   Deichman, Seymour J. LIMITED WAR AND AMERICAN DEFENSE
        POLICY. Cambridge: M.I.T. Press, 1964. 273 p.

        A study of the problems of the American military system, and
        the application of that system to limited war.

1492   DeWeerd, Harvey A. "Is It Time U.S. Appraised its Nuclear Weapons
        Policies?" ARMY 27 (1977): 14–19.

        Traces American nuclear weapons policy since World War II
        and suggests that ways are being sought to control its uses.

1493   Donovan, James A. MILITARISM, USA. New York: Scribner, 1970.
        265 p.

        By a retired Marine colonel. Argues military grown too power-
        ful, and policy makers cannot help using this awesome power.

1494   Englebardt, Stanley L. STRATEGIC DEFENSES. New York: Crowell,
        1966. 168 p.

        A guide to American nuclear defenses, focusing on the inte-
        grated nature of the system.

1495   Enthoven, Alain C., and Smith, K. Wayne. HOW MUCH IS ENOUGH?:
        SHAPING THE DEFENSE PROGRAM, 1961-1969. New York: Harper,
        1971. 364 p.

        Analysis of defense policy that considers roles of secretary of
        defense, joint chiefs of staff and system analyses.

1496   Evans, Gordon. "The New Military Strategy." CURRENT HISTORY
        47 (1964): 77–80.

        Discusses the concept of damage-limiting strategy as marking
        the end of the era of massive retaliation.

1497   Ezell, Edward C. "Cracks in the Post-War Anglo-American Alliance:
        The Great Rifle Controversy, 1947-1957." MILITARY AFFAIRS 38
        (1974): 138–41.

        Discusses how even the matter of a standard rifle for North
        Atlantic Treaty Organization forces turned out to be a politi-
        cal "hot potato."

1498   Falk, Stanley L. "The National Security Council Under Truman,
        Eisenhower, and Kennedy." POLITICAL SCIENCE QUARTERLY 79
        (1964): 403-34.

        Traces the development of the National Security Council un-
        der three presidents. Concludes it has been an effective in-
        strument for presidents.

1499   Fitzsimons, Louise. THE KENNEDY DOCTRINE. New York: Random,
        1972. 275 p.

        Pictures Kennedy administration as captive of Cold War ide-
        ology.

1500   Fox, J. Ronald. ARMING AMERICA: HOW THE U.S. BUYS WEAP-
        ONS. Cambridge, Mass.: Harvard Business School, 1974. 484 p.

        A major study of weapons acquisition, depicting much waste
        and inefficiency in the procurement process.

1501   Fox, William T., and Fox, Annette B. NATO AND THE RANGE OF
        AMERICAN CHOICE. New York: Columbia University Press, 1967.
        352 p.

        Besides assessing North Atlantic Treaty Organization's role in
        American foreign and military policy, the work focuses on
        significant strategic issues involving North Atlantic Treaty
        Organization.

1502   Fulbright, J. William. THE ARROGANCE OF POWER. New York:
        Random, 1967. 264 p.

        Argues America showed arrogance of power that destroyed na-
        tions of the past. Arrogance dictated Cold War policy, es-
        pecially in Vietnam.

1503   Furniss, Edgar S., Jr. AMERICAN MILITARY POLICY: STRATEGIC
        ASPECTS OF WORLD POLITICAL GEOGRAPHY. New York: Rine-
        hart, 1951. 494 p.

        A collection of essays by author on the subject of the military
        component of American statecraft.

1504   Gavin, James M. WAR AND PEACE IN THE SPACE AGE. New
        York: Harper, 1958. 304 p.

        By former general. Strongly critical of cumbersome Defense
        Department and the failure to develop a more flexible mili-
        tary policy without relying exclusively on nuclear forces.

1505 Gilpatric, Roswell. "Our Defense Needs." FOREIGN AFFAIRS 42
      (1964): 366-78.

      Surveys American defense posture as of 1964 and suggests no
      contradiction between a policy of detente and one of in-
      creasing American defenses.

1506 Gimbel, John. THE AMERICAN OCCUPATION OF GERMANY: POL-
      ITICS AND THE MILITARY, 1945-49. Stanford, Calif.: Stanford
      University Press, 1968. 335 p.

      Argues that American policy, rather than ambivalent, was
      guided by a broad range of interests that gave policy con-
      sistency and continuity.

1507 Ginsburg, Robert H. U.S. MILITARY STRATEGY IN THE SIXTIES.
      New York: Norton, 1965. 160 p.

      Described as a "primer" but actually a useful discussion of
      strategy and recent American strategic policies and problems.

1508 Goldwin, Robert A., ed. AMERICA ARMED: ESSAYS ON AMERI-
      CAN MILITARY POLICY. Chicago: Rand McNally, 1963. 140 p.

      Conflicting essays on America's nuclear policy. Both sides of
      the issue represented by such writers as Millis and Kahn.

1509 Green, Philip. DEADLY LOGIC: THE THEORY OF NUCLEAR DE-
      TERRENCE. Columbus: Ohio State University Press, 1966. 361 p.

      A critique of the theory and theorists of nuclear deterrence.
      Particularly critical of Herman Kahn.

1510 Greenwood, John, comp. AMERICAN DEFENSE POLICY SINCE 1945:
      A PRELIMINARY BIBLIOGRAPHY. Lawrence: University Press of
      Kansas, 1973. 317 p.

      Approximately three thousand entries that focus on topic areas
      of U.S. military programs.

1511 Grodzins, Morton, and Rabinowich, Eugene, eds. THE ATOMIC AGE:
      SCIENTISTS IN NATIONAL AND WORLD AFFAIRS. New York:
      Basic Books, 1963. 640 p.

      Essays by prominent scientists who deal with the failures, per-
      ils, fears, and hopes in the field of nuclear weapons.

1512 Hahn, Walter F., and Neff, J.C., eds. AMERICAN STRATEGY FOR
      THE NUCLEAR AGE. Garden City, N.Y.: Doubleday, 1960. 455 p.

      Collection of essays by authorities on nuclear strategy.
      Strongly anti-Communist.

1513   Hammond, Paul Y. "NSC-68: Prologue to Rearmament." In STRATEGY,
POLITICS AND DEFENSE BUDGETS, edited by Warner R. Schilling et al.,
pp. 267-378. New York: Columbia University Press, 1962.

Until declassified in the Nixon era, Hammond's article was
the only knowledge we had of the famous National Security
Council study that recommended a massive arms buildup.

1514   _____. ORGANIZING FOR DEFENSE: THE AMERICAN MILITARY
ESTABLISHMENT IN THE 20TH CENTURY. Princeton, N.J.: Princeton University Press, 1961. 403 p.

Focuses on the politics of defense policy and on the organization of the defense establishment.

1515   Haynes, Richard F. THE AWESOME POWER: HARRY S. TRUMAN
AS COMMANDER IN CHIEF. Baton Rouge: Louisiana State University Press, 1973. 359 p.

Comprehensive description of Truman's efforts as commander-
in-chief. Deals with decision to drop the bomb, unification
of the military and the Korean War.

1516   Head, Richard G., and Rokke, Ervin J., eds. AMERICAN DEFENSE
POLICY. Baltimore: Johns Hopkins University Press, 1973. 676 p.

Collection of essays on the striking changes in American defense posture after World War II.

1517   Hitch, Charles J. DECISION-MAKING FOR DEFENSE. Berkeley
and Los Angeles: University of California Press, 1965. 83 p.

Lectures by former assistant secretary of defense with emphasis
on organizational aspects of defense policy.

1518   Hitch, Charles J., and McKean, Roland N. THE ECONOMICS OF
DEFENSE IN THE NUCLEAR AGE. Cambridge, Mass.: Harvard University Press, 1960. 422 p.

Technical economic analysis of American defense policy from
the RAND Corporation.

1519   Howard, Michael. "Civil-Military Relations in Great Britain and the
United States, 1945-1958." POLITICAL SCIENCE QUARTERLY 75
(1960): 35-46.

Compares how both nations maintain civilian authority over
the military.

1520   Hubler, Richard G. SAC: THE STRATEGIC AIR COMMAND. New

York: Duell, 1958. 280 p.

Covers the budgetary and technical problems of Strategic Air
Command.

1521　Huntington, Samuel P. THE COMMON DEFENSE: STRATEGIC PRO-
GRAMS OF NATIONAL POLITICS. New York: Columbia University
Press, 1962. 500 p.

Analyzes patterns of decision making, centering around strategic policy. Focuses on strategic programs and weapons innovation.

1522　_____. "Strategic Planning and the Political Process." FOREIGN
AFFAIRS 38 (1960): 285-99.

Views the making of strategic policy in the context of the
American political system.

1523　Kahan, Jerome, and Lang, Anne K. "The Cuban Missile Crisis: A
Study of its Strategic Context." POLITICAL SCIENCE QUARTERLY
87 (1972): 564-90.

Argues that the interaction of Soviet and American strategic
policies in the early 1960s served to precipitate the Cuban
missile crisis.

1524　Kahn, Herman. ON THERMONUCLEAR WAR. Princeton, N.J.:
Princeton University Press, 1960. 651 p.

A landmark in the literature of military strategy. Analyzes
how national and military policy can be applied to the nuclear dilemma. Kahn believes both United States and
USSR can survive a nuclear war.

1525　Kanter, Arnold. "Congress and the Defense Budget, 1960-70."
AMERICAN POLITICAL SCIENCE REVIEW 66 (1972): 129-41.

Argues that literature suggests that Congress has not had an
active, nor even a policy making, role in creating defense
budgets.

1526　Kaufman, Richard F. THE WAR PROFITEERS. Indianapolis: Bobbs-
Merrill, 1970. 282 p.

An attack on American military procurement policies. Accuses government contractors of milking the government of
millions of dollars. In the muckraking tradition.

1527　Kaufmann, William W. THE McNAMARA STRATEGY. New York:
Harper, 1964. 330 p.

Presents a sympathetic although analytical account of America's nuclear strategy as devised by McNamara when he was
secretary of defense.

1528 _____, ed. MILITARY POLICY AND NATIONAL SECURITY.
Princeton, N.J.: Princeton University Press, 1956. 247 p.

Eight essays by such authors as Gordon Craig and Klaus Knorr
discussing various strategic doctrines including American military policy. Dated but still useful.

1529 Kelley, George A. "Arms Control and the Military Establishment."
MILITARY REVIEW 41 (1961): 62-72.

Argues military establishment must prepare for peace as well
as war.

1530 Kent, Sherman. STRATEGIC INTELLIGENCE FOR AMERICAN WORLD
POLICY. Princeton, N.J.: Princeton University Press, 1949. 226 p.

Former member of the Office of Strategic Services uses intelligence experience to construct an account which deromanti-
cizes intelligence gathering. Dated but still useful.

1531 Kinnard, Douglas. PRESIDENT EISENHOWER AND STRATEGY MAN-
AGEMENT: A STUDY IN DEFENSE POLITICS. Lexington: University
of Kentucky Press, 1977. 169 p.

Argues that contrary to the general view that Eisenhower was
dominated by strong personalities, the president was active
and effective in making defense policy.

1532 Kirkpatrick, Lyman B., Jr. THE REAL CIA. New York: Macmillan,
1968. 312 p.

Account by an eighteen-year veteran of the CIA, dealing
mainly with organization and administrative developments,
bureaucratic infighting, and departmental jealousies. In the
end, favorable view presented.

1533 _____. THE U.S. INTELLIGENCE COMMUNITY: FOREIGN POL-
ICY AND DOMESTIC ACTIVITIES. New York: Hill and Wang, 1973.
212 p.

Contains much information on intelligence gathering but little
analysis. Sometimes excessively defensive.

1534 Kissinger, Henry A. "Force and Diplomacy in the Nuclear Age."
FOREIGN AFFAIRS 34 (1956): 349-66.

Critical of Dulles's policy of massive retaliation. Advocates flexible response. Significant for views of a future national security advisor.

1535 _____. "Military Policy and Defense of the 'Grey Areas.'" FOR-EIGN AFFAIRS 33 (1955): 416–28.

Critical of Dulles's "massive retaliation." Argued this policy would not help United States to defend the peripheral or "grey" areas around USSR and China.

1536 _____. THE NECESSITY FOR CHOICE. New York: Harper, 1961. 370 p.

Covers such topics as strategy of deterrence, limited war. Revises slightly his conclusions in NUCLEAR WEAPONS AND FOREIGN POLICY (see below).

1537 _____. NUCLEAR WEAPONS AND FOREIGN POLICY. New York: Harper, 1957. 455 p.

Best selling study of the relationship between nuclear strategy and the issues of total and limited wars. Focuses on the policy implications of nuclear strategy.

1538 _____. "Strategy and Organization." FOREIGN AFFAIRS 35 (1957): 379–94.

Argues the need to establish a strategic doctrine before proceeding to organize America's defense establishment.

1539 Kolodziej, Edward A. THE UNCOMMON DEFENSE AND CONGRESS, 1945–1963. Columbus: Ohio State University Press, 1966. 630 p.

Exhaustive narrative account of Congress, participation in post World War II military policy making.

1540 Lapp, Ralph E. AIMS BEYOND DOUBT: THE TYRANNY OF WEAPONS TECHNOLOGY. New York: Cowles, 1970. 210 p.

Account traces the arms race from the debates over the Nike-Ajax to the MIRV controversy. A well-known Cassandra of the arms race. This book fits the pattern. Excessively hard on the Pentagon.

1541 _____. THE WEAPONS CULTURE. New York: Norton, 1968. 230 p.

Thesis is that "the United States' dedication to arms making constitutes a national danger." Implies a large conspiracy

involving business, military, and politicians. Useful explan-
ation of weapons technology.

1542   Lawrence, Richard, and Record, Jeffrey. U.S. FORCE STRUCTURE
       IN NATO: AN ALTERNATIVE. Washington, D.C.: Brookings Insti-
       tution, 1976. 136 p.

       Argues that short intense wars are now most likely in Europe
       and NATO forces are not prepared to fight such wars.

1543   Levine, Robert A. THE ARMS DEBATE. Cambridge, Mass.: Harvard
       University Press, 1963. 347 p.

       Useful survey of various viewpoints on arms policy. Estab-
       lished a five-point typology from decision-making theory.

1544   Licklider, Roy E. THE PRIVATE NUCLEAR STRATEGISTS. Columbus:
       Ohio State University Press, 1971. 213 p.

       Profiles nongovernmental analysts of nuclear strategy through
       the use of questionnaires. Finds most are academic political
       scientists.

1545   Lincoln, George A.; Stone, William S.; and Harvey, Thomas H., eds.
       ECONOMICS OF NATIONAL SECURITY. New York: Prentice-Hall,
       1950. 601 p.

       An early, but still useful account which surveys in nontechni-
       cal language the scope and nature of economic problems in-
       volved in military policy.

1546   Lowe, George E. THE AGE OF DETERRENCE. Boston: Little, Brown,
       1964. 324 p.

       Foreign service officer's discussion of strategy and defense
       theory debates in the United States since 1952. Reduces
       various positions to a dualism: Utopians versus Traditionalists.

1547   Luttwak, Edward. "Nuclear Strategy: The New Debate." COM-
       MENTARY 57 (1974): 53-59.

       Traces the development of the strategy of mutual assured des-
       truction, and suggests that the Nixon administration tried to
       change the doctrine to one of detente.

1548   McClintock, Robert. THE MEANING OF LIMITED WAR. New York:
       Houghton-Mifflin, 1967. 233 p.

       Argues that limited wars are appropriate instruments of policy
       in the age of nuclear weapons.

1549   Mansfield, Edwin, ed. DEFENSE, SCIENCE AND PUBLIC POLICY.
        New York: Norton, 1968. 192 p.

        Various experts discuss a variety of topics relating to science,
        technology, and defense.

1550   Margin, Lawrence. ARMS AND STRATEGY: THE WORLD POWER
        STRUCTURE. New York: McKay, 1973. 320 p.

        Contains significant chapter on U.S. strategy in nontechnical
        language.

1551   May, Ernest R. "The Development of Political-Military Consultation
        in the U.S." POLITICAL SCIENCE QUARTERLY 70 (1955): 161-80.

        Historical survey of the way in which Americans have devel-
        oped a method of weighing political and military factors
        through the National Security Council.

1552   Melman, Seymour. PENTAGON CAPITALISM: THE POLITICAL ECON-
        OMY OF WAR. New York: McGraw-Hill, 1970. 290 p.

        Impassioned indictment of expansion of Pentagon into Ameri-
        can life, leading to a garrison state.

1553   Millis, Walter. "Military Problems in the New Administration."
        FOREIGN AFFAIRS 31 (1953): 215-24.

        General discussion of American military policy, 1945-53,
        focusing on the contradictory goals of Eisenhower's statements
        on military policy.

1554   Morgenstern, Oscar. THE QUESTION OF NATIONAL DEFENSE.
        New York: Random, 1959. 306 p.

        Develops a theoretical perspective on nuclear strategy in
        space rather than on earth.

1555   Moulton, Harland B. FROM SUPERIORITY TO PARITY: THE U.S.
        AND THE STRATEGIC ARMS RACE, 1961-1971. Westport, Conn.:
        Greenwood, 1973. 333 p.

        Authoritative study of U.S. nuclear defense policy by a di-
        rector at the National War College. Focuses on the McNa-
        mara era.

1556   Mrozek, Donald J. "A New Look At 'Balanced Forces': Defense
        Continuities From Truman to Eisenhower." MILITARY AFFAIRS 38
        (1974): 145-51.

        Rejects view that the Eisenhower administration created a "new look" defense and emphasizes continuity in Truman and Eisenhower policies.

1557 Murdock, Clark A. DEFENSE POLICY FORMULATION: A COMPARATIVE ANALYSIS OF THE McNAMARA ERA. New York: State University of New York Press, 1974. 209 p.

Compares Eisenhower and McNamara procedures. Comprehensible, though specialized, approach.

1558 Newhouse, John. U.S. TROOPS IN EUROPE: ISSUES, COSTS AND CHOICES. Washington, D.C.: Brookings Institution, 1971. 177 p.

A searching and speculative review of American defense policy and possible alternatives.

1559 Nitze, Paul H. "Atoms, Strategy and Policy." FOREIGN AFFAIRS 34 (1956): 187-98.

Argues against strategy of "massive retaliation." Says American "action" policy should be "graduated deterrence."

1560 Olson, Robert A. "Air Mobility for the Army: A Case Study of Policy Evolution in Relation to Changing Strategy." MILITARY AFFAIRS 28 (1964): 163-73.

Discusses the vicissitudes of the post-war army and how its fate rested on each administration's strategic policy. The army held to a policy of limited war and air mobility and found a home in the Kennedy administration.

1561 Osgood, Robert E. LIMITED WAR, THE CHALLENGE TO AMERICAN STRATEGY. Chicago: University of Chicago Press, 1957. 315 p.

Argues limited war answer to the dilemma of employing the irrational power of nuclear weapons.

1562 Owen, David. THE POLITICS OF DEFENSE. New York: Taplinger, 1972. 249 p.

Second part deals with strategic relationships between the United States and North Atlantic Treaty Organization. Supports transferring more nuclear capability to England and France.

1563 Owen, Henry. "NATO Strategy: What is Past is Prologue." FOREIGN AFFAIRS 43 (1965): 682-90.

Cites lessons to be learned from pre-World War I and pre-World War II war plans. Argues all strategy, including North

Atlantic Treaty Organization strategy, needs to take into account "unintended" as well as "deliberate" attack.

1564   Paul, Roland A. AMERICAN MILITARY COMMITMENTS ABROAD.
New Brunswick, N.J.: Rutgers University Press, 1973. 237 p.

A former chief counsel to the Senate Foreign Relations Committee describes but does not analyze the U.S. overseas commitments.

1565   Pipes, Richard. "Why the Soviet Union Thinks It Could Fight and
Win a Nuclear War." COMMENTARY 64 (1977): 21-34.

Discusses the differences between Russian and American strategic traditions, the former accepting the realities of conflict
and violence, the latter rejecting them. Thus, while the
United States believes there will be no winner in a nuclear
war, the Soviets hold that, if sufficently prepared, one side
will win.

1566   Poole, Walter S. "From Conciliation to Containment: The Joint
Chiefs of Staff and the Coming of the Cold War." MILITARY AF-
FAIRS 42 (1978): 12-16.

Account of when and why the Joint Chiefs of Staff decided
that the Soviet Union was a menace to American security.
Immediately after the war that attitude was sanguine, but by
autumn 1945 JCS views had turned hostile.

1567   Powers, Patrick W. A GUIDE TO NATIONAL DEFENSE: THE OR-
GANIZATION AND OPERATIONS OF THE U.S. MILITARY ESTAB-
LISHMENT. New York: Praeger, 1964. 326 p.

Describes most aspects of America's national defense system
from basic policies to the structure of several branches.

1568   Proxmire, William. REPORT FROM THE WASTELAND: AMERICA'S
MILITARY INDUSTRIAL COMPLEX. New York: Praeger, 1970.
284 p.

Well-known senator and opponent of military spending discusses intimate relationships between military services and
military contractors. Evidence from author's senatorial investigation on military budgets.

1569   Quade, E.S., ed. ANALYSIS FOR MILITARY DECISIONS. New
York: Rand McNally, 1964. 382 p.

Essays by experts in nuclear strategy, focuses on aspects of
the use of system analysis in military decisions.

1570 Quester, George H. NUCLEAR DIPLOMACY: THE FIRST TWENTY-FIVE YEARS. New York: Dunellen, 1970. 327 p.

Discusses sociological and economic aspects of nuclear strategy in terms of weapons development.

1571 Ranson, Harry H. THE INTELLIGENCE ESTABLISHMENT. Cambridge, Mass.: Harvard University Press, 1970. 309 p.

Account of intelligence gathering focusing on the CIA, and also the role of secrecy in a democratic state.

1572 Rapoport, Roger. THE GREAT AMERICAN BOMB MACHINE. New York: Dutton, 1971. 160 p.

Discusses issues and problems of maintaining a nuclear weapons capability, then proceeds to attack the system.

1573 Reinhardt, George C. AMERICAN STRATEGY IN THE ATOMIC AGE. Norman: University of Oklahoma Press, 1955. 236 p.

Explores problem of how to devise a strategic policy that will be both democratic and militarily sound.

1574 Robert, Chalmers. THE NUCLEAR YEARS: THE ARMS RACE AND ARMS CONTROL, 1945-1970. New York: Praeger, 1970. 159 p.

Journalistic summary of nuclear arms and the efforts to control them after World War II.

1575 Russett, Bruce M. WHAT PRICE VIGILANCE? THE BURDENS OF NATIONAL DEFENSE. New Haven, Conn.: Yale University Press, 1970. 261 p.

Focuses on the factors that determine the overall size of the military. Based on much data and analysis. Believes Congress and the military-industrial complex determine defense policy.

1576 Salkeld, Robert. WAR AND SPACE. New York: Prentice-Hall, 1970. 195 p.

Argues that because of past Soviet duplicity, United States should be prepared to fight nuclear war in space should SALT talks fail.

1577 Sander, Alfred D. "Truman and the National Security Council: 1945-1947." JOURNAL OF AMERICAN HISTORY 59 (1972): 369-88.

Argues Truman avoided using the NSC as an advisory council

until forced to by the Korean War.

1578 Schelling, Thomas C., and Halperin, Morton H. STRATEGY AND ARMS CONTROL. New York: Twentieth Century Fund, 1961. 148 p.

Detailed, complex study of the relationship between arms control and military strategy. Suggest possibilities of arms control reducing war dangers.

1579 Schick, Jack M. "The Berlin Crisis of 1961 and U.S. Military Strategy." ORBIS 8 (1965): 816–31.

Proposes that the Berlin crisis was a matter of military strategy more than it was a matter of diplomacy. Argues that American strategy was only partially successful.

1580 Schilling, Warner R., et al. STRATEGY, POLITICS AND DEFENSE. New York: Columbia University Press, 1962. 532 p.

Three essays by authorities dealing with military spending and the national economy.

1581 Schlesinger, James R. THE POLITICAL ECONOMY OF NATIONAL SECURITY: A STUDY OF THE ECONOMIC ASPECTS OF THE CONTEMPORARY POWER STRUGGLE. New York: Praeger, 1960. 292 p.

A pioneering book which deals with the rapidly changing economics of national defense.

1582 Schwarz, Urs. AMERICAN STRATEGY: A NEW PERSPECTIVE. Garden City, N.Y.: Doubleday, 1966. 178 p.

Combination of a history of American strategic thought and an analysis of new strategic theories since World War II. Argues Americans have overcome reluctance to use power.

1583 Schwiebert, Ernest G. A HISTORY OF THE U.S. AIR FORCE BALLISTIC MISSILES. New York: Praeger, 1965. 264 p.

A journalistic account, with much sympathy toward the Air Force point of view.

1584 Smith, Jean E. DEFENSE OF BERLIN. Baltimore: Johns Hopkins University Press, 1963. 431 p.

A clear narrative of American responses to Russian policies in Berlin after World War II by an American official. Criticizes U.S. policy as too "soft."

1585 _____, ed. THE PAPERS OF GENERAL LUCIUS D. CLAY: GER-
MANY, 1945-1949. 2 vols. Bloomington: Indiana University Press,
1974.

Indicates Clay's problems as pro-consul of Germany and his
reactions. Shows Clay as a tough administrator but also a
good diplomat.

1586 Smith, Mark E. III, and Johns, Claude J., Jr., eds. AMERICAN
DEFENSE POLICY. Baltimore: Johns Hopkins University Press, 1968.
551 p.

Essays by experts and students of post-World War II defense
policy.

1587 Stanley, Timothy W. AMERICAN DEFENSE AND NATIONAL SECUR-
ITY. Washington, D.C.: Public Affairs, 1956. 202 p.

Analysis of America's defense structure, focusing on the significant developments leading to the National Security Act
of 1957.

1588 Taylor, Maxwell. RESPONSIBILITY AND RESPONSE. New York:
Harper, 1967. 84 p.

Taylor's statement how U.S. national security policy should
deal with "wars of liberation."

1589 _____. THE UNCERTAIN TRUMPET. New York: Harper, 1960.
Reprint. Westport, Conn.: Greenwood, 1977. 203 p.

Critical of the Eisenhower "new look" defense policy and the
machinery of national security. Suggests a "National Military Program" which became a basis for Kennedy's "flexible
response."

1590 Tillema, Herbert K. APPEAL TO FORCE: AMERICAN MILITARY IN-
TERVENTION IN THE ERA OF CONTAINMENT. New York: Crowell, 1973. 260 p.

Deals with four interventions--South Korea, Lebanon, South
Vietnam, and Dominican Republic--from the point of view of
theoretical models.

1591 Twining, Nathan F. NEITHER LIBERTY NOR SAFETY: A HARD
LOOK AT U.S. MILITARY POLICY AND STRATEGY. New York:
Holt, Rinehart and Winston, 1966. 320 p.

Account critical of American military policy by a hard line,
former ranking general who wants a defense system that can
win any kind of war against the Communists.

1592 Wohlstetter, Albert. "The Delicate Balance of Terror." FOREIGN
AFFAIRS 37 (1959): 211-34.

Pathbreaking article. Argued that Americans must expect the
possibility of an attack by USSR and therefore must construct
a strategic deterrence force to prevent such a catastrophe.
Early warning by a political scientist working for RAND Corporation.

1593 Wohlstetter, Roberta. "Cuba and Pearl Harbor: Hindsight and Foresight." FOREIGN AFFAIRS 43 (1965): 691-707.

Employs same analysis method on Cuba as author did in PEARL
HARBOR (see entry 1426). Concludes prior intelligence data in
both cases was ambiguous and incomplete.

1594 Yanarella, Ernest J. THE MISSILE DEFENSE CONTROVERSY: TECH-
NOLOGY, AND POLITICS, 1955-1972. Lexington: University Press
of Kentucky, 1977. 236 p.

Account of United States policy on ballistic missile defense
from Eisenhower through Nixon. Argues that the United
States developed its policy not on what the Russians were do-
ing but on the imperatives of weapons technology.

Chapter 8
THE MILITARY AND LIMITED WARS

A. THE KOREAN WAR

1595   Alberts, Robert C. "Profile of a Soldier: Matthew B. Ridgway."
AMERICAN HERITAGE 27 (1976): 4–7, 73–82.

Important narrative taken from interviews with Ridgway in
1975.

1596   Appleman, Ray E. SOUTH TO THE NAKTONG, NORTH TO THE
YALU. U.S. Army in the Korean War Series. Washington, D.C.:
Government Printing Office, 1961. 831 p.

Details the first five months of the war, focusing on Mac-
Arthur's landing at Tuchon and his drive northward to the
Yalu River.

1597   Berger, Carl. THE KOREA KNOT: A MILITARY-POLITICAL HISTORY.
Philadelphia: University of Pennsylvania Press, 1957. 206 p.

Traces the sequence of events leading to the Korean War and
attempts to analyze its outcome. Impartial on such controversial issues as the decision to intervene.

1598   Biderman, Albert D. MARCH TO CALUMNY: THE STORY OF AMER-
ICAN POW'S IN THE KOREAN WAR. New York: Macmillan, 1963.
Reprint. New York: Arno, 1979. 326 p.

A defense of American prisoner behavior in Korean War. Refutes the view that the "misbehavior" revealed alarming weakness in American character. Argues that American soldiers
fought and behaved as well as American soldiers in past wars.

1599   Blanchard, Carroll H., Jr. KOREAN WAR BIBLIOGRAPHY. Albany,
N.Y.: Korean Conflict Research Foundation, 1964. 181 p.

1600   Bodron, Margaret M. "U.S. Intervention in Lebanon, 1958." MILI-
        TARY REVIEW 56 (1976): 66-76.

        Traces the development of the intervention in Lebanon, citing
        it as an example of the use of limited war and applied di-
        plomacy.

1601   Clark, Mark W. FROM THE DANUBE TO THE YALU. New York:
        Harper, 1954. Reprint. Westport, Conn.: Greenwood, 1977. 369 p.

        Recollects his role in the Korean war, with emphasis on the
        truce negotiations.

1602   Collins, J. Lawton. WAR IN PEACETIME: THE HISTORY AND LES-
        SONS OF KOREA. Boston: Houghton-Mifflin, 1969. 416 p.

        Account of the war from its inception through the armistice
        negotiations by a former chief of staff. Presents the war as
        seen from the top.

1603   Dean, William F. GENERAL DEAN'S STORY: AS TOLD TO WIL-
        LIAM WORDEN. Westport, Conn.: Greenwood, 1977. 305 p.

        Dean's recollection of the ordeal of his imprisonment in North
        Korea with interesting detail.

1604   Fehrenbach, T.R. THIS KIND OF WAR. New York: Macmillan,
        1963. 688 p.

        Heavy with details on military operations. Makes special
        plea for a larger professional army. Includes section on
        POW's.

1605   Fredericks, Edgar J. MacARTHUR: HIS MISSION AND MEANING.
        Philadelphia: Whitmore, 1968. 91 p.

        Accepts MacArthur's claim that the Korean War was necessary
        to prove America's willingness to use force in Asia. Short
        on historical analysis.

1606   Gardner, Lloyd C., ed. THE KOREAN WAR. New York: New View-
        points, 1972. 244 p.

        A collection of articles from the NEW YORK TIMES analyz-
        ing the war from the point of view of observers.

1607   Heinl, Robert D., Jr. VICTORY AT HIGH TIDE: THE INCHON-
        SEOUL CAMPAIGN. New York: Lippincott, 1968. 315 p.

        Light, breezy style which focuses on interservice rivalry dur-
        ing a Korean War campaign that made possible the crossing
        of the 38th Parallel.

1608   Heller, Francis H., ed. THE KOREAN WAR: A 25-YEAR PERSPEC-
        TIVE. Lawrence: Regents Press of Kansas, 1977. 251 p.

        Collection of papers from a conference sponsored by the Tru-
        man Library in 1975. Major participants in the Korean War
        and also diplomatic historians read papers. Most important
        contribution is a selected bibliographic essay with suggestions
        for future research by Richard Leopold.

1609   Hermes, Walter G. "The Military Role in the Korean Truce Negotia-
        tions." MILITARY REVIEW 44 (1964): 14-23.

        Describes the important role of the military negotiator in
        bringing the Korean War to a close.

1610   _____. TRUCE TENT AND FIGHTING FRONT. Washington, D.C.:
        Government Printing Office, 1966. 571 p.

        Account of the intricate truce negotiations between July
        1951 and July 1953. Also deals with bitter fighting going
        on along with the negotiations.

1611   Higgins, Marguerite. WAR IN KOREA: THE REPORT OF A WOMAN
        COMBAT CORRESPONDENT. Garden City, N.Y.: Doubleday,
        1951. 233 p.

        A first-hand account that is especially useful on combat de-
        scription.

1612   Higgins, Trumbull. KOREA AND THE FALL OF MacARTHUR: A
        PRECIS IN LIMITED WAR. New York: Oxford University Press,
        1960. 229 p.

        Account of the major strategic issues of the Korean War, fo-
        cusing on the recall of MacArthur. Argues that MacArthur
        brought trouble on himself.

1613   Kahn, E.J., Jr. THE PECULIAR WAR; IMPRESSIONS OF A REPORTER
        IN KOREA. New York: Random, 1952. 211 p.

        Impressions of a reporter in Korea for three months, intended
        for home consumption. Useful for reporter's observations.

1614   Kinkead, Eugene. IN EVERY WAR BUT ONE. New York: Norton,
        1959. 219 p.

        Thesis that, in all wars except the Korean War, American
        prisoners acted honorably and with courage. Why the Korean
        War? Implies society at fault but never really answers why.

1615   Krasner, Michael A. "Decision to Cross the 38th Parallel." MILI-
        TARY REVIEW 52 (1972): 17-26.

        Argues that the decision was made on the assumption that the
        Chinese would not intervene and, in turn, that was based on
        a misunderstanding of the Chinese government.

1616   Kriebel, Wesley P. "Korea: The Military Armistice Commission."
        MILITARY AFFAIRS 36 (1972): 96-99.

        Story of the ten men (five from each side) responsible for
        supervising the terms of the Korean Armistice. Argues that
        the commission is a sound instrument for maintaining North-
        South contacts.

1617   Leckie, Robert. CONFLICT: THE HISTORY OF THE KOREAN WAR,
        1950-53. New York: Putnam, 1962. 448 p.

        Account by a combat reporter. Because of lack of sources,
        contains only intelligent speculations.

1618   McGovern, James. TO THE YALU: FROM THE CHINESE INVASION
        OF KOREA TO MacARTHUR'S DISMISSAL. New York: Morrow,
        1972. 225 p.

        Conventional retelling of the story of MacArthur's dismissal.

1619   Marshall, S.L.A. PORT CHOP HILL: THE AMERICAN FIGHTING
        MAN IN ACTION IN KOREA, SPRING 1953. New York: Morrow,
        1956. 315 p.

        Based on interviews with combat infantrymen, discusses a typ-
        ical small unit action in Korea.

1620   _____. THE RIVER AND THE GAUNTLET: DEFEAT OF THE EIGHTH
        ARMY BY THE CHINESE COMMUNIST FORCES NOV. 1950 IN THE
        BATTLE OF THE CHONGCHON RIVER, KOREA. New York: Mor-
        row, 1953. 385 p.

        Account of how the Chinese intervention struck terror into the
        2d and 25th U.S. Divisions.

1621   Maurer, Maurer. "The Korean Conflict Was a War." MILITARY AF-
        FAIRS 24 (1960): 137-45.

        Discusses legal and constitutional aspects of the war.

1622   Meade, Edward G. AMERICAN MILITARY GOVERNMENT IN KOREA.
        New York: Crown, 1951. 281 p.

        Covers period, 1945-46. Examines and analyzes American
        civil affairs officers in Korea.

1623 Middleton, Harry J. THE COMPACT HISTORY OF THE KOREAN
WAR. New York: Hawthorn, 1965. 255 p.

Short, objective account for the general reader.

1624 Miller, John, et al. KOREA, 1951-1953. Washington, D.C.: U.S.
Office of Military History, 1956. 328 p.

Pictorial account of photographs and cartoons of the Korean
War.

1625 Norman, John. "MacArthur's Blockade Proposals Against Red China."
PACIFIC HISTORICAL REVIEW 26 (1957): 161-74.

Discusses how the Truman administration undercut MacArthur's
main charge against it by showing his blockade proposal to
be too ineffectual and impractical.

1626 Paige, Glenn D. THE KOREAN DECISION JUNE 24-30, 1950.
New York: Free Press, 1968. 394 p.

Account of U.S. decision to intervene, aimed at extracting
a general hypothesis concerning American foreign policy.

1627 Rees, David. KOREA: THE LIMITED WAR. New York: St. Martin's, 1964. 511 p.

Argues that the decision to limit the war sprang from Truman's
containment policy. Covers all aspects of the war, including
disputes among the military.

1628 Ridgway, Matthew B. THE KOREA WAR. Garden City, N.Y.: Doubleday, 1967. 291 p.

History of the Korean War by a major participant. Provides
perceptive interpretations and insights nowhere else available.
Concludes all warfare henceforth must be limited.

1629 _____. SOLDIER: THE MEMOIRS OF MATTHEW B. RIDGWAY.
New York: Harper, 1956. 371 p.

Focuses on his experience with interpersonal relations in the
American Army, particularly discipline and morale.

1630 Sawyer, Robert K. MILITARY ADVISORS IN KOREA: KMAG IN
PEACE AND WAR. Washington, D.C.: Government Printing Office,
1963. 216 p.

Account of the problems faced by the first military advisory
group to try to create an effective army in a politically and
economically divided nation.

1631   Schnabel, James F. POLICY AND DIRECTION: THE FIRST YEAR.
       U.S. Army in Korean War series. Washington, D.C.: Government
       Printing Office, 1972. 443 p.

       Outlines the developments in Korea from August 1945 to June
       1950, and then explores major policy decisions in Washington
       and Japan through June 1951.

1632   Sheldon, Walt. HELL ON HIGH WATER: MacARTHUR'S LANDING
       AT INCHON. New York: Macmillan, 1968. 340 p.

       Narrative of how MacArthur overcame military opposition to
       the Inchon landing and how the operation overcame handicaps
       to achieve success.

1633   Spanier, John W. THE TRUMAN-MacARTHUR CONTROVERSY AND
       THE KOREAN WAR. New York: Norton, 1965. 311 p.

       Discusses the controversy from point of view of civil-military
       relations, relationship of foreign and military policy and mod-
       ern limitations placed on commanders. Supports MacArthur's
       dismissal.

1634   Stewart, James T., ed. AIRPOWER: THE DECISIVE FORCE IN
       KOREA. New York: Van Nostrand, 1957. 320 p.

       Series of essays by various authors describing the role of the
       Air Force in Korea. Highly specialized account.

1635   Westover, John G., ed. THE UNITED STATES ARMY IN THE KO-
       REAN CONFLICT: COMBAT SUPPORT IN KOREA. Washington,
       D.C.: Combat Forces Press, 1955. 254 p.

       Prepared under the direction of the Chief of Military History,
       Department of the Army. Collection of interviews concerning
       the experiences of officers and enlisted men who served in
       Korea, 1950-1953.

1636   White, William L. BACK DOWN THE RIDGE. New York: Harcourt
       Brace, 1953. 182 p.

       Narrative of the medical and sanitary affairs of the Korean
       War.

1637   _____. THE CAPTIVES OF KOREA: AN UNOFFICIAL WHITE PA-
       PER ON THE TREATMENT OF WAR PRISONERS. New York: Scrib-
       ner, 1957. 347 p.

       A semischolarly study of the prisoner-of-war problems arising
       from the Korean War. Hard on the Communists, less so on
       American officials.

1638   Wiltz, John. "Truman and MacArthur: The Wake Island Meeting."
        MILITARY AFFAIRS 62 (1978): 169-76.

        Argues that, contrary to conventional view, no important de-
        cisions were made at the Wake meeting, and that Truman did
        not intend that it would produce any major decisions.

1639   Wittner, Lawrence, ed. MacARTHUR. Great Lives Observed Series.
        Prentice Hall, 1971. 186 p.

        Excerpts from MacArthur's writings and speeches, and com-
        ments from those who knew him.

1640   Wuhhen, H.H. "American Prisoners of War: A Second Look At the
        'Something New in History' Theme." AMERICAN QUARTERLY 22
        (1970): 3-19.

        Argues that behavior of Korean War POWs was not histori-
        cally different than how American POWs had behaved in other
        wars.

B. THE VIETNAM WAR

1641   Adler, Bill, ed. LETTERS FROM VIETNAM. New York: Dutton,
        1967. 212 p.

        Soldiers who were fighting and who had fought in Vietnam
        relate graphically the hell that was Vietnam: they felt
        strongly about the killing of civilians and even the scenic
        beauty of the country.

1642   Bator, Victor. VIETNAM, A DIPLOMATIC TRAGEDY: THE ORIGINS
        OF U.S. INVOLVEMENT. New York: Oceana, 1965. 271 p.

        Maintains not enough diplomatic endeavors were used. United
        States relied too heavily on military means.

1643   Baxter, Gordon. 13/13 VIETNAM: SEARCH AND DESTROY. New
        York: World, 1967. 120 p.

        Description of the effect of war on Vietnam and American
        participants, focusing on a thirteen-day search and destroy
        mission in February 1967.

1644   Bond, Thomas C. "Fragging: A Study." ARMY 67 (1977): 45-47.

        Covers the incidence of officer killing in Vietnam.

1645   Brown, Weldon A. THE LAST CHOPPER: THE DENOUEMENT OF

THE AMERICAN ROLE IN VIETNAM, 1963-1975. Port Washington, N.Y.: Kennikat, 1976. 371 p.

Makes an effort at objectivity, but his story of the final days in Vietnam basically an anti-Communist polemic.

1646 _____. PRELUDE TO DISASTER: THE AMERICAN ROLE IN VIET-NAM, 1940-1963. Port Washington, N.Y.: Kennikat, 1975. 278 p.

Analyzes the background for the American involvement in Vietnam. Concludes it was an effort to avoid another Munich.

1647 Caputo, Philip. A RUMOR OF WAR. New York: Holt, Rinehart, Winston, 1977. 346 p.

A sensitive account of the personal experiences of a young combat officer in the Vietnam War.

1648 Corson, William R. THE BETRAYAL. New York: Norton, 1968. 318 p.

Historical and thematic account of the U.S. government's pacification effort by a former commander of one hundred such programs. Highly critical of America's failure to exploit pacification, chosing instead the kill and destroy strategy.

1649 Duncanson, Dennis J. GOVERNMENT AND REVOLUTION IN VIET-NAM. New York: Oxford University Press, 1968. 442 p.

Analyzes French and American influences in Vietnam and seeks to explain why Americans failed to realize their aims by 1968.

1650 Fall, Bernard B. LAST REFLECTIONS ON A WAR. Garden City, N.Y.: Doubleday, 1967. 288 p.

A collection of tape recordings, and heretofore unpublished essays and articles by the well-known authority on Vietnam.

1651 _____. STREET WITHOUT JOY: INSURGENCY IN INDOCHINA, 1946-1964. Harrisburg, Pa.: Stackpole, 1964. 408 p.

Indispensible for background to American intervention. Deals with French-Vietminh struggle.

1652 Fitzgerald, Frances. FIRE IN THE LAKE: THE VIETNAMESE AND THE AMERICANS IN VIETNAM. New York: Little, Brown, 1972. 491 p.

Account of the nature and character of Vietnam's encounter with the West, focusing on its relations with the United States. Particularly critical of America's pacification efforts, claiming that they simply fostered corruption in the Vietnam army and bureaucracy.

1653 Flood, Charles B. THE WAR OF THE INNOCENTS. New York: McGraw-Hill, 1970. 480 p.

Account by a reporter of the day-to-day operations in Vietnam, expressing graphically the frustrations and dangers facing American soldiers in Vietnam.

1654 Galloway, John. THE GULF OF TONKIN RESOLUTION. Rutherford, N.J.: Fairleigh-Dickinson University Press, 1970. 578 p.

Concludes that attack on naval ships was imaginary but nevertheless allowed Johnson to obtain authority for unlimited retaliation.

1655 Goldstein, Joseph, et al., eds. THE MY LAI MASSACRE AND ITS COVER-UP: BEYOND THE REACH OF LAW? New York: Free Press, 1976. 586 p.

Volume 1 of the Peers Commission Report, the official investigation of the My Lai incident, along with some documentation of the trials.

1656 Herbert, Anthony B., and Wooten, James I. SOLDIER. New York: Holt, Rinehart and Winston, 1973. 498 p.

Memoirs of author's military career focusing on corruption and negligence of the U.S. Army in Vietnam. Mixture of autobiography and diatribe.

1657 Hersh, Seymour. MY LAI 4: A REPORT ON THE MASSACRE AND ITS AFTERMATH. New York: Random, 1970. 210 p.

Straightforward, yet moving description of the background, the massacre, the cover-up and the widespread reaction when the story of the incident was uncovered.

1658 Kahin, George, and Lewis, John. THE UNITED STATES IN VIETNAM. New York: Dial, 1967. 465 p.

After a brief survey of Vietnam history, authors focus on the post World War II period. Highly critical of American involvement.

1659 Kinnard, Douglas. "Vietnam Reconsidered: An Attitudinal Survey of

U.S. Army General Officers." PUBLIC OPINION QUARTERLY (1975): 445-56.

Argues that general officers who participated in Vietnam hold mixed feelings about the war and its necessity.

1660 _____. "The Vietnam War in Retrospect: The Army Generals' Views." JOURNAL OF POLITICAL AND MILITARY SOCIOLOGY 5 (1976): 17-28.

Surveyed 173 general officers and found a noteworthy lack of consensus on most aspects of the war, particularly on whether or not it was a worthwhile endeavor.

1661 _____. THE WAR MANAGERS. Hanover, N.H.: University Press of New England, 1977. 216 p.

Assessment of the Vietnam War from the point of view of the principal U.S. commanders by a retired general. Study based on a sixty-item questionnaire and interviews of 173 general officers.

1662 Kirk, Donald. TELL IT TO THE DEAD: MEMORIES OF A WAR. Chicago: Nelson-Hall, 1977. 215 p.

Recollections of Vietnam as Kirk observed it in 1965. A skeptical point of view.

1663 Kriegel, Ricahrd C. "Tet Offensive: Victory or Defeat?" MARINE CORPS GAZETTE 52 (1968): 24-28.

Not surprisingly concludes it was a victory. Useful narrative on the subject.

1664 Kutger, Joseph P. "Irregular War in Transition." MILITARY AFFAIRS 24 (1960): 113-23.

Survey of the successes and failures of guerrilla warfare in the twentieth century.

1665 Lake, Anthony, ed. THE VIETNAM LEGACY: THE WAR, AMERICAN SOCIETY AND THE FUTURE OF AMERICAN FOREIGN POLICY. New York: New York University Press, 1976. 440 p.

Twenty-two essays by scholars, politicians, and bureaucrats on the domestic impact of the war. Sponsored by the Council on Foreign Relations.

1666 Lansdale, Edward G. IN THE MIDST OF WARS: AN AMERICAN MISSION TO SOUTHEAST ASIA. New York: Harper and Row, 1972. 386 p.

American agent involved in counterinsurgency and counterintelligence recounts his experiences in Southeast Asia, focusing on efforts to halt the spread of communism in South Vietnam in the early 1960s.

1667 _____. "Vietnam: Do We Understand Revolution?" FOREIGN AFFAIRS 43 (1964): 75-86.

Argues Americans were seeking to establish democratic society in Vietnam. Important as an example of the attitude of a major participant.

1668 Leitenberg, Milton, and Burns, Richard D. THE VIETNAM CONFLICT: THE GEOGRAPHICAL DIMENSIONS, POLITICAL TRAUMAS AND MILITARY DEVELOPMENTS. Santa Barbara, Calif.: ABC-Clio, 1973. 164 p.

Comprehensive bibliography of the Vietnam conflict.

1669 Liska, George. WAR AND ORDER: REFLECTIONS ON VIETNAM AND HISTORY. Baltimore: Johns Hopkins Press, 1968. 115 p.

Argues in support of American intervention in order to maintain world order.

1670 Littauer, Raphael, and Uploff, Norman, eds. THE AIR WAR IN INDOCHINA. Boston: Beacon Press, 1972. 289 p.

Account filled with data from graphs, tables, photographs, published and unpublished sources, and interviews aimed at covering the impact of the air war on Vietnam.

1671 McCarthy, Mary. VIETNAM. New York: Harcourt, Brace and World, 1967. 106 p.

Undisquised antiwar attack on U.S. intervention in Vietnam.

1672 Marshall, S.L.A. BATTLES IN THE MONSOON. New York: Morrow, 1967. 408 p.

This book and the following by Marshall are all an attempt by the famous retired officer-reporter to capture the nature and character of combat in Vietnam in much the same fashion as he did in the Korean War (see entry 1619). Unconcerned with the larger issues of the war, author describes the problems of the firing line and command problems from the point of view of the combatants.

1673 _____. WEST TO CAMBODIA. New York: Cowles, 1968. 253 p.

1674 _____. BIRD: THE CHRISTMASTIDE BATTLE. New York: Cowles, 1968. 206 p.

1675 _____. AMBUSH. New York: Cowles, 1969. 217 p.

1676 _____. THE FIELDS OF BAMBOO. New York: Dial, 1971. 242 p.

1677 Millett, Allan R., ed. A SHORT HISTORY OF THE VIETNAM WAR. Foreword by Major General Edward G. Lansdale. Bloomington: Indiana University Press, 1978. 165 p.

Collection of articles printed in the Washington POST, mostly from a supplement on Vietnam on January 28, 1973, which probed the causes, the history and the effects of the war.

1678 Oberdorfer, Don. TET! Garden City, N.Y.: Doubleday, 1971. 385 p.

Account of a critical operation in the Vietnam War when Communists attacked one hundred cities simultaneously. Based on extensive interviews and captured documents.

1679 O'Brien, Tim. IF I DIE IN A COMBAT ZONE: BOX ME UP AND SHIP ME HOME. New York: Delacorte, 1973 p.

Personal account of the foot soldier's daily life in the rice paddies and foxholes of Vietnam. Not particularly profound, but a moving description of one man's frustrations.

1680 PENTAGON PAPERS: THE DEFENSE DEPARTMENT HISTORY OF UNITED STATES DECISION-MAKING ON VIETNAM. 5 vols. The Senator Gravel Edition. Boston: Beacon, 1971.

The indispensible primary source on the Vietnam War. Volume five contains critical antiwar essays.

1681 Polner, Murray. NO VICTORY PARADES: THE RETURN OF THE VIETNAM VETERAN. New York: Holt, Rinehart, and Winston, 1971. 169 p.

Study of the impact of the Vietnam War on a group of nine men from lower-middle and working-class families. Based on interviews.

1682 Salisbury, Harrison E. BEHIND THE LINES: HANOI, DECEMBER 1966-JANUARY, 1967. New York: Harper, 1967. 243 p.

One of first to note that bombing was counter-productive, that it was strengthening, not weakening, Hanoi's will.

1683   Savage, Paul, and Gabriel, Richard. "Cohesion and Disintegration
        in the American Army: An Alternative Perspective." ARMED FORCES
        AND SOCIETY 2 (1976): 340-76.

        Using much data, authors argue that there was sufficient evi-
        dence for disintegration of the army in Vietnam: desertion,
        fragging, mutiny, drugs, and an ineffectual officer corps
        held in contempt by its troops.

1684   Schell, Jonathan. THE MILITARY HALF. New York: Knopf, 1968.
        212 p.

        Follows the path of destruction of an army task force moving
        through two provinces in Vietnam in 1966. Critical of indis-
        criminate use of American firepower.

1685   Shaplen, Robert. THE LOST REVOLUTION: THE U.S. IN VIETNAM,
        1946-1966. New York: Harper and Row, 1966. 404 p.

        Describes and analyzes American involvement in IndoChina
        since World War II, attempting to show how early involve-
        ments led inextricably to Vietnam.

1686   _____. THE ROAD FROM WAR: VIETNAM, 1965-1970. New York:
        Harper, 1970. 300 p.

        Originally published in NEW YORKER, author's reports from
        Vietnam. Conveys immediacy and tragedy.

1687   Smith, William A., Jr. "The Strategic Hamlet Program in Vietnam."
        MILITARY REVIEW 44 (1964): 17-23.

        Member of the Strategic Hamlets Division argues for the suc-
        cess of the program.

1688   Taylor, Maxwell D. SWORDS AND PLOWSHARES. New York: Nor-
        ton, 1972. 422 p.

        An account of Taylor's experiences with the Kennedy admin-
        istration's Vietnam policy. Criticizes policy of gradualism
        and advocates forceful decisive action in future "small" wars.

1689   Van Alstyne, Richard W. "The Vietnam War in Historical Perspective."
        CURRENT HISTORY 65 (1973): 241-46.

1690   Walt, Lewis W. STRANGE WAR, STRANGE STRATEGY. New York:
        Funk and Wagnall, 1972. 208 p.

        Professional account of the experiences of the marine com-
        mander in Vietnam 1965-68, providing important impressions

of Hue and Danang where the marines met North Vietnam regulars in large unit actions.

1691   West, Francis J., Jr. SMALL UNIT ACTION IN VIETNAM: SUMMER, 1966. New York: Significant, 1967. 123 p.

Firsthand account of patrol duty in Vietnam involving various units of the Marine Corps.

1692   Westmoreland, William C. A SOLDIER REPORTS. Garden City, N.Y.: Doubleday, 1976. 446 p.

A kind of apologia but useful for a picture of the Vietnam War from the point of view of its leading commander.

1693   Windchy, Eugene G. TONKIN GULF. Garden City, N.Y.: Doubleday, 1971. 358 p.

Account by a former officer of the U.S. Information Agency in Japan describing the Tokin Gulf incident and the aftermath. Conspiratorial in tone, accuses officials of deliberate deception.

C. POST-VIETNAM MILITARY ESTABLISHMENT

1694   Alciano, Richard. "The American Military: A Reappraisal." MILITARY REVIEW 52 (1972): 51-57.

Appraises the meaning of what are becoming military cliches: "new militarism," "power elite," "military-industrial-complex."

1695   Bachman, Jerald, and Blair, John. "'Citizen-Force' or 'Career-Force'?: Implications for Ideology in the All-Volunteer Army." ARMED FORCES AND SOCIETY 2 (1975): 81-96.

Concludes that without conscripted citizen soldiers, the all-volunteer army is undergoing attitudinal changes.

1696   Bletz, Donald F. THE ROLE OF THE MILITARY PROFESSIONAL IN U.S. FOREIGN POLICY. New York: Praeger, 1972. 320 p.

Author argues that high-ranking officers should be trained to understand political factors in military decisions because since World War II officers are called upon more than ever to deal with political problems.

1697   Bradford, Zeb B., and Brown, Frederick. THE UNITED STATES ARMY IN TRANSITION. Beverly Hills, Calif.: Sage, 1973. 385 p.

Examines the post-Vietnam army and suggests reorganizational solutions to the very real human problems of the new army.

1698   Busch, Terry J., and Stupak, Ronald J. "The U.S. Military: Patterns of Adaptation for the 1970's." ORBIS 16 (1973): 990-1007.

Believes that the military establishment is undergoing sweeping changes brought on by new social awareness, technological advancements, and the war in Vietnam. Argues that the military is successfully adapting.

1699   Chodes, John J. THE MYTH OF AMERICA'S MILITARY POWER. Boston: Braden, 1973. 224 p.

Critical of American military policy and techniques since World War II. Attacks air power, fire power, and armored power theories as ineffective and leading to self-destructive thinking.

1700   Cortright, David. SOLDIERS IN REVOLT: THE AMERICAN MILITARY TODAY. Garden City, N.Y.: Doubleday, 1975. 317 p.

Discusses the discontent that has sapped the vitality from the American Army. "Today" means the Vietnam era.

1701   Donovan, James A., and Shoup, David M. MILITARISM, U.S.A. New York: Scribner, 1970. 265 p.

Account by a retired Marine colonel contends that American military more powerful and wasteful than need be. Cites Vietnam, nuclear struggle, and Dominican fiasco as evidence of costly misadventures caused by being overly powerful.

1702   Ferria, William R. "The Enlisted Man: Army Folklore." NEW YORK FOLKLORE 2 (1976): 229-37.

Relates that the jokes and cartoons that today's enlisted man tells on his officers reflect his dissatisfaction with army life.

1703   Gard, Robert G. "The Military and American Society." FOREIGN AFFAIRS 49 (1971): 698-710.

Argues for more intensive effort to encourage civilian-military contact and cooperation: "a close association of the armed forces with civilian society is necessary to insure that military resources will be employed in a manner consistent with American societal values."

1704   Gates, Thomas S. THE REPORT OF THE PRESIDENT'S COMMISSION ON AN ALL-VOLUNTEER ARMED FORCE. New York: Macmillan, 1970. 218 p.

The Gates report that led Nixon to propose and Congress to pass the act creating the All-Volunteer Force.

1705   Hauser, William L. AMERICA'S ARMY IN CRISIS: A STUDY IN CIVIL MILITARY RELATIONS. Baltimore: Johns Hopkins University Press, 1973. 242 p.

Discusses army's social problems during 1971, its problems of drug abuse, discipline and moral. Contends social problems are a reflection of post-industrial mass consumption society. Suggests two armies: a professional one and a citizen support army.

1706   Hickman, Martin B., comp. THE MILITARY AND AMERICAN SOCIETY. Beverly Hills, Calif.: Glencoe Press, 1971. 167 p.

A collection of essays dealing with such topics as the "new" American militarism by David Shoup and several on the military-industrial complex. Generally antimilitary in tone.

1707   Janowitz, Morris. "The Decline of the Mass Army." MILITARY REVIEW 52 (1972): 10-16.

Argues that the mass army was the result of industrialism and nationalism and with the maturing of these two developments, the mass army will be replaced by a smaller professional one.

1708   _____. "Volunteer Armed Forces and Military Purposes." FOREIGN AFFAIRS 50 (1972): 427-33.

Argues that to carry out its military purposes the all-volunteer force must incorporate a constabulary type of strategy and develop a higher level of professionalism.

1709   _____, ed. THE NEW MILITARY: CHANGING PATTERNS OF ORGANIZATION. New York: Sage, 1964. 369 p.

Sociological essays covering managerial organization, social cohesion and career commitment in the present military establishment.

1710   Janowitz, Morris, and Moskos, Charles C. "Racial Composition in the All-Volunteer Force." ARMED FORCES AND SOCIETY 1 (1974): 109-24.

Argues that democratic society must be broadly represented in the Armed Forces and All-Volunteer Force is not achieving that goal.

1711   Jesse, W.L. "The New Military Professional." U.S. NAVAL INSTITUTE PROCEEDINGS 101 (1975): 25-31.

Argues that traditional separation of military and political
issues now impossible. Contends that military must play a
larger role in policy decisions.

1712   Kim, K.H., et al. THE ALL-VOLUNTEER ARMY: AN ANALYSIS
OF DEMAND AND SUPPLY. New York: Praeger, 1971. 208 p.

Technical account of the economic and statistical aspects of
the All-Volunteer Force, served as data for Gates study.

1713   King, Edward L. THE DEATH OF THE ARMY: A PRE-MORTEM.
New York: Saturday Review Press, 1972. 246 p.

A 23-year veteran's attack on the U.S. Army establishment
(especially its officer promotion system) after the Vietnam debacle. Mostly polemical.

1714   Klare, Michael T. WAR WITHOUT END: AMERICAN PLANNING
FOR THE NEXT VIETNAMS. New York: Knopf, 1972. 464 p.

Contends United States already prepared for future limited
wars. Draws on records of the Pentagon and State Department. Interpreted from a Marxist point of view.

1715   Knoll, Erwin, and McFadden, Judith. AMERICAN MILITARISM, 1970.
New York: Viking, 1969. 150 p.

Dialogue on the role of the military in foreign affairs.

1716   Kohn, Richard. "The All-Volunteer Army: Too High a Price?" U.S.
NAVAL INSTITUTE PROCEEDINGS 100 (1974): 35-43.

Argues All-Volunteer Army policy will not achieve an effective, efficient military force.

1717   Lang, Kurt. "Trends in Military Occupational Structure and Their Political Implications." JOURNAL OF POLITICAL AND MILITARY SO-
CIOLOGY 1 (1973): 1-18.

Argues that tactical operations for officers are being replaced
by desk jobs and this is partly a cause for the bureaucratiza-
tion of the trend toward civilianization of the military.

1718   Loory, Stuart. DEFEATED: INSIDE AMERICA'S MILITARY MACHINE.
New York: Random, 1973. 405 p.

Discussion of author's view that America's military establishment has been deteriorating since World War II and this trend
has increased since Vietnam.

1719   Lovell, John P., and Kronenberg, Philip S., eds. NEW CIVIL-
       MILITARY RELATIONS: THE AGONIES OF ADJUSTMENT TO POST-
       VIETNAM REALITIES. New York: Dutton, 1974. 352 p.

       A collection of essays by prominent political scientists and
       historians on the military adjustment to post-Vietnam condi-
       tions.

1720   Margiotta, Franklin D. THE CHANGING WORLD OF THE AMERICAN
       MILITARY. Boulder, Colo.: Westview Press, 1978. 415 p.

       A collection of articles presented by civilian scholars and
       military men of all services and ranks on the organizational
       and technological changes in the present American military
       establishment.

1721   Marmion, Harry A. THE CASE AGAINST A VOLUNTEER ARMY.
       Chicago: Quadrangle, 1971. 107 p.

       Polemic on the order of a lawyer's brief. Argues all-volun-
       teer force would be manned by blacks and the poor.

1722   Middleton, Drew. CAN AMERICA WIN THE NEXT WAR? New York:
       Scribner, 1975. 271 p.

       Author worried about the development of the All-Volunteer
       Army and its problems--racism, drugs, and apathetic American
       public. The answer to the title questions is: "No."

1723   Moskos, Charles C., Jr. THE AMERICAN ENLISTED MAN: THE
       RANK AND FILE IN TODAY'S MILITARY. New York: Sage, 1970.
       274 p.

       An account of the attitudes and styles of life in the U.S.
       Army's "enlisted" culture based on interviews with American
       soldiers.

1724   _____. "From Institution to Occupational: Trends in Military Organ-
       ization." ARMED FORCES AND SOCIETY 4 (1977): 41-49.

       Argues that "the American military is moving from an institu-
       tional format to one more and more resembling that of an oc-
       cupation," perhaps bringing into question military legitimacy.

1725   _____, ed. PUBLIC OPINION AND THE MILITARY ESTABLISHMENT.
       Beverly Hills, Calif.: Sage, 1971. 274 p.

       Sociological essays with general thesis that armed forces must
       remain broadly representative of American society.

1726   Norman, Lloyd. "The Military Chiefs and Defense Policy: Is Anyone

Listening?" ARMY 28 (1978): 14–25.

Argues every administration for past thirty years has tried to reorganize the Defense Department. Discusses Carter's efforts.

1727 Oppenheimer, Martin, ed. THE AMERICAN MILITARY. Chicago: Aldine, 1971. 180 p.

Essays, originally published in TRANS-ACTION, by political scientists and sociologists dealing with post-Vietnam military life and affairs.

1728 Polner, Murray. NO MORE PARADES: THE RETURN OF THE VIET-NAM VETERAN. New York: Holt, Rinehart and Winston, 1971. 169 p.

Argues that unlike veterans of other American wars, Vietnam vets will be alienated by their military experience.

1729 Reedy, George. WHO WILL DO OUR FIGHTING FOR US? New York: World, 1970. 126 p.

Brief against an all-volunteer force and for a conscript armed force. Containing many documents on the issue.

1730 Reeves, Thomas, and Hess, Karl. THE END OF THE DRAFT. New York: Random, 1970. 200 p.

Argument against conscription on basis that it is incompatible with freedom. Only a volunteer force acceptable in a demo-cratic state.

1731 Rosser, Richard F. "Civil-Military Relations in the 1980's." MILI-TARY REVIEW 52 (1972): 26–31.

Argues that the trend is a drift away from militarism brought on by a restricted role for the military and the privacy of domestic politics.

1732 Sandsberry, U.C. "Civilianism, Civilianization and the Military Serv-ices." U.S. NAVAL INSTITUTE PROCEEDINGS 98 (1972): 62–67.

Argues that trends toward civilianism, greater civilian partici-pation, the conversion of military positions to civilian-like ones, are just as dangerous to civil-military relations as mil-itarism and militarization.

1733 Sarkesian, Sam C. "Political Soldiers: Perspectives on Professionalism in the U.S. Military." MID-WEST JOURNAL OF POLITICAL SCI-ENCE 26 (1972): 239–58.

Argues that a political dimension of military professionalism must be added to the traditional ones of the managerial role and the diminished heroic leader.

1734 _____. THE PROFESSIONAL OFFICER IN A CHANGING SOCIETY. Chicago: Nelson-Hall, 1975. 264 p.

Covers the multifaceted dimension of military life--from the military family to the All-Volunteer Army--in present day society.

1735 Schexnider, Alvin, and Butler, John. "Race and the All-Volunteer System: A Reply to Janowitz and Moskos." ARMED FORCES AND SOCIETY 2 (1976): 421-32.

Argue that "representativeness" in the armed forces is a code word for racial quotas. They suggest more openness in re-cruitment for the All-Volunteer Force. Critical of the Jano-witz-Moskos thesis (see entry 1710).

1736 Stapp, Andy. UP AGAINST THE BRASS. New York: Simon and Schuster, 1970. 192 p.

Autobiography of an attempt to create the American Service-men's Union.

1737 Starr, Paul, et al. THE DISCARDED ARMY: THE NADER REPORT ON VIETNAM VETERANS AND THE VETERANS ADMINISTRATION. New York: Charterhouse, 1973. 304 p.

Sees America's indifference to Vietnam vets as a sordid story. Blames Veterans' Administration.

1738 Summers, Harry G. "Another View of the All-Volunteer Army." MILITARY REVIEW 52 (1972): 75-79.

Disagrees with Syrett and Kohn (below) concerning the All-Volunteer Army. Believes they exaggerate the possibility of a military coup.

1739 Syrett, David, and Kohn, Richard. "The Dangers of An All-Volunteer Army." MILITARY REVIEW 52 (1972): 70-74.

Argues that an All-Volunteer Force could pose a tremendous threat to civilian control and may create the conditions for a military coup.

1740 Thorne, David, and Butler, George, eds. THE NEW SOLDIER. New York: Macmillan, 1971. 174 p.

Account of the Vietnam Veterans Against the War. Mainly collected statements by members who testified before a congressional committee.

1741 Wool, Harold. THE MILITARY SPECIALIST: SKILLED MANPOWER FOR THE ARMED FORCES. Baltimore: Johns Hopkins University Press, 1969. 219 p.

Describes the need for skills in a more technologically oriented armed forces. Also provides insights into the effectiveness of an all-volunteer force.

1742 Yarmolinsky, Adam. "Picking Up the Pieces: Impact of Vietnam on the Military Establishment." YALE REVIEW 61 (1972): 481-95.

Discusses lessons the military ought to learn from the Vietnam War and argues that this may be difficult because the military has serious morale problems today.

1743 _____, ed. "The Military and American Society." ANNALS OF THE AMERICAN ACADEMY OF POLITICAL AND SOCIAL SCIENCES 406 (1973): 1-172.

Essays by leading social scientists who are authorities on American military affairs, covering such topics as the military and national power and the military as an institution in American society.

ADDENDUM

Adams, Michael C. OUR MASTERS THE REBELS: A SPECULATION ON UNION FAILURE IN THE EAST, 1861-1865. Cambridge, Mass.: Harvard University Press, 1978. 256 p.

Argues that the Union Army failed to subdue the Confederate forces because Northerners were victims of a cultural myth: they thought Southern society produced superior soldiers, better disciplined and better fighters. These qualities give the South a psychological advantage early in the war.

Anderson, Martin, ed. CONSCRIPTION: A SELECTED AND ANNOTATED BIBLIOGRAPHY. Stanford, Calif.: Hoover Institute Press, 1976. 245 p.

Selective but fairly comprehensive. Useful because of its thorough and perceptive annotations.

Averell, William W. TEN YEARS IN THE SADDLE: THE MEMOIR OF WILLIAM W. AVERELL. Edited by Edward Eckert and Nicholas Amato. San Rafael, Calif.: Presidio, 1978. 443 p.

Personal account, written in 1890s, of a military professional who served on the frontier, in the Mexican War and in the Civil War. A Democrat, he was highly critical of Republican leadership.

Bernstein, Barton J. "The Quest for Security: American Foreign Policy and International Control of Atomic Energy, 1942-1946." JOURNAL OF AMERICAN HISTORY 60 (1974): 1003-44.

Argues that "the stalemate on atomic energy was a symbol of the mutual distrust in Soviet-American relations. The dispute over atomic energy was both a cause and a consequence of the Cold War."

Boyle, Richard. FLOWER OF THE DRAGON: THE BREAKDOWN OF THE U.S. ARMY IN VIETNAM. New York: RAMPARTS, 1972. 288 p.

Presents the GI's view of the Vietnam War. Tells story of soldiers going into combat high on drugs. Also describes fragging, mutiny and the use of heroin.

Brodie, Bernard. WAR AND POLITICS. New York: Macmillan, 1973. 496 p.

Collection of essays by Brodie that explores the relationship between strategy and politics in America's twentieth century wars. Contains a particularly perceptive chapter on the Vietnam War. Other topics include attitudes toward war; causes of war; meaning of "vital interests"; and a discussion of those who plan war.

Brown, Richard C. SOCIAL ATTITUDES OF AMERICAN GENERALS, 1898–1940. New York: Arno, 1979.

Often used Ph.D. dissertation (University of Wisconsin, 1951) that furnished data for studies on military attitudes in the twentieth century. Probes the background careers and experiences of five hundred army generals.

Erney, Richard A. THE PUBLIC LIFE OF HENRY DEARBORN. New York: Arno, 1979.

Study of one of the founders of the American Army who served as a general in the War of 1812 and as Jefferson's Secretary of War. Covers not only the controversial general but Jefferson's military policy as well. Originally a Ph.D. dissertation, Columbia University, 1957.

Essame, Hubert. PATTON: A STUDY IN COMMAND. New York: Scribner's, 1974. 280 p.

Patton's career during World War II studied from the sympathetic point of view of a professional English officer. Examines all major battles in which Patton was involved concluding that the controversial general should have been given much more freedom of decision.

Flynn, George Q. THE MESS IN WASHINGTON: MANPOWER MOBILIZATION IN WORLD WAR II. Westport, Conn.: Greenwood, 1979. 294 p.

Scholarly study of manpower mobilization during World War II that deals with the question of the right to conscript citizens and the efforts to install a national service, one that would allow the government to conscript for a war task.

Frassanito, William A. ANTIETAM: THE PHOTOGRAPHIC LEGACY OF AMERICA'S BLOODIEST DAY. New York: Scribner's, 1978. 304 p.

Definitive collection of photographs of a major Civil War battle, along with maps, modern views of the battlefield, and a brief narrative.

Garal, Jaya K. THE PENTAGON AND THE MAKING OF U.S. FOREIGN POLICY: A CASE STUDY OF VIETNAM, 1960-68. New York: Humanities, 1978. 333 p.

Effort to analyze the role of the Department of Defense in shaping American foreign policy. Emphasis on the politics of war in Vietnam.

Gavin, James M. "Bloody Huertgen: The Battle That Should Have Never Been Fought." AMERICAN HERITAGE 31 (1979): 32-44.

Personal account and narrative history by the commander of the 82nd Airborne Division who had traversed the Huertgen Forest and saw the difficult terrain, but claims the high command was ignorant of this fact.

Griffin, Robert K., Jr. "Quality Not Quantity: The Volunteer Army During the Depression." MILITARY AFFAIRS 63 (1979): 171-77.

Discusses army recruiting efforts in the 1920s and the 1930s indicating how the economic malaise not recruiting methods brought in a higher quality soldier in the 1930s.

Kohn, Richard H., ed. ANGLO-AMERICAN ANTIMILITARY TRACTS, 1697-1830. New York: Arno, 1979.

Collection of six essays which the author claims proves the persistence of American antimilitarism. Includes essays by John Trenchard and Alan Partridge.

_____. MILITARY LAWS OF THE UNITED STATES FROM THE CIVIL WAR THROUGH THE POWER ACT OF 1973. New York: Arno, 1973.

A collection of national military laws selected from PUBLIC STATUTES AT LAW, 1862-1963. Includes legislation on manpower, procurement, and veterans affairs.

Koistinen, Paul. THE HAMMER AND THE SWORD: LABOR, THE MILITARY AND INDUSTRIAL MOBILIZATION, 1920-1945. New York: Arno, 1979.

Explores the relationship between labor and the military during World War II, focusing on the government's manpower policy and labor's and the military's reaction to it. Originally a Ph.D. dissertation, University of California, 1964.

Lovell, John P. NEITHER ATHENS NOR SPARTA: THE AMERICAN SERVICE ACADEMIES IN TRANSITION. Bloomington: Indiana University Press, 1979. 384 p.

Analyzes America's contemporary service academies--the Military, Naval, and Air Force Academies--by employing structural organizational theory.

Manders, Eric I. THE BATTLE OF LONG ISLAND. New York: Freneau, 1978. 64 p.

Short narrative of the battle with emphasis on the British and American plans, movement of troops and frequent small engagements. Uses eyewitness accounts but not many other sources.

Moulton, Harland B. FROM SUPERIORITY TO PARITY: THE UNITED STATES AND THE STRATEGIC ARMS ACT, 1960-1971. Westport, Conn.: Greenwood, 1973. 333 p.

Technical study of U.S. nuclear strategy during the decade of the 1960s. Discounts claims of past missile gaps and blames America for making arms limitations more difficult.

Parks, Robert J. "The Development of Segregation in U.S. Army Hospitals, 1940-1942." MILITARY AFFAIRS 37 (1974): 145-50.

Parrish, Noel F. BEHIND THE SHELTERING BOMB: MILITARY INDECISION FROM ALAMOGORDO TO KOREA. New York: Arno, 1979.

Although a participant in the decision on nuclear policy, author writes in a detached way, basing his interpretation on solid research in printed and manuscript sources. Focuses on the military attempt to adjust its defense thinking from conventional to nuclear war. Originally a Ph.D. dissertation, Rich University, 1968.

Rutman, Darrett B. A MILITANT NEW WORLD, 1607-1640: AMERICA'S FIRST GENERATION: ITS MARTIAL SPIRIT, ITS TRADITION OF ARMS, ITS MILITIA ORGANIZATION, ITS WARS. New York: Arno, 1979.

Explores the origins of the American military experience in the early colonial period and how the colonists found their own ways of organization and fighting. Originally a Ph.D. dissertation, University of Virginia, 1959.

Schaffer, Ronald, ed. THE UNITED STATES IN WORLD WAR I: A SELECTED BIBLIOGRAPHY. Santa Barbara, Calif.: Clio Books, 1978. 224 p.

Divided into sections which included military, political, social, and economic sources. Unannotated but well-indexed.

Schlesinger, Arthur M., Jr., and Rovere, Richard. THE GENERAL AND THE PRESIDENT. New York: Farrar, Straus, 1951. 336 p.

Study by a political writer and a historical scholar of the character and career of Gen. Douglas MacArthur and his confrontation with President Truman.

Skelton, William B. "Officers and Politicians: The Origins of Army Politics in the United States Before the Civil War." ARMED FORCES AND SOCIETY 6 (1979): 22-48.

Argues that military professionals' ideology rejected political partisanship but not politics. Officers in the pre-Civil War period politicked for professional goals which had an impact on American civil military relations.

Starr, Paul. THE DISCARDED ARMY: VETERANS AFTER VIETNAM. Nader Report on Vietnam Veterans and the Veterans Administration. New York: Charterhouse, 1974. 304 p.

Examines the problems of the Vietnam veteran, focusing on the ineffectiveness of the Veterans Administration in providing for the needs of the veterans of America's latest war. Author concludes VA was too concerned with veterans of previous wars.

Steffen, Randy. THE HORSE SOLDIERS, 1776-1943. 3 vols. Norman: University of Oklahoma Press, 1977-79.

Three volumes of a projected four-volume study of the U.S. cavalry. This definitive history also contains authentic drawings by the author.

Stockfisch, J.A. PLOWSHARES INTO SWORDS: MANAGING THE AMERICAN DEFENSE ESTABLISHMENT. New York: Mason and Lipscomb, 1973. 360 p.

Analyzes management problems arising from a large, complex military establishment; focusing on bureaucratic struggles and the role of civilian in the decision-making process of military policy and weapons procurement.

Tustin, Joseph A., ed. DIARY OF THE AMERICAN WAR: A HESSIAN JOURNAL. New Haven, Conn.: Yale University Press, 1979. 480 p.

Diary of English captain, Johann Ewald, who was present at several battles, from Brandywine to the seige of Charleston. Written with sensitivity and humor. Useful on British tactics and strategies.

Vaugh, Stephen L. HOLDING THE INNER LINE: DEMOCRACY, NATIONALISM, AND THE COMMITTEE ON PUBLIC SAFETY. Chapel Hill: University of North Carolina Press, 1979. 420 p.

Study of the major propaganda agency of World War I. Author critical of the committee, arguing that its tactics weakened democratic government and encouraged the development of an imperial presidency. Argues also that the committee was not far wrong in warning against German militarism.

Addendum

Wakin, Malham M., ed. WAR, MORALITY AND THE MILITARY PROFES-
SION. Boulder, Colo.: Praeger, 1979. 531 p.

Anthology connects two major topics: the military as a profession
and the morality of war. Topics include just war, theory of war
crimes and laws of war.

AUTHOR INDEX

This index includes all authors, editors, and compilers to works cited in the text. References are to entry numbers and alphabetization is letter by letter.

A

Abel, Elie 1463
Ackley, Charles W. 67, 1464
Adams, Benson D. 1465
Adams, Charles F. 68
Adams, George R. 672
Adams, George W. 799
Adams, Henry 609
Adams, Henry H. 1237
Adams, Randolph G. 377, 378, 557
Adams, Reid M.B. 610
Addington, Larry H. 176
Adler, Bill 1641
Agnew, James B. 260
Alberts, Robert C. 1595
Albion, Robert G. 1
Alciano, Richard 1694
Alden, John R. 379-82
Alexander, Arthur 383-87
Alexander, Robert 1110
Alger, Russell A. 1056-57
Amann, William F., ed. 800
Ambrose, Stephen 69, 110, 177-79,
  801-3, 1238-39, 1268
American Battle Monuments Commission
  1111
American Military Institute 180
Amrine, Michael 1240
Anders, Leslie 2
Anderson, James 221

Anderson, Robert 719
Andrist, Ralph K. 990
Ansell, Samuel 181
Applegate, Howard L. 388
Appleman, Ray E. 1596
Armacost, Michael H. 1466
Armstrong, Anne 1241
Armstrong, John 611
Amhym, Albert 1382
Arnold, Henry H. 1242
Art, Robert J. 1427
Asprey, Robert 1112
Athearn, Robert G. 991-92
Augur, Helen 389
Ayer, Fred 1243

B

Bachman, Jerald 1695
Bachus, Electus 720
Bacon, Eugene H. 3
Bacon, Robert 1058
Bailey, Thomas 721
Bakeless, John 558
Baker, Newton D. 111
Baker-Crothers, Hayes 301
Baldwin, Hanson 1244-46, 1467-68
Ballard, Colin R. 804
Bandel, Eugene 559
Barbeau, Arthur 1114
Barnet, Richard J. 1469-71

Author Index

Author Index

Author Index

Author Index

Author Index

Margiotta, Franklin D. 1720
Margolin, Leo J. 1357
Margulies, Herbert F. 228
Marmion, Harry A. 1721
Marquis, Thomas B. 1934
Marshall, George C. 1185
Marshall, S.L.A. 1035, 1186,
  1358-60, 1619-20, 1672-76
Masland, John 38, 226, 229
Maslowski, Pete 910
Mason, Philip 655
Matloff, Maurice 40, 1187
Matthews, William 41
Mauldin, William H. 1361
Maurer, Maurer 483, 1621
Maxim, Hudson 93
May, Ernest 42, 157, 1551
Mayo, Lida 1362
Mazuzan, George T. 1363
Mead, Spencer P. 344
Meade, Edward G. 1622
Meade, George G. 765
Meck, Basil 586
Meiwold, Robert D. 230
Melman, Seymour 1552
Merrill, James M. 43, 912
Metzger, Charles 484
Meyers, Robert M. 913
Meyers, William S.L. 766
Michie, Peter 231
Middleton, Drew 1722
Middleton, Harry J. 1623
Miers, Earl S. 914-15
Miles, Nelson A. 1036
Miley, John D. 1091
Miller, John C. 485-86, 1624
Miller, John R. 1364
Millett, Allan 232, 279-82, 1092-
  94, 1188, 1677
Millett, John D. 1365
Milligan, John D. 916
Millis, Walter 44, 94, 158, 283,
  1095, 1189, 1366, 1553
Mitchell, Broadus 487
Mitchell, Joseph B. 488
Mitchell, William 1190
Mock, James R. 1191
Molender, Earl A. 159
Moley, Raymond, Jr. 45
Monaghan, James 917

Montross, Lynn 489-90
Mook, Telfer H. 345
Mooney, Chase C. 1192
Moore, Albert B. 918
Moore, Frank 491
Moore, Robert 197
Morgan, Gwenda 346
Morganstern, George E. 1367
Morgenstern, Oscar 1554
Morison, Elting E. 1368
Morison, Samuel E. 160, 1369
Morris, Robert B. 419
Morrison, James L. 233
Morton, Louis 95, 227, 234, 284-
  87, 347-48, 1370
Moskos, Charles C. 161, 1710,
  1723-25
Motte, Jacob Rhett 587
Moulton, Harland B. 1555
Mrozek, Donald J. 1444, 1556
Muller, Charles 656
Murdock, Clark A. 1557
Murdock, Eugene 919-20
Murdock, Harold 492
Murfin, James V. 921
Murphy, Andie 1372
Murphy, Orville T. 493

N

Nalty, Bernard C. 39
Nardin, Terry 1454
Nash, Gerald D. 1193
Neff, J.C. 1512
Nell, William C. 494
Nelson, Donald M. 1373
Nelson, Keith L. 162
Nelson, Otto 235
Nelson, Paul D. 288, 495, 497,
  588-89
Neninger, Timothy K. 236
Nevins, Allan 46, 767, 922-23
Newhouse, John 1558
Newman, Ralph G. 857
Nichols, Edward J. 768
Nichols, F.T. 349
Nichols, Roger L. 590-91, 699
Nickerson, Hoffman 498
Nitze, Paul H. 1559
Niven, John 924

Author Index

Randall, James G. 934-35
Rankin, Hugh F. 420, 512-15, 521
Ransom, Edward 241, 1097-98
Ranson, Harry H. 1571
Rapoport, Roger 1572
Rawley, James A. 936
Raymond, Jack 1447
Record, Jeffrey 1542
Reed, John 516
Reedy, George 1729
Rees, David 1627
Reeves, Ira L. 242
Reeves, Thomas 1730
Reilly, Robin 661
Reinhardt, George C. 54, 1573
Reuss, John 277
Rice, Berkeley 1448
Rice, Howard 517
Richter, William 937
Rickey, Don, Jr. 1040-41
Ridgway, Matthew B. 1628-29
Ries, John C. 1449
Riker, William 243
Ripley, Roswell S. 772
Risch, Erna 244
Rister, Carl C. 1042
Rives, George L. 773
Robert, Chalmers 1574
Roberts, Kenneth L. 518
Robertson, James I. 906, 938-39
Robinett, Paul 290
Robinson, Fayette 55
Robinson, Ralph 662
Rodberg, Leonard S. 1450
Rodenbaugh, Theophilus 245
Rodenbaugh, Thomas F. 21
Rogers, J. Alan 361-62
Rogow, Arnold A. 1451
Roherty, James M. 1452
Rokke, Ervin J. 1516
Roland, Charles P. 940
Roosevelt, Theodore 1099
Ropp, Theodore 291
Ross, Davis R. 1385
Rosser, Richard F. 1731
Rossie, Jonathan G. 519
Rowland, Eron O. 663
Rundell, Walter 1386
Rupp, Lelia J. 1387
Russett, Bruce M. 1575

Rutkowski, Edwin H. 1388
Ryan, Cornelius 1389-91

S

Salisbury, Harrison E. 1682
Salkeld, Robert 1576
Sander, Alfred D. 1577
Sandler, Stanley 292
Sandsberry, U.C. 1732
Sanger, Donald B. 941
Sapin, Burton M. 164
Sapio, Victor 664
Sargent, Herbert H. 1100
Sarkesian, Sam C. 165, 1733-34
Savage, Paul 1683
Sawyer, Robert K. 1630
Scheer, George F. 521
Scheips, Paul J. 293
Schell, Jonathan 1684
Schelling, Thomas C. 1578
Schexnider, Alvin 1735
Schick, Jack M. 1579
Schiller, Herbert I. 166, 1453
Schilling, Warner R. 1513, 1580
Schlesinger, Arthur M. 1208
Schlesinger, James R. 1581
Schlessel, Lillian 167
Schmitt, Martin F. 1043
Schnabel, James F. 1631
Schneider, George A. 1044
Schoenberger, Walter S. 1392
Schoff, Morris 246
Schonberger, Howard 168
Schroeder, John 774
Schwarz, Urs. 1582
Schwiebert, Ernest G. 1583
Scisco, Louis 363
Scott, James B. 247, 1058
Scott, Robert L. 1393
Scott, Winfield 775
Scribner, Benjamin F. 776
Seager, Robert 13
Sedgwick, John 777
Sefton, James E. 942-43
Seldes, George 1209
Sellen, Robert Walker 100
Sexton, William T. 1101
Shannon, Fred A. 944-48

Author Index

SUBJECT INDEX

References are to entry numbers. Alphabetization is letter by letter.

A

Ainsworth, Fred 1140
Airmobile Warfare 18
Allen, Ethan 467
American Expeditionary Force 1128,
  1133, 1139, 1162, 1174, 1184,
  1195, 1205, 1214
  French view of 1174
  history of 1120, 1216, 1229, 1232
American Legion 45
Amherst, Lord Jeffery 330, 339
Antietam 921
Anzio 1254
Apache Indians 993, 1012, 1030,
  1047-48
Army Air Force
  history 8
  World War I 1166-68, 1222
  World War II 1242, 1282, 1300,
    1305, 1334, 1382, 1388
Army Engineers 688, 691
Army General Staff
  history 213, 215
  National security 235
  World War I 1126, 1184, 1214
Army logistics 216
Army officers
  biographical register 193
  general officer selection 206
  on the frontier 677, 708
  post-World War I 190, 218-19
  professionalization 249

sketches 24
See also biographies and personal
  accounts of officers
Army War College 238
Arnhem 1389
Arnold, Benedict 406, 441, 479,
  522, 544
Artillery
  Civil War 852
  coastal defense 241
  creation of 567
  history 14, 52, 176
  Mexican War 419, 737, 739
  World War I 1141
Atkinson, Henry 572, 699
Atlanta 815, 893, 905
Atomic bomb. See World War II

B

Bacon's Rebellion 374
Baker, Newton 111, 1117-18,
  1136, 1147, 1198
Baltimore 622, 656, 662
Banks, Nathaniel 895
Baruch, Bernard 114-15, 1129,
  1235
Bastogne 1358
Battles, history of American 53
Battles of the Civil War
  Antietam 921
  Appomattox 840

Subject Index

Atlanta 315, 893, 905
Bull Run 844
Chancellorsville 807
Chickamauga 963
Gettysburg 826, 852, 878, 925, 942, 964–65
Shenandoah Valley 958
Shiloh 902, 957
Vicksburg 914
Wilderness 955
See also Civil War, history
Battles of the Korean War
Chonchou River 1620
Inchon 1607, 1632
Pork Chop Hill 1619
See also Korean War, history
Battles of the Mexican War
Monterey 720
Buena Vista 727, 756
Mexico City 728, 794
See also Mexican War, history
Battles of the Revolutionary War
Boston 447
Bunker Hill 470, 472
Charleston 492
Concord 444, 492
Cowpens 513
Lexington 492
Manhattan 401
Saratoga 434, 497
Ticonderoga 416, 448
Quebec 327, 368
Yorktown 377, 415, 424, 439, 452
See also Revolutionary War, history
Battles of the Spanish-American War
Santiago 1060, 1071, 1100, 1107
See also Spanish-American War, history
Battles of the Vietnam War
history of 1673–76
Tet 1663, 1678
Battles of the War of 1812
Baltimore 622, 656, 662
Canada 667
Chippewa 645
Detroit 627
New Orleans 610, 617, 619, 621, 623, 629, 651, 663

Niagara 626
Washington 648, 650, 656
See also War of 1812, history
Battles of World War II
Anzio 1254
Arnhem 1389
Bastogne 1358
Berlin 1238, 1390, 1408
Bulge 1291, 1407
Burma 1377, 1393
Corregidor 1249, 1419
Huertgen Forest 1352
Kasserine Pass 1257
New Guinea 1362
Normandy 1256, 1292, 1360, 1391, 1412
North Africa 1272
Okinawa 1250
Philippines 1248
Pearl Harbor 1298, 1426
Rapido 1255
See also World War II, history
Battles with Indians
Apaches 993, 1012, 1030, 1047–48
Little Bighorn 999, 1013, 1018, 1034
Modock 1005
Navajo 1033
Nez Perce 1025
Plains 1035
Red River 1020
Sioux 1019, 1044, 1051
Washita 1021
Beauregard, P.T.G. 798, 986
Berlin 1228, 1390, 1408, 1579, 1504
Bibliographies 6, 9, 27, 31, 46, 57, 237, 290
Blackhawk War 683, 695, 713
Black soldiers
Civil War 806, 836, 854, 859, 885, 932, 944, 978, 981
documents 39
history 200, 202, 208
integration 251
Seminole War 705
Spanish-American War 1073
West Point 201
World War I 114, 1163
World War II 1283, 1312, 1355

Subject Index

Subject Index

Subject Index